AT&T

VOLUME 2

SYSTEM CALLS AND LIBRARY ROUTINES

UNIX*
programmer's manual

CBS COLLEGE PUBLISHING'S
UNIX SYSTEM LIBRARY

* Trademark of AT&T.

AT&T

VOLUME 2

SYSTEM CALLS AND LIBRARY ROUTINES

UNIX*

programmer's manual

CBS COLLEGE PUBLISHING'S
UNIX SYSTEM LIBRARY

Steven V. Earhart: Editor

HOLT, RINEHART AND WINSTON
New York Chicago San Francisco Philadelphia
Montreal Toronto London Sydney Tokyo
Mexico City Rio de Janeiro Madrid

* Trademark of AT&T.

IMPORTANT NOTE TO USERS

While every effort has been made to ensure the accuracy of all information in this document, AT&T assumes no liability to any party for any loss or damage caused by errors or omissions or statements of any kind in the *UNIX* Programmer's Manual*, its updates, supplements, or special editions, whether such errors are omissions or statements resulting from negligence, accident, or any other cause. AT&T further assumes no liability arising out of the application or use of any product or system described herein; nor any liability for incidental or consequential damages arising from the use of this document. AT&T disclaims all warranties regarding the information contained herein, whether expressed, implied or statutory, including implied warranties of merchantability or fitness for a particular purpose.

AT&T reserves the right to make changes without further notice to any products herein to improve reliability, function or design.

This document was set on an AUTOLOGIC, Inc. APS-5 phototypesetter driven by the TROFF formatter operating under the UNIX system on an AT&T 3B20 computer.

---

* Trademark of AT&T.

Address correspondence to:
383 Madison Avenue
New York, NY 10017

Library of Congress Cataloging-in-Publication Data

UNIX programmer's manual.

At head of title: AT&T
Includes index.
Contents: v. 1. Commands and utilities — v. 2. System calls and library routines — v. 3. System administration facilities.
1. UNIX (Computer operating system) I. Earhart, Steven V. II. American Telephone and Telegraph Company.
QA76.76.063U548 1986 005.4′3 86-311

Select Code 320-032
ISBN 0-03-009314-7

Printed in the United States of America

Published simultaneously in Canada

678 090 98765432

CBS COLLEGE PUBLISHING
Holt, Rinehart and Winston
The Dryden Press
Saunders College Publishing

PREFACE

The *UNIX Programmer's Manual* describes most of features of UNIX System V. It does not provide a general overview of the UNIX system nor details of the implementation of the system.

Not all commands, features, or facilities described in this series are available in every UNIX system implementation. For specific questions on a machine implementation of the UNIX system, consult your system administrator.

The *UNIX Programmer's Manual* is available in several volumes.

- Volume 1 contains the Commands and Utilities (sections 1 and 6).

- Volume 2 contains the System Calls and Library Routines (sections 2, 3, 4, and 5).

- Volume 3 contains the System Administration Facilities (section 1M, 7, and 8).

TRADEMARKS

UNIX, TELETYPE, and DOCUMENTER'S WORKBENCH are trademarks of AT&T.

DEC, VAX, PDP, and MASSBUS are trademarks of Digital Equipment Corporation.

HP is a trademark of Hewlett-Packard, Inc.

TEKTRONIX is a registered trademark of Tektronix, Inc.

INTRODUCTION

The *UNIX Programmer's Manual Volume 2: System Calls and Library Routines* is divided into four sections:

2–System Calls

3–Library Routines

4–File Formats

5–Miscellaneous Facilities

Section 2 (*System Calls*) describes the entries into the UNIX system kernel, including the C language interface.

Section 3 (*Library Routines*) describes the library routines available on most systems. The binary versions usually reside in various system libraries in the directories **/lib** and **/usr/lib**. See *intro*(3) for descriptions of these libraries and the files in which they are stored. **Section 3** is divided into the following libraries:

3C. C and Assembler Library Routines

3S. Standard I/O Library Routines

3M. Mathematical Library Routines

3X. Miscellaneous Routines

3F. FORTRAN Library Routines

Section4 (*File Formats*) documents the structure of particular kinds of files; for example, the format of the output of the link editor is given in *a.out*(4). Excluded are files used by only one command. In general, the C language **struct** declarations corresponding to these formats can be found in the directories **/usr/include** and **.usr/include/sys**.

Section5 (*Miscellaneous Facilities*) contains a variety of things. Included are descriptions of character sets, macro packages, etc.

Each section consists of a number of independent entries of a page or so each. The name of the entry appears in the upper corners of its page(s). Entries within each section are alphabetized, with the exception of the introductory entry that begins each section. Some entries may describe several routines, commands, etc. In such cases, the entry appears only once, under its "major" name.

All entries use a common format, not all of whose parts always appear:

The **NAME** part gives the name(s) of the entry and briefly states its purpose.

The **SYNOPSIS** part summarizes the use of the program described. A few conventions are used:

Boldface strings are literals and are typed just as they appear.

Italic strings usually represent substitutable argument prototypes and program names found elsewhere in the *UNIX Programmer's Manual.*

Square brackets **[ ]** around an argument prototype indicate that the argument is optional. When an argument prototype is given as "name" or "file", it always refers to a *file* name.

Ellipses **...** are used to show that the previous argument prototype may be repeated.

A final convention is used by the commands themselves. An argument beginning with minus –, plus **+**, or equal sign **=** is often taken to be a flag argument, even if it appears in a position where a file name could appear. Files that begin with –, **+**, or **=** should therefore be avoided.

The **DESCRIPTION** part discusses the subject.

The **EXAMPLE(S)** part provides example(s) of usage.

The **FILES** part shows the file names that are built into the program.

The **DIAGNOSTICS** part discusses the diagnostic indications that may be produced. Messages that are self-explanatory are not listed.

The **BUGS** section describes known deficiencies that exist on some implementations.

The **SEE ALSO** section suggests related utilities or information to consult.

The **WARNINGS** part describes potential pitfalls.

A table of contents and a permuted index precede Section 2. The table of contents lists each major entry with a brief description and the page number that the entry begins on.

The permuted index is used by searching the middle column for a key word or phrase. The right column contains the name of the utility along with the section number. The left column of the permuted index contains additional useful information about the utility or command.

Throughout this volume references to sections 1 and 6 can be found in *UNIX Programmer's Manual Volume 1: Commands and Utilities.* References to sections 1M, 7, and 8 will be found in the *UNIX Programmer's Manual Volume 3: System Administration Facilities.*

TABLE OF CONTENTS

2. System Calls

3. Library Routines

3C. C and Assembler Library Routines

3S. Standard I/O Library Routines

3M. Mathematical Library Routines

3X. Miscellaneous Routines

3F. FORTRAN Library Routines

4. File Formats

5. Miscellaneous Facilities

PERMUTED INDEX

NAME

intro − introduction to system calls and error numbers

SYNOPSIS

#include <errno.h>

DESCRIPTION

This section describes all of the system calls. Most of these calls have one or more error returns. An error condition is indicated by an otherwise impossible returned value. This is almost always −1; the individual descriptions specify the details. An error number is also made available in the external variable *errno*. *Errno* is not cleared on successful calls, so it should be tested only after an error has been indicated.

Each system call description attempts to list all possible error numbers. The following is a complete list of the error numbers and their names as defined in **<errno.h>**.

1 EPERM Not owner
: Typically this error indicates an attempt to modify a file in some way forbidden except to its owner or super-user. It is also returned for attempts by ordinary users to do things allowed only to the super-user.

2 ENOENT No such file or directory
: This error occurs when a file name is specified and the file should exist but doesn't, or when one of the directories in a path name does not exist.

3 ESRCH No such process
: No process can be found corresponding to that specified by *pid* in *kill* or *ptrace*.

4 EINTR Interrupted system call
: An asynchronous signal (such as interrupt or quit), which the user has elected to catch, occurred during a system call. If execution is resumed after processing the signal, it will appear as if the interrupted system call returned this error condition.

5 EIO I/O error
: Some physical I/O error has occurred. This error may in some cases occur on a call following the one to which it actually applies.

6 ENXIO No such device or address
: I/O on a special file refers to a subdevice which does not

exist, or beyond the limits of the device. It may also occur when, for example, a tape drive is not on-line or no disk pack is loaded on a drive.

7 E2BIG Arg list too long
An argument list longer than 5,120 bytes is presented to a member of the *exec* family.

8 ENOEXEC Exec format error
A request is made to execute a file which, although it has the appropriate permissions, does not start with a valid magic number [see *a.out*(4)].

9 EBADF Bad file number
Either a file descriptor refers to no open file, or a read (respectively, write) request is made to a file which is open only for writing (respectively, reading).

10 ECHILD No child processes
A *wait* was executed by a process that had no existing or unwaited-for child processes.

11 EAGAIN No more processes
A *fork* failed because the system's process table is full or the user is not allowed to create any more processes.

12 ENOMEM Not enough space
During an *exec*, *brk*, or *sbrk*, a program asks for more space than the system is able to supply. This is not a temporary condition; the maximum space size is a system parameter. The error may also occur if the arrangement of text, data, and stack segments requires too many segmentation registers, or if there is not enough swap space during a *fork*.

13 EACCES Permission denied
An attempt was made to access a file in a way forbidden by the protection system.

14 EFAULT Bad address
The system encountered a hardware fault in attempting to use an argument of a system call.

15 ENOTBLK Block device required
A non-block file was mentioned where a block device was required, e.g., in *mount*.

16 EBUSY Device or resource busy
An attempt was made to mount a device that was already mounted or an attempt was made to dismount a device on which there is an active file (open file, current directory, mounted-on file, active text segment). It will also occur if an attempt is made to enable accounting when it is already enabled. The device or resource is currently unavailable.

17 EEXIST File exists
An existing file was mentioned in an inappropriate context, e.g., *link*.

18 EXDEV Cross-device link
A link to a file on another device was attempted.

19 ENODEV No such device
An attempt was made to apply an inappropriate system call to a device; e.g., read a write-only device.

20 ENOTDIR Not a directory
A non-directory was specified where a directory is required, for example in a path prefix or as an argument to *chdir*(2).

21 EISDIR Is a directory
An attempt was made to write on a directory.

22 EINVAL Invalid argument
Some invalid argument (e.g., dismounting a non-mounted device; mentioning an undefined signal in *signal*, or *kill*; reading or writing a file for which *lseek* has generated a negative pointer) was attempted. The math functions described in the (3M) entries of this manual causes the invalid argument to be set.

23 ENFILE File table overflow
The system file table is full, and temporarily no more *opens* can be accepted.

24 EMFILE Too many open files
No process may have more than 20 file descriptors open at a time. When a record lock is being created with *fcntl*, there are too many files with record locks on them.

25 ENOTTY Not a character device
An attempt was made to *ioctl*(2) a file that is not a special character device.

26 ETXTBSY Text file busy
An attempt was made to execute a pure-procedure program that is currently open for writing. Also an attempt to open for writing a pure-procedure program that is being executed.

27 EFBIG File too large
The size of a file exceeded the maximum file size (1,082,201,088 bytes) or ULIMIT; see *ulimit*(2).

28 ENOSPC No space left on device
During a *write* to an ordinary file, there is no free space left on the device. In *fcntl*, the setting or removing of record locks on a file cannot be accomplished because there are no more record entries left on the system.

29 ESPIPE Illegal seek
An *lseek* was issued to a pipe.

30 EROFS Read-only file system
An attempt to modify a file or directory was made on a device mounted read-only.

31 EMLINK Too many links
An attempt to make more than the maximum number of links (1000) to a file.

32 EPIPE Broken pipe
A write on a pipe for which there is no process to read the data. This condition normally generates a signal; the error is returned if the signal is ignored.

33 EDOM Math argument
The argument of a function in the math package (3M) is out of the domain of the function.

34 ERANGE Result too large
The value of a function in the math package (3M) is not representable within machine precision.

35 ENOMSG No message of desired type
An attempt was made to receive a message of a type that does not exist on the specified message queue; see *msgop*(2).

36 EIDRM Identifier Removed

This error is returned to processes that resume execution due to the removal of an identifier from the file system's name space [see *msgctl*(2), *semctl*(2), and *shmctl*(2)].

45 EDEADLK Deadlock

A deadlock situation was detected and avoided.

DEFINITIONS

Process ID

Each active process in the system is uniquely identified by a positive integer called a process ID. The range of this ID is from 1 to 30,000.

Parent Process ID

A new process is created by a currently active process; see *fork*(2). The parent process ID of a process is the process ID of its creator.

Process Group ID

Each active process is a member of a process group that is identified by a positive integer called the process group ID. This ID is the process ID of the group leader. This grouping permits the signaling of related processes; see *kill*(2).

Tty Group ID

Each active process can be a member of a terminal group that is identified by a positive integer called the tty group ID. This grouping is used to terminate a group of related processes upon termination of one of the processes in the group; see *exit*(2) and *signal*(2).

Real User ID and Real Group ID

Each user allowed on the system is identified by a positive integer called a real user ID.

Each user is also a member of a group. The group is identified by a positive integer called the real group ID.

An active process has a real user ID and real group ID that are set to the real user ID and real group ID, respectively, of the user responsible for the creation of the process.

Effective User ID and Effective Group ID

An active process has an effective user ID and an effective group ID that are used to determine file access permissions (see below). The effective user ID and effective group ID are equal to the process's real user ID and real group ID respectively, unless the process or one of its ancestors evolved from a file that had the set-user-ID bit or set-group ID bit set; see *exec*(2).

Super-user

A process is recognized as a ***super-user*** process and is granted special privileges if its effective user ID is 0.

Special Processes

The processes with a process ID of 0 and a process ID of 1 are special processes and are referred to as *proc0* and *proc1*.

Proc0 is the scheduler. *Proc1* is the initialization process (*init*). Proc1 is the ancestor of every other process in the system and is used to control the process structure.

File Descriptor

A file descriptor is a small integer used to do I/O on a file. The value of a file descriptor is from 0 to 19. A process may have no more than 20 file descriptors (0-19) open simultaneously. A file descriptor is returned by system calls such as *open*(2), or *pipe*(2). The file descriptor is used as an argument by calls such as *read*(2), *write*(2), *ioctl*(2), and *close*(2).

File Name

Names consisting of 1 to 14 characters may be used to name an ordinary file, special file, or directory.

These characters may be selected from the set of all character values excluding \0 (null) and the ASCII code for / (slash).

Note that it is generally unwise to use *, ?, [, or] as part of file names because of the special meaning attached to these characters by the shell. See *sh*(1). Although permitted, it is advisable to avoid the use of unprintable characters in file names.

Path Name and Path Prefix

A path name is a null-terminated character string starting with an optional slash (/), followed by zero or more directory names separated by slashes; optionally followed by a file name.

More precisely, a path name is a null-terminated character string constructed as follows:

<path-name>::=<file-name>|<path-prefix><file-name>|/
<path-prefix>::=<rtprefix>|/<rtprefix>
<rtprefix>::=<dirname>/|<rtprefix><dirname>/

where <file-name> is a string of 1 to 14 characters other than the ASCII slash and null, and <dirname> is a string of 1 to 14 characters with the same restrictions) that names a directory.

If a path name begins with a slash, the path search begins at the *root* directory. Otherwise, the search begins from the current working directory.

A slash by itself names the root directory.

Unless specifically stated otherwise, the null path name is treated as if it named a non-existent file.

Directory

Directory entries are called links. By convention, a directory contains at least two links, . and .., referred to as *dot* and *dot-dot* respectively. Dot refers to the directory itself and dot-dot refers to its parent directory.

Root Directory and Current Working Directory

Each process has associated with it a concept of a root directory and a current working directory for the purpose of resolving path name searches. The root directory of a process need not be the root directory of the root file system.

File Access Permissions

Read, write, and execute/search permissions on a file are granted to a process if one or more of the following are true:

The effective user ID of the process is super-user.

The effective user ID of the process matches the user ID of the owner of the file and the appropriate access bit of the "owner" portion (0700) of the file mode is set.

The effective user ID of the process does not match the user ID of the owner of the file, and the effective group ID of the process matches the group of the file and the appropriate access bit of the "group" portion (070) of the file mode is set.

The effective user ID of the process does not match the user ID of the owner of the file, and the effective group ID of the process does not match the group ID of the file, and the appropriate access bit of the "other" portion (07) of the file mode is set.

Otherwise, the corresponding permissions are denied.

Message Queue Identifier

A message queue identifier (msqid) is a unique positive integer created by a *msgget*(2) system call. Each msqid has a message queue and a data structure associated with it. The data structure is referred to as *msqid_ds* and contains the following members:

```
struct    ipc_perm msg_perm;   /* operation permission struct */
ushort    msg_qnum;            /* number of msgs on q */
ushort    msg_qbytes;          /* max number of bytes on q */
ushort    msg_lspid;           /* pid of last msgsnd operation */
ushort    msg_lrpid;           /* pid of last msgrcv operation */
time_t    msg_stime;           /* last msgsnd time */
time_t    msg_rtime;           /* last msgrcv time */
time_t    msg_ctime;           /* last change time */
                               /* Times measured in secs since */
                               /* 00:00:00 GMT, Jan. 1, 1970 */
```

Msg_perm is an ipc_perm structure that specifies the message operation permission (see below). This structure includes the following members:

```
ushort   cuid;      /* creator user id */
ushort   cgid;      /* creator group id */
ushort   uid;       /* user id */
ushort   gid;       /* group id */
ushort   mode;      /* r/w permission */
```

Msg_qnum is the number of messages currently on the queue. **Msg_qbytes** is the maximum number of bytes allowed on the queue. **Msg_lspid** is the process id of the last process that performed a *msgsnd* operation. **Msg_lrpid** is the process id of the last process that performed a *msgrcv* operation. **Msg_stime** is the time of the last *msgsnd* operation, **msg_rtime** is the time of the last *msgrcv* operation, and **msg_ctime** is the time of the last *msgctl*(2) operation that changed a member of the above structure.

Message Operation Permissions

In the *msgop*(2) and *msgctl*(2) system call descriptions, the permission required for an operation is given as "{token}", where "token" is the type of permission needed interpreted as follows:

00400	Read by user
00200	Write by user
00060	Read, Write by group
00006	Read, Write by others

Read and Write permissions on a msqid are granted to a process if one or more of the following are true:

The effective user ID of the process is super-user.

The effective user ID of the process matches **msg_perm.[c]uid** in the data structure associated with *msqid* and the appropriate bit of the "user" portion (0600) of **msg_perm.mode** is set.

The effective user ID of the process does not match **msg_perm.[c]uid** and the effective group ID of the process matches **msg_perm.[c]gid** and the appropriate bit of the "group" portion (060) of **msg_perm.mode** is set.

The effective user ID of the process does not match **msg_perm.[c]uid** and the effective group ID of the process does not match **msg_perm.[c]gid** and the appropriate bit of the "other" portion (06) of **msg_perm.mode** is set.

Otherwise, the corresponding permissions are denied.

Semaphore Identifier

A semaphore identifier (semid) is a unique positive integer created by a *semget*(2) system call. Each semid has a set of semaphores and a data structure associated with it. The data structure is referred to as *semid_ds* and contains the following members:

```
struct   ipc_perm sem_perm;   /* operation permission struct */
ushort   sem_nsems;           /* number of sems in set */
time_t   sem_otime;           /* last operation time */
time_t   sem_ctime;           /* last change time */
                              /* Times measured in secs since */
                              /* 00:00:00 GMT, Jan. 1, 1970 */
```

Sem_perm is an ipc_perm structure that specifies the semaphore operation permission (see below). This structure includes the following members:

```
ushort   cuid;     /* creator user id */
ushort   cgid;     /* creator group id */
ushort   uid;      /* user id */
ushort   gid;      /* group id */
ushort   mode;     /* r/a permission */
```

The value of **sem_nsems** is equal to the number of semaphores in the set. Each semaphore in the set is referenced by a positive integer referred to as a *sem_num*. Sem_num values run sequentially from 0 to the value of sem_nsems minus 1. **Sem_otime** is the time of the last *semop*(2) operation, and **sem_ctime** is the time of the last *semctl*(2) operation that changed a member of the above structure.

A semaphore is a data structure that contains the following members:

```
ushort   semval;     /* semaphore value */
short    sempid;     /* pid of last operation  */
ushort   semncnt;    /* # awaiting semval > cval */
ushort   semzcnt;    /* # awaiting semval = 0 */
```

Semval is a non-negative integer. **Sempid** is equal to the process ID of the last process that performed a semaphore operation on this semaphore. **Semncnt** is a count of the number of processes that are currently suspended awaiting this semaphore's semval to become greater than its current value. **Semzcnt** is a count of the number of processes that are currently suspended awaiting this semaphore's semval to become zero.

Semaphore Operation Permissions

In the *semop*(2) and *semctl*(2) system call descriptions, the permission required for an operation is given as "{token}", where "token" is the type of permission needed interpreted as follows:

00400	Read by user
00200	Alter by user
00060	Read, Alter by group
00006	Read, Alter by others

Read and Alter permissions on a semid are granted to a process if one or more of the following are true:

The effective user ID of the process is super-user.

The effective user ID of the process matches **sem_perm.[c]uid** in the data structure associated with *semid* and the appropriate bit of the "user" portion (0600) of **sem_perm.mode** is set.

The effective user ID of the process does not match **sem_perm.[c]uid** and the effective group ID of the process matches **sem_perm.[c]gid** and the appropriate bit of the "group" portion (060) of **sem_perm.mode** is set.

The effective user ID of the process does not match **sem_perm.[c]uid** and the effective group ID of the process does not match **sem_perm.[c]gid** and the appropriate bit of the "other" portion (06) of **sem_perm.mode** is set.

Otherwise, the corresponding permissions are denied.

Shared Memory Identifier

A shared memory identifier (shmid) is a unique positive integer created by a *shmget*(2) system call. Each shmid has a segment of memory (referred to as a shared memory segment) and a data structure associated with it. The data structure is referred to as *shmid_ds* and contains the following members:

```
struct   ipc_perm shm_perm;   /* operation permission struct */
int      shm_segsz;           /* size of segment */
ushort   shm_cpid;            /* creator pid */
ushort   shm_lpid;            /* pid of last operation */
short    shm_nattch;          /* number of current attaches */
time_t   shm_atime;           /* last attach time */
time_t   shm_dtime;           /* last detach time */
time_t   shm_ctime;           /* last change time */
                              /* Times measured in secs since */
                              /* 00:00:00 GMT, Jan. 1, 1970 */
```

Shm_perm is an ipc_perm structure that specifies the shared memory operation permission (see below). This structure includes the following members:

```
ushort   cuid;     /* creator user id */
ushort   cgid;     /* creator group id */
ushort   uid;      /* user id */
ushort   gid;      /* group id */
ushort   mode;     /* r/w permission */
```

Shm_segsz specifies the size of the shared memory segment. **Shm_cpid** is the process id of the process that created the shared memory identifier. **Shm_lpid** is the process id of the last process that performed a *shmop*(2) operation. **Shm_nattch** is the number of processes that currently have this segment attached. **Shm_atime** is the time of the last *shmat* operation, **shm_dtime** is the time of the last *shmdt* operation, and **shm_ctime** is the time of the last *shmctl*(2) operation that changed one of the members of the above structure.

Shared Memory Operation Permissions

In the *shmop*(2) and *shmctl*(2) system call descriptions, the permission required for an operation is given as "{token}", where "token" is the type of permission needed interpreted as follows:

00400	Read by user
00200	Write by user

00060	Read, Write by group
00006	Read, Write by others

Read and Write permissions on a shmid are granted to a process if one or more of the following are true:

The effective user ID of the process is super-user.

The effective user ID of the process matches **shm_perm.[c]uid** in the data structure associated with *shmid* and the appropriate bit of the "user" portion (0600) of **shm_perm.mode** is set.

The effective user ID of the process does not match **shm_perm.[c]uid** and the effective group ID of the process matches **shm_perm.[c]gid** and the appropriate bit of the "group" portion (060) of **shm_perm.mode** is set.

The effective user ID of the process does not match **shm_perm.[c]uid** and the effective group ID of the process does not match **shm_perm.[c]gid** and the appropriate bit of the "other" portion (06) of **shm_perm.mode** is set.

Otherwise, the corresponding permissions are denied.

SEE ALSO

close(2), ioctl(2), open(2), pipe(2), read(2), write(2), intro(3).

NAME

access — determine accessibility of a file

SYNOPSIS

int access (path, amode)
char *path;
int amode;

DESCRIPTION

Path points to a path name naming a file. *Access* checks the named file for accessibility according to the bit pattern contained in *amode*, using the real user ID in place of the effective user ID and the real group ID in place of the effective group ID. The bit pattern contained in *amode* is constructed as follows:

04	read
02	write
01	execute (search)
00	check existence of file

Access to the file is denied if one or more of the following are true:

[ENOTDIR]	A component of the path prefix is not a directory.
[ENOENT]	Read, write, or execute (search) permission is requested for a null path name.
[ENOENT]	The named file does not exist.
[EACCES]	Search permission is denied on a component of the path prefix.
[EROFS]	Write access is requested for a file on a read-only file system.
[ETXTBSY]	Write access is requested for a pure procedure (shared text) file that is being executed.
[EACCESS]	Permission bits of the file mode do not permit the requested access.
[EFAULT]	*Path* points outside the allocated address space for the process.

The owner of a file has permission checked with respect to the "owner" read, write, and execute mode bits Members of the file's group other than the owner have permissions checked with respect to the "group" mode bits, and all others have permissions checked with respect to the "other" mode bits.

RETURN VALUE

If the requested access is permitted, a value of 0 is returned. Otherwise, a value of −1 is returned and *errno* is set to indicate the error.

SEE ALSO

chmod(2), stat(2).

NAME

acct − enable or disable process accounting

SYNOPSIS

int acct (path)
char *path;

DESCRIPTION

Acct is used to enable or disable the system process accounting routine. If the routine is enabled, an accounting record will be written on an accounting file for each process that terminates. Termination can be caused by one of two things: an *exit* call or a signal; see *exit*(2) and *signal*(2). The effective user ID of the calling process must be super-user to use this call.

Path points to a path name naming the accounting file. The accounting file format is given in *acct*(4).

The accounting routine is enabled if *path* is non-zero and no errors occur during the system call. It is disabled if *path* is zero and no errors occur during the system call.

Acct will fail if one or more of the following are true:

[EPERM]	The effective user of the calling process is not super-user.
[EBUSY]	An attempt is being made to enable accounting when it is already enabled.
[ENOTDIR]	A component of the path prefix is not a directory.
[ENOENT]	One or more components of the accounting file path name do not exist.
[EACCES]	A component of the path prefix denies search permission.
[EACCES]	The file named by *path* is not an ordinary file.
[EACCES]	*Mode* permission is denied for the named accounting file.
[EISDIR]	The named file is a directory.
[EROFS]	The named file resides on a read-only file system.
[EFAULT]	*Path* points to an illegal address.

RETURN VALUE

Upon successful completion, a value of 0 is returned. Otherwise, a value of −1 is returned and *errno* is set to indicate the error.

SEE ALSO

exit(2), signal(2), acct(4).

NAME

alarm — set a process alarm clock

SYNOPSIS

unsigned alarm (sec)
unsigned sec;

DESCRIPTION

Alarm instructs the alarm clock of the calling process to send the signal **SIGALRM** to the calling process after the number of real time seconds specified by *sec* have elapsed; see *signal*(2).

Alarm requests are not stacked; successive calls reset the alarm clock of the calling process.

If *sec* is 0, any previously made alarm request is canceled.

RETURN VALUE

Alarm returns the amount of time previously remaining in the alarm clock of the calling process.

SEE ALSO

pause(2), signal(2).

NAME

brk, sbrk — change data segment space allocation

SYNOPSIS

```
int brk (endds)
char *endds;

char *sbrk (incr)
int incr;
```

DESCRIPTION

Brk and *sbrk* are used to change dynamically the amount of space allocated for the calling process's data segment; see *exec*(2). The change is made by resetting the process's break value and allocating the appropriate amount of space. The break value is the address of the first location beyond the end of the data segment. The amount of allocated space increases as the break value increases. The newly allocated space is set to zero.

Brk sets the break value to *endds* and changes the allocated space accordingly.

Sbrk adds *incr* bytes to the break value and changes the allocated space accordingly. *Incr* can be negative, in which case the amount of allocated space is decreased.

Brk and *sbrk* will fail without making any change in the allocated space if one or more of the following are true:

> Such a change would result in more space being allocated than is allowed by a system-imposed maximum (see *ulimit*(2)). [ENOMEM]
>
> Such a change would result in the break value being greater than or equal to the start address of any attached shared memory segment (see *shmop*(2)).

RETURN VALUE

Upon successful completion, *brk* returns a value of 0 and *sbrk* returns the old break value. Otherwise, a value of −1 is returned and *errno* is set to indicate the error.

SEE ALSO

exec(2), shmop(2), ulimit(2).

NAME

chdir – change working directory

SYNOPSIS

int chdir (path)
char *path;

DESCRIPTION

Path points to the path name of a directory. *Chdir* causes the named directory to become the current working directory, the starting point for path searches for path names not beginning with /.

Chdir will fail and the current working directory will be unchanged if one or more of the following are true:

[ENOTDIR]	A component of the path name is not a directory.
[ENOENT]	The named directory does not exist.
[EACCES]	Search permission is denied for any component of the path name.
[EFAULT]	*Path* points outside the allocated address space of the process.

RETURN VALUE

Upon successful completion, a value of 0 is returned. Otherwise, a value of −1 is returned and *errno* is set to indicate the error.

SEE ALSO

chroot(2).

NAME

chmod — change mode of file

SYNOPSIS

int chmod (path, mode)
char *path;
int mode;

DESCRIPTION

Path points to a path name naming a file. *Chmod* sets the access permission portion of the named file's mode according to the bit pattern contained in *mode*.

Access permission bits are interpreted as follows:

04000	Set user ID on execution.
02000	Set group ID on execution.
01000	Save text image after execution.
00400	Read by owner.
00200	Write by owner.
00100	Execute (search if a directory) by owner.
00070	Read, write, execute (search) by group.
00007	Read, write, execute (search) by others.

The effective user ID of the process must match the owner of the file or be super-user to change the mode of a file.

If the effective user ID of the process is not super-user, mode bit 01000 (save text image on execution) is cleared.

If the effective user ID of the process is not super-user and the effective group ID of the process does not match the group ID of the file, mode bit 02000 (set group ID on execution) is cleared.

If an executable file is prepared for sharing then mode bit 01000 prevents the system from abandoning the swap-space image of the program-text portion of the file when its last user terminates. Thus, when the next user of the file executes it, the text need not be read from the file system but can simply be swapped in, saving time.

Chmod will fail and the file mode will be unchanged if one or more of the following are true:

[ENOTDIR] A component of the path prefix is not a directory.

[ENOENT] The named file does not exist.

[EACCES]	Search permission is denied on a component of the path prefix.
[EPERM]	The effective user ID does not match the owner of the file and the effective user ID is not super-user.
[EROFS]	The named file resides on a read-only file system.
[EFAULT]	*Path* points outside the allocated address space of the process.

RETURN VALUE

Upon successful completion, a value of 0 is returned. Otherwise, a value of −1 is returned and *errno* is set to indicate the error.

SEE ALSO

chown(2), mknod(2).

NAME

chown − change owner and group of a file

SYNOPSIS

int chown (path, owner, group)
char *path;
int owner, group;

DESCRIPTION

Path points to a path name naming a file. The owner ID and group ID of the named file are set to the numeric values contained in *owner* and *group* respectively.

Only processes with effective user ID equal to the file owner or super-user may change the ownership of a file.

If *chown* is invoked by other than the super-user, the set-user-ID and set-group-ID bits of the file mode, 04000 and 02000 respectively, will be cleared.

Chown will fail and the owner and group of the named file will remain unchanged if one or more of the following are true:

[ENOTDIR] A component of the path prefix is not a directory.

[ENOENT] The named file does not exist.

[EACCES] Search permission is denied on a component of the path prefix.

[EPERM] The effective user ID does not match the owner of the file and the effective user ID is not super-user.

[EROFS] The named file resides on a read-only file system.

[EFAULT] *Path* points outside the allocated address space of the process.

RETURN VALUE

Upon successful completion, a value of 0 is returned. Otherwise, a value of −1 is returned and *errno* is set to indicate the error.

SEE ALSO

chmod(2).
chown(1) in the *UNIX Programmer's Manual—Volume 1: Commands and Utilities.*

NAME

chroot − change root directory

SYNOPSIS

int chroot (path)
char *path;

DESCRIPTION

Path points to a path name naming a directory. *Chroot* causes the named directory to become the root directory, the starting point for path searches for path names beginning with /. The user's working directory is unaffected by the *chroot* system call.

The effective user ID of the process must be super-user to change the root directory.

The .. entry in the root directory is interpreted to mean the root directory itself. Thus, .. cannot be used to access files outside the subtree rooted at the root directory.

Chroot will fail and the root directory will remain unchanged if one or more of the following are true:

[ENOTDIR] Any component of the path name is not a directory.

[ENOENT] The named directory does not exist.

[EPERM] The effective user ID is not super-user.

[EFAULT] *Path* points outside the allocated address space of the process.

RETURN VALUE

Upon successful completion, a value of 0 is returned. Otherwise, a value of −1 is returned and *errno* is set to indicate the error.

SEE ALSO

chdir(2).

NAME

close − close a file descriptor

SYNOPSIS

int close (fildes)
int fildes;

DESCRIPTION

Fildes is a file descriptor obtained from a *creat*, *open*, *dup*, *fcntl*, or *pipe* system call. *Close* closes the file descriptor indicated by *fildes*. All outstanding record locks owned by the process (on the file indicated by *fildes*) are removed.

Close will fail if *fildes* is not a valid open file descriptor.

RETURN VALUE

Upon successful completion, a value of 0 is returned. Otherwise, a value of −1 is returned and *errno* is set to indicate the error.

SEE ALSO

creat(2), dup(2), exec(2), fcntl(2), open(2), pipe(2).

NAME

creat — create a new file or rewrite an existing one

SYNOPSIS

int creat (path, mode)
char *path;
int mode;

DESCRIPTION

Creat creates a new ordinary file or prepares to rewrite an existing file named by the path name pointed to by *path*.

If the file exists, the length is truncated to 0 and the mode and owner are unchanged. Otherwise, the file's owner ID is set to the effective user ID, of the process the group ID of the process is set to the effective group ID, of the process and the low-order 12 bits of the file mode are set to the value of *mode* modified as follows:

> All bits set in the process's file mode creation mask are cleared. See *umask*(2).
>
> The "save text image after execution bit" of the mode is cleared. See *chmod*(2).

Upon successful completion, the file descriptor is returned and the file is open for writing, even if the mode does not permit writing. The file pointer is set to the beginning of the file. The file descriptor is set to remain open across *exec* system calls. See *fcntl*(2). No process may have more than 20 files open simultaneously. A new file may be created with a mode that forbids writing.

Creat will fail if one or more of the following are true:

[ENOTDIR]	A component of the path prefix is not a directory.
[ENOENT]	A component of the path prefix does not exist.
[EACCES]	Search permission is denied on a component of the path prefix.
[ENOENT]	The path name is null.
[EACCES]	The file does not exist and the directory in which the file is to be created does not permit writing.
[EROFS]	The named file resides or would reside on a read-only file system.
[ETXTBSY]	The file is a pure procedure (shared text) file that is being executed.

[EACCES]	The file exists and write permission is denied.
[EISDIR]	The named file is an existing directory.
[EMFILE]	Twenty (20) file descriptors are currently open.
[EFAULT]	*Path* points outside the allocated address space of the process.
[ENFILE]	The system file table is full.

RETURN VALUE

Upon successful completion, a non-negative integer, namely the file descriptor, is returned. Otherwise, a value of −1 is returned and *errno* is set to indicate the error.

SEE ALSO

chmod(2), close(2), dup(2), fcntl(2), lseek(2), open(2), read(2), umask(2), write(2).

NAME

dup − duplicate an open file descriptor

SYNOPSIS

int dup (fildes)
int fildes;

DESCRIPTION

Fildes is a file descriptor obtained from a *creat*, *open*, *dup*, *fcntl*, or *pipe* system call. *Dup* returns a new file descriptor having the following in common with the original:

Same open file (or pipe).

Same file pointer (i.e., both file descriptors share one file pointer).

Same access mode (read, write or read/write).

The new file descriptor is set to remain open across *exec* system calls. See *fcntl*(2).

The file descriptor returned is the lowest one available.

Dup will fail if one or more of the following are true:

[EBADF] *Fildes* is not a valid open file descriptor.

[EMFILE] Twenty (20) file descriptors are currently open.

RETURN VALUE

Upon successful completion a non-negative integer, namely the file descriptor, is returned. Otherwise, a value of −1 is returned and *errno* is set to indicate the error.

SEE ALSO

creat(2), close(2), exec(2), fcntl(2), open(2), pipe(2).

NAME

execl, execv, execle, execve, execlp, execvp — execute a file

SYNOPSIS

```
int execl (path, arg0, arg1, ..., argn, 0)
char *path, *arg0, *arg1, ..., *argn;

int execv (path, argv)
char *path, *argv[ ];

int execle (path, arg0, arg1, ..., argn, 0, envp)
char *path, *arg0, *arg1, ..., *argn, *envp[ ];

int execve (path, argv, envp)
char *path, *argv[ ], *envp[ ];

int execlp (file, arg0, arg1, ..., argn, 0)
char *file, *arg0, *arg1, ..., *argn;

int execvp (file, argv)
char *file, *argv[ ];
```

DESCRIPTION

Exec in all its forms transforms the calling process into a new process. The new process is constructed from an ordinary, executable file called the *new process file*. This file consists of a header (see *a.out*(4)), a text segment, and a data segment. The data segment contains an initialized portion and an uninitialized portion (bss). There can be no return from a successful *exec* because the calling process is overlaid by the new process.

When a C program is executed, it is called as follows:

```
main (argc, argv, envp)
int argc;
char **argv, **envp;
```

where *argc* is the argument count and *argv* is an array of character pointers to the arguments themselves. As indicated, *argc* is conventionally at least one and the first member of the array points to a string containing the name of the file.

Path points to a path name that identifies the new process file.

File points to the new process file. The path prefix for this file is obtained by a search of the directories passed as the *environment* line "PATH =" (see *environ*(5)). The environment is supplied by the shell (see *sh*(1)).

Arg0, *arg1*, ..., *argn* are pointers to null-terminated character strings. These strings constitute the argument list available to the new process. By convention, at least *arg0* must be present and point to a string that is the same as *path* (or its last component).

Argv is an array of character pointers to null-terminated strings. These strings constitute the argument list available to the new process. By convention, *argv* must have at least one member, and it must point to a string that is the same as *path* (or its last component). *Argv* is terminated by a null pointer.

Envp is an array of character pointers to null-terminated strings. These strings constitute the environment for the new process. *Envp* is terminated by a null pointer. For *execl* and *execv*, the C run-time start-off routine places a pointer to the environment of the calling process in the global cell:

```
extern char **environ;
```

and it is used to pass the environment of the calling process to the new process.

File descriptors open in the calling process remain open in the new process, except for those whose close-on-exec flag is set; see *fcntl*(2). For those file descriptors that remain open, the file pointer is unchanged.

Signals set to terminate the calling process will be set to terminate the new process. Signals set to be ignored by the calling process will be set to be ignored by the new process. Signals set to be caught by the calling process will be set to terminate new process; see *signal*(2).

If the set-user-ID mode bit of the new process file is set (see *chmod*(2)), *exec* sets the effective user ID of the new process to the owner ID of the new process file. Similarly, if the set-group-ID mode bit of the new process file is set, the effective group ID of the new process is set to the group ID of the new process file. The real user ID and real group ID of the new process remain the same as those of the calling process.

The shared memory segments attached to the calling process will not be attached to the new process (see *shmop*(2)).

Profiling is disabled for the new process; see *profil*(2).

The new process also inherits the following attributes from the calling process:

nice value (see *nice*(2))
process ID
parent process ID
process group ID
semadj values (see *semop*(2))
tty group ID (see *exit*(2) and *signal*(2))
trace flag (see *ptrace*(2) request 0)
time left until an alarm clock signal (see *alarm*(2))
current working directory
root directory
file mode creation mask (see *umask*(2))
file size limit (see *ulimit*(2))
utime, *stime*, *cutime*, and *cstime* (see *times*(2))

Exec will fail and return to the calling process if one or more of the following are true:

[ENOENT] One or more components of the new process path name of the file do not exist.

[ENOTDIR] A component of the new process path of the file prefix is not a directory.

[EACCES] Search permission is denied for a directory listed in the new process file's path prefix.

[EACCES] The new process file is not an ordinary file.

[EACCES] The new process file mode denies execution permission.

[ENOEXEC] The exec is not an *execlp* or *execvp*, and the new process file has the appropriate access permission but an invalid magic number in its header.

[ETXTBSY] The new process file is a pure procedure (shared text) file that is currently open for writing by some process.

[ENOMEM] The new process requires more memory than is allowed by the system-imposed maximum MAXMEM.

[E2BIG] The number of bytes in the new process's argument list is greater than the system-imposed limit of 5120 bytes.

[EFAULT]	The new process file is not as long as indicated by the size values in its header.
[EFAULT]	*Path*, *argv*, or *envp* point to an illegal address.

RETURN VALUE

If *exec* returns to the calling process an error has occurred; the return value will be −1 and *errno* will be set to indicate the error.

SEE ALSO

alarm(2), exit(2), fork(2), nice(2), ptrace(2), semop(2), signal(2), times(2), ulimit(2), umask(2), a.out(4), environ(5).
sh(1) in the *UNIX Programmer's Manual—Volume 1: Commands and Utilities*.

NAME

exit, _exit – terminate process

SYNOPSIS

void exit (status)
int status;
void _exit (status)
int status;

DESCRIPTION

Exit terminates the calling process with the following consequences:

All of the file descriptors open in the calling process are closed.

If the parent process of the calling process is executing a *wait*, it is notified of the calling process's termination and the low order eight bits (i.e., bits 0377) of *status* are made available to it; see *wait* (2).

If the parent process of the calling process is not executing a *wait*, the calling process is transformed into a zombie process. A *zombie process* is a process that only occupies a slot in the process table. It has no other space allocated either in user or kernel space. The process table slot that it occupies is partially overlaid with time accounting information (see **<sys/proc.h>**) to be used by *times*.

The parent process ID of all of the calling process's existing child processes and zombie processes is set to 1. This means the initialization process (see *intro* (2)) inherits each of these processes.

Each attached shared memory segment is detached and the value of **shm_nattach** in the data structure associated with its shared memory identifier is decremented by 1.

For each semaphore for which the calling process has set a semadj value (see *semop* (2)), that semadj value is added to the semval of the specified semaphore.

If the process has a process, text, or data lock, an *unlock* is performed (see *plock* (2)).

An accounting record is written on the accounting file if the system's accounting routine is enabled; see *acct* (2).

If the process ID, tty group ID, and process group ID of the calling process are equal, the **SIGHUP** signal is sent to each process that has a process group ID equal to that of the calling process.

The C function *exit* may cause cleanup actions before the process exits. The function *_exit* circumvents all cleanup.

SEE ALSO

acct(2), intro(2), plock(2), semop(2), signal(2), wait(2).

WARNING

See *WARNING* in *signal*(2).

NAME

fcntl − file control

SYNOPSIS

#include <fcntl.h>

int fcntl (fildes, cmd, arg)
int fildes, cmd, arg;

DESCRIPTION

Fcntl provides for control over open files. *Fildes* is an open file descriptor obtained from a *creat*, *open*, *dup*, *fcntl*, or *pipe* system call.

The *commands* available are:

F_DUPFD Return a new file descriptor as follows:

Lowest numbered available file descriptor greater than or equal to *arg*.

Same open file (or pipe) as the original file.

Same file pointer as the original file (i.e., both file descriptors share one file pointer).

Same access mode (read, write, or read/write).

Same file status flags (i.e., both file descriptors share the same file status flags).

The close-on-exec flag associated with the new file descriptor is set to remain open across *exec*(2) system calls.

F_GETFD Get the close-on-exec flag associated with the file descriptor *fildes*. If the low-order bit is **0** the file will remain open across *exec*, otherwise the file will be closed upon execution of *exec*.

F_SETFD Set the close-on-exec flag associated with *fildes* to the low-order bit of *arg* (**0** or **1** as above).

F_GETFL Get *file* status flags.

F_SETFL Set *file* status flags to *arg*. Only certain flags can be set; see *fcntl*(5).

F_GETLK Get the first lock which blocks the lock description given by the variable of type *struct flock* pointed to by *arg*. The information retrieved overwrites the information passed to *fcntl* in the *flock* structure. If no lock is found that would prevent this lock from being created, then the structure is passed back unchanged except for the lock type which will be set to F_UNLCK.

F_SETLK
Set or clear a file segment lock according to the variable of type *struct flock* pointed to by *arg* [see *fcntl*(5)]. The *cmd* F_SETLK is used to establish read (F_RDLCK) and write (F_WRLCK) locks, as well as remove either type of lock (F_UNLCK). If a read or write lock cannot be set, *fcntl* will return immediately with an error value of −1.

F_SETLKW
This *cmd* is the same as F_SETLK except that if a read or write lock is blocked by other locks, the process will sleep until the segment is free to be locked.

A read lock prevents any process from write locking the protected area. More than one read lock may exist for a given segment of a file at a given time. The file descriptor on which a read lock is being placed must have been opened with read access.

A write lock prevents any process from read locking or write locking the protected area. Only one write lock may exist for a given segment of a file at a given time. The file descriptor on which a write lock is being placed must have been opened with write access.

The structure *flock* describes the type (*l_type*), starting offset (*l_whence*), relative offset (*l_start*), size (*l_len*), and process id (*l_pid*) of the segment of the file to be affected. The process id field is only used with the F_GETLK *cmd* to return the value for a block in lock. Locks may start and extend beyond the current end of a file, but may not be negative relative to the beginning of the file. A lock may be set to always extend to the end of file by setting *l_len* to zero (0). If such a lock also has *l_start* set to zero (0), the whole file will be locked. Changing or unlocking a segment from the middle of a larger locked segment leaves two smaller segments for either end. Locking a segment that is already locked by the calling process causes the old lock type to be removed and the new lock type to take affect. All locks associated with a file for a given process are removed when a file descriptor for that file is closed by that process or the process holding that file descriptor terminates. Locks are not inherited by a child process in a *fork*(2) system call.

Fcntl will fail if one or more of the following are true:

[EBADF]	*Fildes* is not a valid open file descriptor.
[EMFILE]	*Cmd* is F_DUPFD and 20 file descriptors are currently open.
[EINFILE]	*Cmd* is F_DUPFD and *arg* is negative or greater than 20.
[EINVAL]	*Cmd* is F_GETLK, F_SETLK, or SETLKW and *arg* or the data it points to is not valid.
[EACCESS]	*Cmd* is F_SETLK the type of lock (*l_type*) is a read (F_RDLCK) or write (F_WRLCK) lock and the segment of a file to be locked is already write locked by another process or the type is a write lock and the segment of a file to be locked is already read or write locked by another process.
[EMFILE]	*Cmd* is F_SETLK or F_SETLKW, the type of lock is a read or write lock and there are no more file locking headers available (too many files have segments locked).
[ENOSPC]	*Cmd* is F_SETLK or F_SETLKW, the type of lock is a read or write lock and there are no more file locking headers available (too many files have segments locked) or there are no more record locks available (too many file segments locked).
[EDEADLK]	*Cmd* is F_SETLK, when the lock is blocked by some lock from another process and sleeping (waiting) for that lock to become free, this causes a deadlock situation.

RETURN VALUE

Upon successful completion, the value returned depends on *cmd* as follows:

F_DUPFD	A new file descriptor.
F_GETFD	Value of flag (only the low-order bit is defined).
F_SETFD	Value other than −1.
F_GETFL	Value of file flags.

F_SETFL	Value other than −1.
F_GETLK	Value other that −1.
F_SETLK	Value other than −1.
F_SETLKW	Value other than −1.

Otherwise, a value of −1 is returned and *errno* is set to indicate the error.

SEE ALSO

close(2), exec(2), open(2), fcntl(5).

NAME

fork — create a new process

SYNOPSIS

int fork ()

DESCRIPTION

Fork causes creation of a new process. The new process (child process) is an exact copy of the calling process (parent process). This means the child process inherits the following attributes from the parent process:

environment
close-on-exec flag (see *exec*(2))
signal handling settings (i.e., **SIG_DFL**, **SIG_ING**, function address)
set-user-ID mode bit
set-group-ID mode bit
profiling on/off status
nice value (see *nice*(2))
all attached shared memory segments (see *shmop*(2))
process group ID
tty group ID (see *exit*(2) and *signal*(2))
trace flag (see *ptrace*(2) request 0)
time left until an alarm clock signal (see *alarm*(2))
current working directory
root directory
file mode creation mask (see *umask*(2))
file size limit (see *ulimit*(2))

The child process differs from the parent process in the following ways:

The child process has a unique process ID.

The child process has a different parent process ID (i.e., the process ID of the parent process).

The child process has its own copy of the parent's file descriptors. Each of the child's file descriptors shares a common file pointer with the corresponding file descriptor of the parent.

All semadj values are cleared (see *semop*(2)).

Process locks, text locks and data locks are not inherited by the child (see *plock*(2)).

The child process's *utime*, *stime*, *cutime*, and *cstime* are set to 0. The time left until an alarm clock signal is reset to 0.

Fork will fail and no child process will be created if one or more of the following are true:

[EAGAIN] The system-imposed limit on the total number of processes under execution would be exceeded.

[EAGAIN] The system-imposed limit on the total number of processes under execution by a single user would be exceeded.

RETURN VALUE

Upon successful completion, *fork* returns a value of 0 to the child process and returns the process ID of the child process to the parent process. Otherwise, a value of −1 is returned to the parent process, no child process is created, and *errno* is set to indicate the error.

SEE ALSO

exec(2), nice(2), plock(2), ptrace(2), semop(2), shmop(2), signal(2), times(2), ulimit(2), umask(2), wait(2).

NAME

getpid, getpgrp, getppid — get process, process group, and parent process IDs

SYNOPSIS

int getpid ()

int getpgrp ()

int getppid ()

DESCRIPTION

Getpid returns the process ID of the calling process.

Getpgrp returns the process group ID of the calling process.

Getppid returns the parent process ID of the calling process.

SEE ALSO

exec(2), fork(2), intro(2), setpgrp(2), signal(2).

NAME

getuid, geteuid, getgid, getegid − get real user, effective user, real group, and effective group IDs

SYNOPSIS

unsigned short getuid ()

unsigned short geteuid ()

unsigned short getgid ()

unsigned short getegid ()

DESCRIPTION

Getuid returns the real user ID of the calling process.

Geteuid returns the effective user ID of the calling process.

Getgid returns the real group ID of the calling process.

Getegid returns the effective group ID of the calling process.

SEE ALSO

intro(2), setuid(2).

NAME

ioctl − control device

SYNOPSIS

ioctl (fildes, request, arg)
int fildes, request;

DESCRIPTION

Ioctl performs a variety of functions on character special files (devices). The write-ups of various devices in Section 7 of the *UNIX Programmer's Manual—Volume 3: System Administration Facilities* discuss how *ioctl* applies to them.

Ioctl will fail if one or more of the following are true:

[EBADF] *Fildes* is not a valid open file descriptor.

[ENOTTY] *Fildes* is not associated with a character special device.

[EINVAL] *Request* or *arg* is not valid. See Section 7 of the *UNIX Programmer's Manual—Volume 3: System Administration Facilities.*

[EINTR] A signal was caught during the *ioctl* system call.

RETURN VALUE

If an error has occurred, a value of −1 is returned and *errno* is set to indicate the error.

SEE ALSO

termio(7) in the *UNIX Programmer's Manual—Volume 3: System Administration Facilities.*

NAME

kill − send a signal to a process or a group of processes

SYNOPSIS

int kill (pid, sig)
int pid, sig;

DESCRIPTION

Kill sends a signal to a process or a group of processes. The process or group of processes to which the signal is to be sent is specified by *pid*. The signal that is to be sent is specified by *sig* and is either one from the list given in *signal*(2), or 0. If *sig* is 0 (the null signal), error checking is performed but no signal is actually sent. This can be used to check the validity of *pid*.

The real or effective user ID of the sending process must match the real or effective user ID of the receiving process, unless the effective user ID of the sending process is super-user.

The processes with a process ID of 0 and a process ID of 1 are special processes (see *intro*(2)) and will be referred to below as *proc0* and *proc1*, respectively.

If *pid* is greater than zero, *sig* will be sent to the process whose process ID is equal to *pid*. *Pid* may equal 1.

If *pid* is 0, *sig* will be sent to all processes excluding *proc0* and *proc1* whose process group ID is equal to the process group ID of the sender.

If *pid* is −1 and the effective user ID of the sender is not super-user, *sig* will be sent to all processes excluding *proc0* and *proc1* whose real user ID is equal to the effective user ID of the sender.

If *pid* is −1 and the effective user ID of the sender is super-user, *sig* will be sent to all processes excluding *proc0* and *proc1*.

If *pid* is negative but not −1, *sig* will be sent to all processes whose process group ID is equal to the absolute value of *pid*.

Kill will fail and no signal will be sent if one or more of the following are true:

[EINVAL] *Sig* is not a valid signal number.

[EINVAL] *Sig* is SIGKILL and *pid* is 1 (proc1).

[ESRCH] No process can be found corresponding to that specified by *pid*.

[EPERM] The user ID of the sending process is not super-user, and its real or effective user ID does not match the real or effective user ID of the receiving process.

RETURN VALUE

Upon successful completion, a value of 0 is returned. Otherwise, a value of −1 is returned and *errno* is set to indicate the error.

SEE ALSO

getpid(2), setpgrp(2), signal(2).
kill(1) in the *UNIX Programmer's Manual—Volume 1: Commands and Utilities*.

NAME

link − link to a file

SYNOPSIS

int link (path1, path2)
char *path1, *path2;

DESCRIPTION

Path1 points to a path name naming an existing file. *Path2* points to a path name naming the new directory entry to be created. *Link* creates a new link (directory entry) for the existing file.

Link will fail and no link will be created if one or more of the following are true:

[ENOTDIR] A component of either path prefix is not a directory.

[ENOENT] A component of either path prefix does not exist.

[EACCES] A component of either path prefix denies search permission.

[ENOENT] The file named by *path1* does not exist.

[EEXIST] The link named by *path2* exists.

[EPERM] The file named by *path1* is a directory and the effective user ID is not super-user.

[EXDEV] The link named by *path2* and the file named by *path1* are on different logical devices (file systems).

[ENOENT] *Path2* points to a null path name.

[EACCES] The requested link requires writing in a directory with a mode that denies write permission.

[EROFS] The requested link requires writing in a directory on a read-only file system.

[EFAULT] *Path* points outside the allocated address space of the process.

[EMLINK] The maximum number of links to a file would be exceeded.

RETURN VALUE

Upon successful completion, a value of 0 is returned. Otherwise, a value of −1 is returned and *errno* is set to indicate the error.

SEE ALSO

unlink(2).

NAME

lseek − move read/write file pointer

SYNOPSIS

long lseek (fildes, offset, whence)
int fildes;
long offset;
int whence;

DESCRIPTION

Fildes is a file descriptor returned from a *creat*, *open*, *dup*, or *fcntl* system call. *Lseek* sets the file pointer associated with *fildes* as follows:

If *whence* is 0, the pointer is set to *offset* bytes.

If *whence* is 1, the pointer is set to its current location plus *offset*.

If *whence* is 2, the pointer is set to the size of the file plus *offset*.

Upon successful completion, the resulting pointer location, as measured in bytes from the beginning of the file, is returned.

Lseek will fail and the file pointer will remain unchanged if one or more of the following are true:

[EBADF] *Fildes* is not an open file descriptor.

[ESPIPE] *Fildes* is associated with a pipe or fifo.

[EINVAL and SIGSYS signal]
Whence is not 0, 1, or 2.

[EINVAL] The resulting file pointer would be negative.

Some devices are incapable of seeking. The value of the file pointer associated with such a device is undefined.

RETURN VALUE

Upon successful completion, a non-negative integer indicating the file pointer value is returned. Otherwise, a value of −1 is returned and *errno* is set to indicate the error.

SEE ALSO

creat(2), dup(2), fcntl(2), open(2).

NAME

mknod − make a directory, or a special or ordinary file

SYNOPSIS

int mknod (path, mode, dev)
char *path;
int mode, dev;

DESCRIPTION

Mknod creates a new file named by the path name pointed to by *path*. The mode of the new file is initialized from *mode*. Where the value of *mode* is interpreted as follows:

- 0170000 file type; one of the following:
  - 0010000 fifo special
  - 0020000 character special
  - 0040000 directory
  - 0060000 block special
  - 0100000 or 0000000 ordinary file
- 0004000 set user ID on execution
- 0002000 set group ID on execution
- 0001000 save text image after execution
- 0000777 access permissions; constructed from the following
  - 0000400 read by owner
  - 0000200 write by owner
  - 0000100 execute (search on directory) by owner
  - 0000070 read, write, execute (search) by group
  - 0000007 read, write, execute (search) by others

The owner ID of the file is set to the effective user ID of the process. The group ID of the file is set to the effective group ID of the process.

Values of *mode* other than those above are undefined and should not be used. The low-order 9 bits of *mode* are modified by the process's file mode creation mask: all bits set in the process's file mode creation mask are cleared. See *umask*(2). If *mode* indicates a block or character special file, *dev* is a configuration-dependent specification of a character or block I/O device. If *mode* does not indicate a block special or character special device, *dev* is ignored.

Mknod may be invoked only by the super-user for file types other than FIFO special.

Mknod will fail and the new file will not be created if one or more of the following are true:

[EPERM] The effective user ID of the process is not super-user.

[ENOTDIR] A component of the path prefix is not a directory.

[ENOENT] A component of the path prefix does not exist.

[EROFS] The directory in which the file is to be created is located on a read-only file system.

[EEXIST] The named file exists.

[EFAULT] *Path* points outside the allocated address space of the process.

RETURN VALUE

Upon successful completion a value of 0 is returned. Otherwise, a value of −1 is returned and *errno* is set to indicate the error.

SEE ALSO

chmod(2), exec(2), umask(2), fs(4).
mkdir(1) in the *UNIX Programmer's Manual—Volume 1: Commands and Utilities*.

NAME

mount — mount a file system

SYNOPSIS

int mount (spec, dir, rwflag)
char *spec, *dir;
int rwflag;

DESCRIPTION

Mount requests that a removable file system contained on the block special file identified by *spec* be mounted on the directory identified by *dir*. *Spec* and *dir* are pointers to path names.

Upon successful completion, references to the file *dir* will refer to the root directory on the mounted file system.

The low-order bit of *rwflag* is used to control write permission on the mounted file system; if **1**, writing is forbidden, otherwise writing is permitted according to individual file accessibility.

Mount may be invoked only by the super-user.

Mount will fail if one or more of the following are true:

[EPERM]	The effective user ID is not super-user.
[ENOENT]	Any of the named files does not exist.
[ENOTDIR]	A component of a path prefix is not a directory.
[ENOTBLK]	*Spec* is not a block special device.
[ENXIO]	The device associated with *spec* does not exist.
[ENOTDIR]	*Dir* is not a directory.
[EFAULT]	*Spec* or *dir* points outside the allocated address space of the process.
[EBUSY]	*Dir* is currently mounted on, is someone's current working directory, or is otherwise busy.
[EBUSY]	The device associated with *spec* is currently mounted.
[EBUSY]	There are no more mount table entries.

RETURN VALUE

Upon successful completion a value of 0 is returned. Otherwise, a value of −1 is returned and *errno* is set to indicate the error.

SEE ALSO

umount(2).

NAME

msgctl − message control operations

SYNOPSIS

#include <sys/types.h>
#include <sys/ipc.h>
#include <sys/msg.h>

int msgctl (msqid, cmd, buf)
int msqid, cmd;
struct msqid_ds *buf;

DESCRIPTION

Msgctl provides a variety of message control operations as specified by *cmd*. The following *cmd*s are available:

IPC_STAT Place the current value of each member of the data structure associated with *msqid* into the structure pointed to by *buf*. The contents of this structure are defined in *intro*(2). {READ}

IPC_SET Set the value of the following members of the data structure associated with *msqid* to the corresponding value found in the structure pointed to by *buf*:

msg_perm.uid
msg_perm.gid
msg_perm.mode /* only low 9 bits */
msg_qbytes

This *cmd* can only be executed by a process that has an effective user ID equal to either that of super user or to the value of **msg_perm.uid** in the data structure associated with *msqid*. Only super user can raise the value of **msg_qbytes**.

IPC_RMID Remove the message queue identifier specified by *msqid* from the system and destroy the message queue and data structure associated with it. This *cmd* can only be executed by a process that has an effective user ID equal to either that of super user or to the value of **msg_perm.uid** in the data structure associated with *msqid*.

Msgctl will fail if one or more of the following are true:

[EINVAL] *Msqid* is not a valid message queue identifier.

[EINVAL] *Cmd* is not a valid command.

[EACCES] *Cmd* is equal to **IPC_STAT** and {READ} operation permission is denied to the calling process (see *intro*(2)).

[EPERM] *Cmd* is equal to **IPC_RMID** or **IPC_SET**. The effective user ID of the calling process is not equal to that of super user and it is not equal to the value of **msg_perm.uid** in the data structure associated with *msqid*.

[EPERM] *Cmd* is equal to **IPC_SET**, an attempt is being made to increase to the value of **msg_qbytes**, and the effective user ID of the calling process is not equal to that of super user.

[EFAULT] *Buf* points to an illegal address.

RETURN VALUE

Upon successful completion, a value of 0 is returned. Otherwise, a value of −1 is returned and *errno* is set to indicate the error.

SEE ALSO

intro(2), msgget(2), msgop(2).

NAME

msgget — get message queue

SYNOPSIS

#include <sys/types.h>
#include <sys/ipc.h>
#include <sys/msg.h>

int msgget (key, msgflg)
key_t key;
int msgflg;

DESCRIPTION

Msgget returns the message queue identifier associated with *key*.

A message queue identifier and associated message queue and data structure (see *intro*(2)) are created for *key* if one of the following are true:

10 *Key* is equal to **IPC_PRIVATE**.

Key does not already have a message queue identifier associated with it, and (*msgflg* & **IPC_CREAT**) is "true".

Upon creation, the data structure associated with the new message queue identifier is initialized as follows:

Msg_perm.cuid, **msg_perm.uid**, **msg_perm.cgid**, and **msg_perm.gid** are set equal to the effective user ID and effective group ID, respectively, of the calling process.

The low-order 9 bits of **msg_perm.mode** are set equal to the low-order 9 bits of *msgflg*.

Msg_qnum, **msg_lspid**, **msg_lrpid**, **msg_stime**, and **msg_rtime** are set equal to 0.

Msg_ctime is set equal to the current time.

Msg_qbytes is set equal to the system limit.

Msgget will fail if one or more of the following are true:

[EACCES] A message queue identifier exists for *key*, but operation permission (see *intro*(2)) as specified by the low-order 9 bits of *msgflg* would not be granted.

[ENOENT] A message queue identifier does not exist for *key* and (*msgflg* & **IPC_CREAT**) is "false".

[ENOSPC] A message queue identifier is to be created but the system-imposed limit on the maximum number of allowed message queue identifiers system wide would be exceeded.

[EEXIST] A message queue identifier exists for *key* but ((*msgflg*& IPC_CREAT) & *msgflg* & IPC_EXCL)) is "true".

RETURN VALUE

Upon successful completion, a non-negative integer, namely a message queue identifier, is returned. Otherwise, a value of −1 is returned and *errno* is set to indicate the error.

SEE ALSO

intro(2), msgctl(2), msgop(2).

NAME

msgop − message operations

SYNOPSIS

#include <sys/types.h>
#include <sys/ipc.h>
#include <sys/msg.h>

int msgsnd (msqid, msgp, msgsz, msgflg)
int msqid;
struct msgbuf *msgp;
int msgsz, msgflg;

int msgrcv (msqid, msgp, msgsz, msgtyp, msgflg)
int msqid;
struct msgbuf *msgp;
int msgsz;
long msgtyp;
int msgflg;

DESCRIPTION

Msgsnd is used to send a message to the queue associated with the message queue identifier specified by *msqid*. {WRITE} *Msgp* points to a structure containing the message. This structure is composed of the following members:

```
long    mtype;      /* message type */
char    mtext[];    /* message text */
```

Mtype is a positive integer that can be used by the receiving process for message selection (see *msgrcv* below). *Mtext* is any text of length *msgsz* bytes. *Msgsz* can range from 0 to a system-imposed maximum.

Msgflg specifies the action to be taken if one or more of the following are true:

> The number of bytes already on the queue is equal to **msg_qbytes** (see *intro*(2)).
>
> The total number of messages on all queues system-wide is equal to the system-imposed limit.

These actions are as follows:

> If (*msgflg* & **IPC_NOWAIT**) is "true", the message will not be sent and the calling process will return immediately.

If (*msgflg* & **IPC_NOWAIT**) is "false", the calling process will suspend execution until one of the following occurs:

The condition responsible for the suspension no longer exists, in which case the message is sent.

Msqid is removed from the system (see *msgctl*(2)). When this occurs, *errno* is set equal to EIDRM, and a value of −1 is returned.

The calling process receives a signal that is to be caught. In this case the message is not sent and the calling process resumes execution in the manner prescribed in *signal*(2)).

Msgsnd will fail and no message will be sent if one or more of the following are true:

[EINVAL] *Msqid* is not a valid message queue identifier.

[EACCES] Operation permission is denied to the calling process (see *intro*(2)).

[EINVAL] *Mtype* is less than 1.

[EAGAIN] The message cannot be sent for one of the reasons cited above and (*msgflg* & **IPC_NOWAIT**) is "true".

[EINVAL] *Msgsz* is less than zero or greater than the system-imposed limit.

[EFAULT] *Msgp* points to an illegal address.

Upon successful completion, the following actions are taken with respect to the data structure associated with *msqid* (see intro (2)).

Msg_qnum is incremented by 1.

Msg_lspid is set equal to the process ID of the calling process.

Msg_stime is set equal to the current time.

Msgrcv reads a message from the queue associated with the message queue identifier specified by *msqid* and places it in the structure pointed to by *msgp*. {READ} This structure is composed of the following members:

```
long    mtype;      /* message type */
char    mtext[];    /* message text */
```

Mtype is the received message's type as specified by the sending process. *Mtext* is the text of the message. *Msgsz* specifies the size in bytes of *mtext*. The received message is truncated to *msgsz* bytes if it is larger than *msgsz* and (*msgflg* & **MSG_NOERROR**) is "true". The truncated part of the message is lost and no indication of the truncation is given to the calling process.

Msgtyp specifies the type of message requested as follows:

> If *msgtyp* is equal to 0, the first message on the queue is received.
>
> If *msgtyp* is greater than 0, the first message of type *msgtyp* is received.
>
> If *msgtyp* is less than 0, the first message of the lowest type that is less than or equal to the absolute value of *msgtyp* is received.

Msgflg specifies the action to be taken if a message of the desired type is not on the queue. These are as follows:

> If (*msgflg* & **IPC_NOWAIT**) is "true", the calling process will return immediately with a return value of −1 and *errno* set to ENOMSG.
>
> If (*msgflg* & **IPC_NOWAIT**) is "false", the calling process will suspend execution until one of the following occurs:
>
> > A message of the desired type is placed on the queue.
> >
> > *Msqid* is removed from the system. When this occurs, *errno* is set equal to EIDRM, and a value of −1 is returned.
> >
> > The calling process receives a signal that is to be caught. In this case a message is not received and the calling process resumes execution in the manner prescribed in *signal*(2)).

Msgrcv will fail and no message will be received if one or more of the following are true:

[EINVAL] *Msqid* is not a valid message queue identifier.

[EACCES] Operation permission is denied to the calling process.

[EINVAL] *Msgsz* is less than 0.

[E2BIG] Mtext is greater than *msgsz* and (*msgflg* & **MSG_NOERROR**) is "false".

[ENOMSG] The queue does not contain a message of the desired type and (*msgtyp* & **IPC_NOWAIT**) is "true".

[EFAULT] *Msgp* points to an illegal address.

Upon successful completion, the following actions are taken with respect to the data structure associated with *msqid* (see intro (2)).

Msg_qnum is decremented by 1.

Msg_lrpid is set equal to the process ID of the calling process.

Msg_rtime is set equal to the current time.

RETURN VALUES

If *msgsnd* or *msgrcv* return due to the receipt of a signal, a value of −1 is returned to the calling process and *errno* is set to EINTR. If they return due to removal of *msqid* from the system, a value of −1 is returned and *errno* is set to EIDRM.

Upon successful completion, the return value is as follows:

Msgsnd returns a value of 0.

Msgrcv returns a value equal to the number of bytes actually placed into *mtext*.

Otherwise, a value of −1 is returned and *errno* is set to indicate the error.

SEE ALSO

intro(2), msgctl(2), msgget(2), signal(2).

NAME

nice − change priority of a process

SYNOPSIS

int nice (incr)
int incr;

DESCRIPTION

Nice adds the value of *incr* to the nice value of the calling process. A process's *nice value* is a positive number for which a more positive value results in lower CPU priority.

A maximum nice value of 39 and a minimum nice value of 0 are imposed by the system. Requests for values above or below these limits result in the nice value being set to the corresponding limit.

[EPERM] *Nice* will fail and not change the nice value if *incr* is negative or greater than 40 and the effective user ID of the calling process is not super-user.

RETURN VALUE

Upon successful completion, *nice* returns the new nicc value minus 20. Otherwise, a value of −1 is returned and *errno* is set to indicate the error.

SEE ALSO

exec(2).
nice(1) in the *UNIX Programmer's Manual—Volume 1: Commands and Utilities.*

NAME

open — open for reading or writing

SYNOPSIS

#include <fcntl.h>
int open (path, oflag [, mode])
char *path;
int oflag, mode;

DESCRIPTION

Path points to a path name naming a file. *Open* opens a file descriptor for the named file and sets the file status flags according to the value of *oflag*. *Oflag* values are constructed by or-ing flags from the following list (only one of the first three flags below may be used):

O_RDONLY Open for reading only.

O_WRONLY Open for writing only.

O_RDWR Open for reading and writing.

O_NDELAY This flag may affect subsequent reads and writes. See *read* (2) and *write* (2).

When opening a FIFO with O_RDONLY or O_WRONLY set:

If O_NDELAY is set:

An *open* for reading-only will return without delay. An *open* for writing-only will return an error if no process currently has the file open for reading.

If O_NDELAY is clear:

An *open* for reading-only will block until a process opens the file for writing. An *open* for writing-only will block until a process opens the file for reading.

When opening a file associated with a communication line:

If O_NDELAY is set:

The open will return without waiting for carrier.

If O_NDELAY is clear:

The open will block until carrier is present.

O_APPEND If set, the file pointer will be set to the end of the file prior to each write.

O_CREAT If the file exists, this flag has no effect. Otherwise, the owner ID of the file is set to the effective user ID of the process, the group ID of the file is set to the effective group ID of the process, and the low-order 12 bits of the file mode are set to the value of *mode* modified as follows (see *creat* (2)):

All bits set in the file mode creation mask of the process are cleared. See *umask* (2).

The "save text image after execution bit" of the mode is cleared. See *chmod* (2).

O_TRUNC If the file exists, its length is truncated to 0 and the mode and owner are unchanged.

O_EXCL If O_EXCL and O_CREAT are set, *open* will fail if the file exists.

The file pointer used to mark the current position within the file is set to the beginning of the file.

The new file descriptor is set to remain open across *exec* system calls. See *fcntl* (2).

The named file is opened unless one or more of the following are true:

[ENOTDIR] A component of the path prefix is not a directory.

[ENOENT] O_CREAT is not set and the named file does not exist.

[EACCES] A component of the path prefix denies search permission.

[EACCES] *Oflag* permission is denied for the named file.

[EISDIR] The named file is a directory and *oflag* is write or read/write.

[EROFS] The named file resides on a read-only file system and *oflag* is write or read/write.

[EMFILE]	Twenty (20) file descriptors are currently open.
[ENXIO]	The named file is a character special or block special file, and the device associated with this special file does not exist.
[ETXTBSY]	The file is a pure procedure (shared text) file that is being executed and *oflag* is write or read/write.
[EFAULT]	*Path* points outside the allocated address space of the process.
[EEXIST]	O_CREAT and O_EXCL are set, and the named file exists.
[ENXIO]	O_NDELAY is set, the named file is a FIFO, O_WRONLY is set, and no process has the file open for reading.
[EINTR]	A signal was caught during the *open* system call.
[ENFILE]	The system file table is full.

RETURN VALUE

Upon successful completion, the file descriptor is returned. Otherwise, a value of −1 is returned and *errno* is set to indicate the error.

SEE ALSO

chmod(2), close(2), creat(2), dup(2), fcntl(2), lseek(2), read(2), umask(2), write(2).

NAME

pause − suspend process until signal

SYNOPSIS

pause ()

DESCRIPTION

Pause suspends the calling process until it receives a signal. The signal must be one that is not currently set to be ignored by the calling process.

If the signal causes termination of the calling process, *pause* will not return.

If the signal is *caught* by the calling process and control is returned from the signal-catching function (see *signal*(2)), the calling process resumes execution from the point of suspension; with a return value of −1 from *pause* and *errno* set to EINTR.

SEE ALSO

alarm(2), kill(2), signal(2), wait(2).

NAME

pipe — create an interprocess channel

SYNOPSIS

int pipe (fildes)
int fildes[2];

DESCRIPTION

Pipe creates an I/O mechanism called a pipe and returns two file descriptors, *fildes*[0] and *fildes*[1]. *Fildes*[0] is opened for reading and *fildes*[1] is opened for writing.

Up to 5120 bytes of data are buffered by the pipe before the writing process is blocked. A read only file descriptor *fildes*[0] accesses the data written to *fildes*[1] on a first-in-first-out (FIFO) basis.

[EMFILE] *Pipe* will fail if 19 or more file descriptors are currently open.

[ENFILE] The system file table is full.

RETURN VALUE

Upon successful completion, a value of 0 is returned. Otherwise, a value of −1 is returned and *errno* is set to indicate the error.

SEE ALSO

read(2), write(2).
sh(1) in the *UNIX Programmer's Manual—Volume 1: Commands and Utilities.*

NAME

plock − lock process, text, or data in memory

SYNOPSIS

#include <sys/lock.h>

int plock (op)
int op;

DESCRIPTION

Plock allows the calling process to lock its text segment (text lock), its data segment (data lock), or both its text and data segments (process lock) into memory. Locked segments are immune to all routine swapping. *Plock* also allows these segments to be unlocked. The effective user ID of the calling process must be super-user to use this call. *Op* specifies the following:

PROCLOCK − lock text and data segments into memory (process lock)

TXTLOCK − lock text segment into memory (text lock)

DATLOCK − lock data segment into memory (data lock)

UNLOCK − remove locks

Plock will fail and not perform the requested operation if one or more of the following are true:

[EPERM] The effective user ID of the calling process is not super-user.

[EINVAL] *Op* is equal to **PROCLOCK** and a process lock, a text lock, or a data lock already exists on the calling process.

[EINVAL] *Op* is equal to **TXTLOCK** and a text lock, or a process lock already exists on the calling process.

[EINVAL] *Op* is equal to **DATLOCK** and a data lock, or a process lock already exists on the calling process.

[EINVAL] *Op* is equal to **UNLOCK** and no type of lock exists on the calling process.

RETURN VALUE

Upon successful completion, a value of 0 is returned to the calling process. Otherwise, a value of −1 is returned and *errno* is set to indicate the error.

SEE ALSO

exec(2), exit(2), fork(2).

NAME

profil − execution time profile

SYNOPSIS

void profil (buff, bufsiz, offset, scale)
char *buff;
int bufsiz, offset, scale;

DESCRIPTION

Buff points to an area of core whose length (in bytes) is given by *bufsiz*. After this call, the user's program counter (pc) is examined each clock tick (60th second); *offset* is subtracted from it, and the result multiplied by *scale*. If the resulting number corresponds to a word inside *buff*, that word is incremented.

The scale is interpreted as an unsigned, fixed-point fraction with binary point at the left: 0177777 (octal) gives a 1-1 mapping of pc's to words in *buff*; 077777 (octal) maps each pair of instruction words together. 02(octal) maps all instructions onto the beginning of *buff* (producing a non-interrupting core clock).

Profiling is turned off by giving a *scale* of 0 or 1. It is rendered ineffective by giving a *bufsiz* of 0. Profiling is turned off when an *exec* is executed, but remains on in child and parent both after a *fork*. Profiling will be turned off if an update in *buff* would cause a memory fault.

RETURN VALUE

Not defined.

SEE ALSO

monitor(3C).
prof(1) in the *UNIX Programmer's Manual—Volume 1: Commands and Utilities.*

NAME

ptrace − process trace

SYNOPSIS

int ptrace (request, pid, addr, data);
int request, pid, addr, data;

DESCRIPTION

Ptrace provides a means by which a parent process may control the execution of a child process. Its primary use is for the implementation of breakpoint debugging; see *sdb*(1). The child process behaves normally until it encounters a signal (see *signal*(2) for the list), at which time it enters a stopped state and its parent is notified via *wait*(2). When the child is in the stopped state, its parent can examine and modify its "core image" using *ptrace*. Also, the parent can cause the child either to terminate or continue, with the possibility of ignoring the signal that caused it to stop.

The *request* argument determines the precise action to be taken by *ptrace* and is one of the following:

0 This request must be issued by the child process if it is to be traced by its parent. It turns on the child's trace flag that stipulates that the child should be left in a stopped state upon receipt of a signal rather than the state specified by *func*; see *signal*(2). The *pid*, *addr*, and *data* arguments are ignored, and a return value is not defined for this request. Peculiar results will ensue if the parent does not expect to trace the child.

The remainder of the requests can only be used by the parent process. For each, *pid* is the process ID of the child. The child must be in a stopped state before these requests are made.

1, 2 With these requests, the word at location *addr* in the address space of the child is returned to the parent process. If I and D space are separated (as on some computers), request **1** returns a word from I space, and request **2** returns a word from D space. If I and D space are not separated (as on the 3B20 computer and some other computers), either request **1** or request **2** may be used with equal results. The *data* argument is ignored. These two requests will fail if *addr* is not the start address of a word, in which case a value of −1 is returned to the parent process and the parent's *errno* is set to EIO.

3 With this request, the word at location *addr* in the child's USER area in the system's address space (see **<sys/user.h>**) is returned to the parent process. Addresses in this area generally range from 0 to 2048 on the 3B20 computer and others. The *data* argument is ignored. This request will fail if *addr* is not the start address of a word or is outside the USER area, in which case a value of −1 is returned to the parent process and the parent's *errno* is set to EIO.

4, 5 With these requests, the value given by the *data* argument is written into the address space of the child at location *addr*. If I and D space are separated (as on some computers) request **4** writes a word into I space, and request **5** writes a word into D space. If I and D space are not separated (as on the 3B20 computer and others), either request **4** or request **5** may be used with equal results. Upon successful completion, the value written into the address space of the child is returned to the parent. These two requests will fail if *addr* is a location in a pure procedure space and another process is executing in that spacc, or *addr* is not thc start address of a word. Upon failure a value of −1 is returned to the parent process and the parent's *errno* is set to EIO.

6 With this request, a few entries in the child's USER area can be written. *Data* gives the value that is to be written and *addr* is the location of the entry. The few entries that can be written are:

the general registers (i.e., registers 0−11 on the 3B20 computer, registers 0−7 on some others, and registers 0−15 on some other machines)

the condition codes of the Processor Status Word on the 3B20 computer

the floating point status register and six floating point registers on some computers certain bits of the Processor Status Word on some computers (i.e, bits 0–4 and 8–11)

certain bits of the Processor Status Longword on the some computers (i.e., bits 0–7, 16–20, and 30–31).

7 This request causes the child to resume execution. If the *data* argument is 0, all pending signals including the one that caused the child to stop are canceled before it resumes execution. If the *data* argument is a valid signal number, the child resumes execution as if it had incurred that signal, and any other pending signals are canceled. The *addr* argument must be equal to 1 for this request. Upon successful completion, the value of *data* is returned to the parent. This request will fail if *data* is not 0 or a valid signal number, in which case a value of −1 is returned to the parent process and the parent's *errno* is set to EIO.

8 This request causes the child to terminate with the same consequences as *exit*(2).

9 This request sets the trace bit in the Processor Status Word of the child (i.e., bit 4 on some computers) and then executes the same steps as listed above for request **7**. The trace bit causes an interrupt upon completion of one machine instruction. This effectively allows single stepping of the child. On the 3B20 computer, there is no trace bit; and this request returns an error.

To forestall possible fraud, *ptrace* inhibits the set-user-id facility on subsequent *exec*(2) calls. If a traced process calls *exec*, it will stop before executing the first instruction of the new image showing signal **SIGTRAP**.

GENERAL ERRORS

Ptrace will in general fail if one or more of the following are true:

[EIO] *Request* is an illegal number.

[ESRCH] *Pid* identifies a child that does not exist or has not executed a *ptrace* with request **0**.

SEE ALSO

exec(2), signal(2), wait(2).
sdb(1) in the *UNIX Programmer's Manual—Volume 1: Commands and Utilities.*

NAME

read − read from file

SYNOPSIS

int read (fildes, buf, nbyte)
int fildes;
char *buf;
unsigned nbyte;

DESCRIPTION

Fildes is a file descriptor obtained from a *creat*, *open*, *dup*, *fcntl*, or *pipe* system call.

Read attempts to read *nbyte* bytes from the file associated with *fildes* into the buffer pointed to by *buf*.

On devices capable of seeking, the *read* starts at a position in the file given by the file pointer associated with *fildes*. Upon return from *read*, the file pointer is incremented by the number of bytes actually read.

Devices that are incapable of seeking always read from the current position. The value of a file pointer associated with such a file is undefined.

Upon successful completion, *read* returns the number of bytes actually read and placed in the buffer; this number may be less than *nbyte* if the file is associated with a communication line (see *ioctl*(2) and *termio*(7)), or if the number of bytes left in the file is less than *nbyte* bytes. A value of 0 is returned when an end-of-file has been reached.

When attempting to read from an empty pipe (or FIFO):

> If O_NDELAY is set, the read will return a 0.
>
> If O_NDELAY is clear, the read will block until data is written to the file or the file is no longer open for writing.

When attempting to read a file associated with a tty that has no data currently available:

> If O_NDELAY is set, the read will return a 0.
>
> If O_NDELAY is clear, the read will block until data becomes available.

Read will fail if one or more of the following are true:

[EBADF] *Fildes* is not a valid file descriptor open for reading.

[EFAULT] *Buf* points outside the allocated address space.

[EINTR] A signal was caught during the *read* system call.

RETURN VALUE

Upon successful completion a non-negative integer is returned indicating the number of bytes actually read. Otherwise, a −1 is returned and *errno* is set to indicate the error.

SEE ALSO

creat(2), dup(2), fcntl(2), ioctl(2), open(2), pipe(2).
termio(7) in the *UNIX Programmer's Manual—Volume 3: System Administration Facilities.*

NAME

semctl – semaphore control operations

SYNOPSIS

```
#include <sys/types.h>
#include <sys/ipc.h>
#include <sys/sem.h>

int semctl (semid, semnum, cmd, arg)
int semid, cmd;
int semnum;
union semun {
      int val;
      struct semid_ds *buf;
      ushort *array;
} arg;
```

DESCRIPTION

Semctl provides a variety of semaphore control operations as specified by *cmd*.

The following *cmd*s are executed with respect to the semaphore specified by *semid* and *semnum:*

GETVAL Return the value of semval (see *intro*(2)). {READ}

SETVAL Set the value of semval to *arg.val*. {ALTER} When this cmd is successfully executed, the semadj value corresponding to the specified semaphore in all processes is cleared.

GETPID Return the value of sempid. {READ}

GETNCNT Return the value of semncnt. {READ}

GETZCNT Return the value of semzcnt. {READ}

The following *cmd*s return and set, respectively, every semval in the set of semaphores.

GETALL Place semvals into array pointed to by *arg.array*. {READ}

SETALL Set semvals according to the array pointed to by *arg.array*. {ALTER} When this cmd is successfully executed the semadj values corresponding to each specified semaphore in all processes are cleared.

The following *cmd*s are also available:

IPC_STAT Place the current value of each member of the data structure associated with *semid* into the structure pointed to by *arg.buf*. The contents of this structure are defined in *intro*(2). {READ}

IPC_SET Set the value of the following members of the data structure associated with *semid* to the corresponding value found in the structure pointed to by *arg.buf*:
sem_perm.uid
sem_perm.gid
sem_perm.mode /* only low 9 bits */

This cmd can only be executed by a process that has an effective user ID equal to either that of super-user or to the value of **sem_perm.uid** in the data structure associated with *semid*.

IPC_RMID Remove the semaphore identifier specified by *semid* from the system and destroy the set of semaphores and data structure associated with it. This cmd can only be executed by a process that has an effective user ID equal to either that of super-user or to the value of **sem_perm.uid** in the data structure associated with *semid*.

Semctl will fail if one or more of the following are true:

[EINVAL] *Semid* is not a valid semaphore identifier.

[EINVAL] *Semnum* is less than zero or greater than **sem_nsems**.

[EINVAL] *Cmd* is not a valid command.

[EACCES] Operation permission is denied to the calling process (see *intro*(2)).

[ERANGE] *Cmd* is **SETVAL** or **SETALL** and the value to which semval is to be set is greater than the system imposed maximum.

[EPERM] *Cmd* is equal to **IPC_RMID** or **IPC_SET** and the effective user ID of the calling process is not equal to that of super-user and it is not equal to the value of **sem_perm.uid** in the data structure associated with *semid*.

[EFAULT] *Arg.buf* points to an illegal address.

RETURN VALUE

Upon successful completion, the value returned depends on *cmd* as follows:

GETVAL	The value of semval.
GETPID	The value of sempid.
GETNCNT	The value of semncnt.
GETZCNT	The value of semzcnt.
All others	A value of 0.

Otherwise, a value of −1 is returned and *errno* is set to indicate the error.

SEE ALSO

intro(2), semget(2), semop(2).

NAME

semget – get set of semaphores

SYNOPSIS

```
#include <sys/types.h>
#include <sys/ipc.h>
#include <sys/sem.h>

int semget (key, nsems, semflg)
key_t key;
int nsems, semflg;
```

DESCRIPTION

Semget returns the semaphore identifier associated with *key*.

A semaphore identifier and associated data structure and set containing *nsems* semaphores (see *intro*(2)) are created for *key* if one of the following are true:

> *Key* is equal to **IPC_PRIVATE**.
>
> *Key* does not already have a semaphore identifier associated with it, and (*semflg* & **IPC_CREAT**) is "true".

Upon creation, the data structure associated with the new semaphore identifier is initialized as follows:

> **Sem_perm.cuid**, **sem_perm.uid**, **sem_perm.cgid**, and **sem_perm.gid** are set equal to the effective user ID and effective group ID, respectively, of the calling process.
>
> The low-order 9 bits of **sem_perm.mode** are set equal to the low-order 9 bits of *semflg*.
>
> **Sem_nsems** is set equal to the value of *nsems*.
>
> **Sem_otime** is set equal to 0 and **sem_ctime** is set equal to the current time.

Semget will fail if one or more of the following are true:

[EINVAL] *Nsems* is either less than or equal to zero or greater than the system-imposed limit.

[EACCES] A semaphore identifier exists for *key*, but operation permission (see *intro*(2)) as specified by the low-order 9 bits of *semflg* would not be granted.

[EINVAL] A semaphore identifier exists for *key*, but the number of semaphores in the set associated with it is less than *nsems* and *nsems* is not equal to zero.

[ENOENT] A semaphore identifier does not exist for *key* and (*semflg* & **IPC_CREAT**) is "false".

[ENOSPC] A semaphore identifier is to be created but the system-imposed limit on the maximum number of allowed semaphore identifiers system wide would be exceeded.

[ENOSPC] A semaphore identifier is to be created but the system-imposed limit on the maximum number of allowed semaphores system wide would be exceeded.

[EEXIST] A semaphore identifier exists for *key* but ((*semflg* & IPC_CREAT) **and** (*semflg* & **IPC_EXCL**)) is "true".

RETURN VALUE

Upon successful completion, a non-negative integer, namely a semaphore identifier, is returned. Otherwise, a value of −1 is returned and *errno* is set to indicate the error.

SEE ALSO

intro(2), semctl(2), semop(2).

NAME

semop — semaphore operations

SYNOPSIS

```
#include <sys/types.h>
#include <sys/ipc.h>
#include <sys/sem.h>

int semop (semid, sops, nsops)
int semid;
struct sembuf **sops;
int nsops;
```

DESCRIPTION

Semop is used to automatically perform an array of semaphore operations on the set of semaphores associated with the semaphore identifier specified by *semid*. *Sops* is a pointer to the array of semaphore-operation structures. *Nsops* is the number of such structures in the array. The contents of each structure includes the following members:

```
short    sem_num;    /* semaphore number */
short    sem_op;     /* semaphore operation */
short    sem_flg;    /* operation flags */
```

Each semaphore operation specified by *sem_op* is performed on the corresponding semaphore specified by *semid* and *sem_num*.

Sem_op specifies one of three semaphore operations as follows:

If *sem_op* is a negative integer, one of the following will occur: {ALTER}

If semval (see *intro*(2)) is greater than or equal to the absolute value of *sem_op*, the absolute value of *sem_op* is subtracted from semval. Also, if (*sem_flg* & **SEM_UNDO**) is "true", the absolute value of *sem_op* is added to the calling process's semadj value (see *exit*(2)) for the specified semaphore.

If semval is less than the absolute value of *sem_op* and (*sem_flg* & **IPC_NOWAIT**) is "true", *semop* will return immediately.

If semval is less than the absolute value of *sem_op* and (*sem_flg* & **IPC_NOWAIT**) is "false", *semop* will increment the semncnt associated with the specified semaphore and suspend execution of the calling process until one of the following conditions occur.

Semval becomes greater than or equal to the absolute value of *sem_op*. When this occurs, the value of semncnt associated with the specified semaphore is decremented, the absolute value of *sem_op* is subtracted from semval and, if (*sem_flg* & **SEM_UNDO**) is "true", the absolute value of *sem_op* is added to the calling process's semadj value for the specified semaphore.

The semid for which the calling process is awaiting action is removed from the system (see *semctl*(2)). When this occurs, *errno* is set equal to EIDRM, and a value of −1 is returned.

The calling process receives a signal that is to be caught. When this occurs, the value of semncnt associated with the specified semaphore is decremented, and the calling process resumes execution in the manner prescribed in *signal*(2).

If *sem_op* is a positive integer, the value of *sem_op* is added to semval and, if (*sem_flg* & **SEM_UNDO**) is "true", the value of *sem_op* is subtracted from the calling process's semadj value for the specified semaphore. {ALTER}

If *sem_op* is zero, one of the following will occur: {READ}

If semval is zero, *semop* will return immediately.

If semval is not equal to zero and (*sem_flg* & **IPC_NOWAIT**) is "true", *semop* will return immediately.

If semval is not equal to zero and (*sem_flg* & **IPC_NOWAIT**) is "false", *semop* will increment the semzcnt associated with the specified semaphore and suspend execution of the calling process until one of the following occurs:

Semval becomes zero, at which time the value of semzcnt associated with the specified semaphore is decremented.

The semid for which the calling process is awaiting action is removed from the system. When this occurs, *errno* is set equal to EIDRM, and a value of −1 is returned.

The calling process receives a signal that is to be caught. When this occurs, the value of semzcnt associated with the specified semaphore is decremented, and the calling process resumes execution in the manner prescribed in *signal*(2).

Semop will fail if one or more of the following are true for any of the semaphore operations specified by *sops*:

[EINVAL] *Semid* is not a valid semaphore identifier.

[EFBIG] *Sem_num* is less than zero or greater than or equal to the number of semaphores in the set associated with *semid*.

[E2BIG] *Nsops* is greater than the system-imposed maximum.

[EACCES] Operation permission is denied to the calling process (see *intro*(2)).

[EAGAIN] The operation would result in suspension of the calling process but (*sem_flg* & **IPC_NOWAIT**) is "true".

[ENOSPC] The limit on the number of individual processes requesting an **SEM_UNDO** would be exceeded.

[EINVAL] The number of individual semaphores for which the calling process requests a **SEM_UNDO** would exceed the limit.

[ERANGE] An operation would cause a semval to overflow the system-imposed limit.

[ERANGE] An operation would cause a semadj value to overflow the system-imposed limit.

[EFAULT] *Sops* points to an illegal address.

Upon successful completion, the value of sempid for each semaphore specified in the array pointed to by *sops* is set equal to the process ID of the calling process.

RETURN VALUE

If *semop* returns due to the receipt of a signal, a value of −1 is returned to the calling process and *errno* is set to EINTR. If it returns due to the removal of a *semid* from the system, a value of −1 is returned and *errno* is set to EIDRM.

Upon successful completion, the value of semval at the time of the call for the last operation in the array pointed to by *sops* is returned. Otherwise, a value of −1 is returned and *errno* is set to indicate the error.

SEE ALSO

exec(2), exit(2), fork(2), intro(2), semctl(2), semget(2).

NAME

setpgrp − set process group ID

SYNOPSIS

int setpgrp ()

DESCRIPTION

Setpgrp sets the process group ID of the calling process to the process ID of the calling process and returns the new process group ID.

RETURN VALUE

Setpgrp returns the value of the new process group ID.

SEE ALSO

exec(2), fork(2), getpid(2), intro(2), kill(2), signal(2).

NAME

setuid, setgid − set user and group IDs

SYNOPSIS

int setuid (uid)
int uid;

int setgid (gid)
int gid;

DESCRIPTION

Setuid (*setgid*) is used to set the real user (group) ID and effective user (group) ID of the calling process.

If the effective user ID of the calling process is super-user, the real user (group) ID and effective user (group) ID are set to *uid* (*gid*).

If the effective user ID of the calling process is not super-user, but its real user (group) ID is equal to *uid* (*gid*), the effective user (group) ID is set to *uid* (*gid*).

If the effective user ID of the calling process is not super-user, but the saved set-user (group) ID from *exec*(2) is equal to *uid* (*gid*), the effective user (group) ID is set to *uid* (*gid*).

Setuid (*setgid*) will fail if the real user (group) ID of the calling process is not equal to *uid* (*gid*) and its effective user ID is not super-user. [EPERM]

The *uid* is out of range. [EINVAL]

RETURN VALUE

Upon successful completion, a value of 0 is returned. Otherwise, a value of −1 is returned and *errno* is set to indicate the error.

SEE ALSO

getuid(2), intro(2).

NAME

shmctl — shared memory control operations

SYNOPSIS

```
#include <sys/types.h>
#include <sys/ipc.h>
#include <sys/shm.h>

int shmctl (shmid, cmd, buf)
int shmid, cmd;
struct shmid_ds *buf;
```

DESCRIPTION

Shmctl provides a variety of shared memory control operations as specified by *cmd*. The following *cmd*s are available:

IPC_STAT Place the current value of each member of the data structure associated with *shmid* into the structure pointed to by *buf*. The contents of this structure are defined in [EINVAL] *intro*(2). {READ}

IPC_SET Set the value of the following members of the data structure associated with *shmid* to the corresponding value found in the structure pointed to by *buf*:
shm_perm.uid
shm_perm.gid
shm_perm.mode /* only low 9 bits */

This *cmd* can only be executed by a process that has an effective user ID equal to either that of super-user or to the value of **shm_perm.uid** in the data structure associated with *shmid*.

IPC_RMID Remove the shared memory identifier specified by *shmid* from the system and destroy the shared memory segment and data structure associated with it. This *cmd* can only be executed by a process that has an effective user ID equal to either that of super-user or to the value of **shm_perm.uid** in the data structure associated with *shmid*.

SHM_LOCK Lock the shared memory segment specified by *shmid* in memory. This *cmd* can only be executed by a process that has an effective usr ID equal to super-user.

SHM_UNLOCK
Unlock the shared memory segment specified by *shmid*. This *cmd* can only be executed by a process that has an effective usr ID equal to super-user.

Shmctl will fail if one or more of the following are true:

Shmid is not a valid shared memory identifier. [EINVAL]

Cmd is not a valid command. [EINVAL]

Cmd is equal to **IPC_STAT** and {READ} operation permission is denied to the calling process [see *intro*(2)]. [EACCES]

Cmd is equal to **IPC_RMID** or **IPC_SET** and the effective user ID of the calling process is not equal to that of super-user and it is not equal to the value of **shm_perm.uid** in the data structure associated with *shmid*. [EPERM]

Cmd is equal to **SHM_LOCK** or **SHM_UNLOCK** and the effective user ID of the calling process is not equal to that of super-user. [EPERM]

Cmd is equal to **SHM_UNLOCK** and the shared-memory segment specified by *shmid* is not locked in memory. [EINVAL] *Buf* points to an illegal address. [EFAULT]

RETURN VALUE

Upon successful completion, a value of 0 is returned. Otherwise, a value of −1 is returned and *errno* is set to indicate the error.

SEE ALSO

shmget(2), shmop(2).

NAME

shmget − get shared memory segment

SYNOPSIS

#include <sys/types.h>
#include <sys/ipc.h>
#include <sys/shm.h>

int shmget (key, size, shmflg)
key_t key;
int size, shmflg;

DESCRIPTION

Shmget returns the shared memory identifier associated with *key*.

A shared memory identifier and associated data structure and shared memory segment of size *size* bytes (see *intro*(2)) are created for *key* if one of the following are true:

> *Key* is equal to **IPC_PRIVATE**.
>
> *Key* does not already have a shared memory identifier associated with it, and (*shmflg* & **IPC_CREAT**) is "true".

Upon creation, the data structure associated with the new shared memory identifier is initialized as follows:

> **Shm_perm.cuid**, **shm_perm.uid**, **shm_perm.cgid**, and **shm_perm.gid** are set equal to the effective user ID and effective group ID, respectively, of the calling process.
>
> The low-order 9 bits of **shm_perm.mode** are set equal to the low-order 9 bits of *shmflg*. **Shm_segsz** is set equal to the value of *size*.
>
> **Shm_lpid**, **shm_nattch**, **shm_atime**, and **shm_dtime** are set equal to 0.
>
> **Shm_ctime** is set equal to the current time.

Shmget will fail if one or more of the following are true:

[EINVAL] *Size* is less than the system-imposed minimum or greater than the system-imposed maximum.

[EACCES] A shared memory identifier exists for *key* but operation permission (see *intro*(2)) as specified by the low-order 9 bits of *shmflg* would not be granted.

[EINVAL] A shared memory identifier exists for *key* but the size of the segment associated with it is less than *size* and *size* is not equal to zero.

[ENOENT] A shared memory identifier does not exist for *key* and (*shmflg* & **IPC_CREAT**) is "false".

[ENOSPC] A shared memory identifier is to be created but the system-imposed limit on the maximum number of allowed shared memory identifiers system wide would be exceeded.

[ENOMEM] A shared memory identifier and associated shared memory segment are to be created but the amount of available physical memory is not sufficient to fill the request.

[EEXIST] A shared memory identifier exists for *key* but ((*shmflg* & **IPC_CREAT**) and (*shmflg* & **IPC_EXCL**)) is "true".

RETURN VALUE

Upon successful completion, a non-negative integer, namely a shared memory identifier is returned. Otherwise, a value of −1 is returned and *errno* is set to indicate the error.

SEE ALSO

intro(2), shmctl(2), shmop(2).

NAME

shmop — shared memory operations

SYNOPSIS

#include <sys/types.h>
#include <sys/ipc.h>
#include <sys/shm.h>

char *shmat (shmid, shmaddr, shmflg)
int shmid;
char *shmaddr
int shmflg;

int shmdt (shmaddr)
char *shmaddr

DESCRIPTION

Shmat attaches the shared memory segment associated with the shared memory identifier specified by *shmid* to the data segment of the calling process. The segment is attached at the address specified by one of the following criteria:

> If *shmaddr* is equal to zero, the segment is attached at the first available address as selected by the system.
>
> If *shmaddr* is not equal to zero and (*shmflg* & **SHM_RND**) is "true", the segment is attached at the address given by (*shmaddr* - (*shmaddr* modulus **SHMLBA**)).
>
> If *shmaddr* is not equal to zero and (*shmflg* & **SHM_RND**) is "false", the segment is attached at the address given by *shmaddr*.

The segment is attached for reading if (*shmflg* & **SHM_RDONLY**) is "true" {READ}, otherwise it is attached for reading and writing {READ/WRITE}.

Shmat will fail and not attach the shared memory segment if one or more of the following are true:

[EINVAL] *Shmid* is not a valid shared memory identifier.

[EACCES] Operation permission is denied to the calling process (see *intro*(2)).

[ENOMEM] The available data space is not large enough to accommodate the shared memory segment.

[EINVAL] *Shmaddr* is not equal to zero, and the value of (*shmaddr* - (*shmaddr* modulus **SHMLBA**)) is an illegal address.

[EINVAL] *Shmaddr* is not equal to zero, (*shmflg* & **SHM_RND**) is "false", and the value of *shmaddr* is an illegal address.

[EMFILE] The number of shared memory segments attached to the calling process would exceed the system-imposed limit.

[EINVAL] *Shmdt* detaches from the calling process's data segment the shared memory segment located at the address specified by *shmaddr*.

[EINVAL] *Shmdt* will fail and not detach the shared memory segment if *shmaddr* is not the data segment start address of a shared memory segment.

RETURN VALUES

Upon successful completion, the return value is as follows:

Shmat returns the data segment start address of the attached shared memory segment.

Shmdt returns a value of 0.

Otherwise, a value of −1 is returned and *errno* is set to indicate the error.

SEE ALSO

exec(2), exit(2), fork(2), intro(2), shmctl(2), shmget(2).

NAME

signal — specify what to do upon receipt of a signal

SYNOPSIS

#include <signal.h>

int (*signal (sig, func))()
int sig;
void (*func)();

DESCRIPTION

Signal allows the calling process to choose one of three ways in which it is possible to handle the receipt of a specific signal. *Sig* specifies the signal and *func* specifies the choice.

Sig can be assigned any one of the following except **SIGKILL**:

SIGHUP	01	hangup
SIGINT	02	interrupt
SIGQUIT	03*	quit
SIGILL	04*	illegal instruction (not reset when caught)
SIGTRAP	05*	trace trap (not reset when caught)
SIGIOT	06*	IOT instruction
SIGEMT	07*	EMT instruction
SIGFPE	08*	floating point exception
SIGKILL	09	kill (cannot be caught or ignored)
SIGBUS	10*	bus error
SIGSEGV	11*	segmentation violation
SIGSYS	12*	bad argument to system call
SIGPIPE	13	write on a pipe with no one to read it
SIGALRM	14	alarm clock
SIGTERM	15	software termination signal
SIGUSR1	16	user-defined signal 1
SIGUSR2	17	user-defined signal 2
SIGCLD	18	death of a child (see *WARNING* below)
SIGPWR	19	power fail (see *WARNING below)*

See below for the significance of the asterisk (*) in the above list.

Func is assigned one of three values: **SIG_DFL**, **SIG_IGN**, or a *function address*. The actions prescribed by these values are as follows:

SIG_DFL — terminate process upon receipt of a signal
Upon receipt of the signal *sig*, the receiving process is

to be terminated with all of the consequences outlined in *exit* (2). In addition a "core image" will be made in the current working directory of the receiving process if *sig* is one for which an asterisk appears in the above list *and* the following conditions are met:

> The effective user ID and the real user ID of the receiving process are equal.
>
> An ordinary file named **core** exists and is writable or can be created. If the file must be created, it will have the following properties:
>
> > a mode of 0666 modified by the file creation mask (see *umask* (2))
> >
> > a file owner ID that is the same as the effective user ID of the receiving process.
> >
> > a file group ID that is the same as the effective group ID of the receiving process

SIG_IGN – ignore signal
The signal *sig* is to be ignored.

Note: the signal **SIGKILL** cannot be ignored.

function address – catch signal
Upon receipt of the signal *sig*, the receiving process is to execute the signal-catching function pointed to by *func*. The signal number *sig* will be passed as the only argument to the signal-catching function. Additional arguments are passed to the signal-catching function for hardware-generated signals. Before entering the signal-catching function, the value of *func* for the caught signal will be set to **SIG_DFL** unless the signal is **SIGILL**, **SIGTRAP**, or **SIGPWR**.

Upon return from the signal-catching function, the receiving process will resume execution at the point it was interrupted.

When a signal that is to be caught occurs during a *read*, a *write*, an *open*, or an *ioctl* system call on a slow device (like a terminal; but not a file), during a *pause* system call, or during a *wait* system call that does not return immediately due to the existence of a previously stopped or zombie process, the signal catching function will be executed and then the interrupted system call may return a −1 to the calling process with *errno* set to EINTR.

Note: The signal **SIGKILL** cannot be caught.

A call to *signal* cancels a pending signal *sig* except for a pending **SIGKILL** signal.

Signal will fail if *sig* is an illegal signal number, including **SIGKILL**. [EINVAL]

RETURN VALUE

Upon successful completion, *signal* returns the previous value of *func* for the specified signal *sig*. Otherwise, a value of −1 is returned and *errno* is set to indicate the error.

SEE ALSO

kill(2), pause(2), ptrace(2), wait(2), setjmp(3C).
kill(1) in the *UNIX Programmer's Manual—Volume 1: Commands and Utilities.*

WARNING

Two other signals that behave differently than the signals described above exist in this release of the system; they are:

SIGCLD	18	death of a child (reset when caught)
SIGPWR	19	power fail (not reset when caught)

There is no guarantee that, in future releases of the UNIX system, these signals will continue to behave as described below; they are included only for compatibility with other versions of the UNIX system. Their use in new programs is strongly discouraged.

For these signals, *func* is assigned one of three values: **SIG_DFL**, **SIG_IGN**, or a *function address*. The actions prescribed by these values of are as follows:

SIG_DFL - ignore signal
The signal is to be ignored.

SIG_IGN - ignore signal
The signal is to be ignored. Also, if *sig* is **SIGCLD**, the calling process's child processes will not create zombie processes when they terminate; see *exit*(2).

function address - catch signal
If the signal is **SIGPWR**, the action to be taken is the

same as that described above for *func* equal to *function address*. The same is true if the signal is **SIGCLD** except, that while the process is executing the signal-catching function, any received **SIGCLD** signals will be queued and the signal-catching function will be continually reentered until the queue is empty.

The **SIGCLD** affects two other system calls (*wait*(2), and *exit*(2)) in the following ways:

wait If the *func* value of **SIGCLD** is set to **SIG_IGN** and a *wait* is executed, the *wait* will block until all of the calling process's child processes terminate; it will then return a value of −1 with *errno* set to ECHILD.

exit If in the exiting process's parent process the *func* value of **SIGCLD** is set to **SIG_IGN**, the exiting process will not create a zombie process.

When processing a pipeline, the shell makes the last process in the pipeline the parent of the proceeding processes. A process that may be piped into in this manner (and thus become the parent of other processes) should take care not to set **SIGCLD** to be caught.

NAME

stat, fstat — get file status

SYNOPSIS

```
#include <sys/types.h>
#include <sys/stat.h>

int stat (path, buf)
char *path;
struct stat *buf;

int fstat (fildes, buf)
int fildes;
struct stat *buf;
```

DESCRIPTION

Path points to a path name naming a file. Read, write, or execute permission of the named file is not required, but all directories listed in the path name leading to the file must be searchable. *Stat* obtains information about the named file.

Similarly, *fstat* obtains information about an open file known by the file descriptor *fildes*, obtained from a successful *open*, *creat*, *dup*, *fcntl*, or *pipe* system call.

Buf is a pointer to a *stat* structure into which information is placed concerning the file.

The contents of the structure pointed to by *buf* include the following members:

```
ushort  st_mode;    /* File mode; see mknod(2) */
ino_t   st_ino;     /* Inode number */
dev_t   st_dev;     /* ID of device containing */
                    /* a directory entry for this file */
dev_t   st_rdev;    /* ID of device */
                    /* This entry is defined only for */
                    /* character special or block special files */
short   st_nlink;   /* Number of links */
ushort  st_uid;     /* User ID of the file's owner */
ushort  st_gid;     /* Group ID of the file's group */
off_t   st_size;    /* File size in bytes */
time_t  st_atime;   /* Time of last access */
time_t  st_mtime;   /* Time of last data modification */
time_t  st_ctime;   /* Time of last file status change */
                    /* Times measured in seconds since */
                    /* 00:00:00 GMT, Jan. 1, 1970 */
```

st_atime Time when file data was last accessed. Changed by the following system calls: *creat*(2), *mknod*(2), *pipe*(2), *utime*(2), and *read*(2).

st_mtime Time when data was last modified. Changed by the following system calls: *creat*(2), *mknod*(2), *pipe*(2), *utime*(2), and *write*(2).

st_ctime Time when file status was last changed. Changed by the following system calls: *chmod*(2), *chown*(2), *creat*(2), *link*(2), *mknod*(2), *pipe*(2), *unlink*(2), *utime*(2), and *write*(2).

Stat will fail if one or more of the following are true:

[ENOTDIR] A component of the path prefix is not a directory.

[ENOENT] The named file does not exist.

[EACCES] Search permission is denied for a component of the path prefix.

[EFAULT] *Buf* or *path* points to an invalid address.

Fstat will fail if one or more of the following are true:

[EBADF] *Fildes* is not a valid open file descriptor.

[EFAULT] *Buf* points to an invalid address.

RETURN VALUE

Upon successful completion a value of 0 is returned. Otherwise, a value of −1 is returned and *errno* is set to indicate the error.

SEE ALSO

chmod(2), chown(2), creat(2), link(2), mknod(2), pipe(2), read(2), time(2), unlink(2), utime(2), write(2).

NAME

stime − set time

SYNOPSIS

int stime (tp)
long *tp;

DESCRIPTION

Stime sets the system's idea of the time and date. *Tp* points to the value of time as measured in seconds from 00:00:00 GMT January 1, 1970.

[EPERM] *Stime* will fail if the effective user ID of the calling process is not super-user.

RETURN VALUE

Upon successful completion, a value of 0 is returned. Otherwise, a value of −1 is returned and *errno* is set to indicate the error.

SEE ALSO

time(2).

NAME

sync − update super-block

SYNOPSIS

void sync ( )

DESCRIPTION

Sync causes all information in memory that should be on disk to be written out. This includes modified super blocks, modified i-nodes, and delayed block I/O.

It should be used by programs which examine a file system, for example *fsck*, *df*, etc. It is mandatory before a boot.

The writing, although scheduled, is not necessarily complete upon return from *sync*.

NAME

time − get time

SYNOPSIS

long time ((long *) 0)

long time (tloc)
long *tloc;

DESCRIPTION

Time returns the value of time in seconds since 00:00:00 GMT, January 1, 1970.

If *tloc* (taken as an integer) is non-zero, the return value is also stored in the location to which *tloc* points.

[EFAULT] *Time* will fail if *tloc* points to an illegal address.

RETURN VALUE

Upon successful completion, *time* returns the value of time. Otherwise, a value of −1 is returned and *errno* is set to indicate the error.

SEE ALSO

stime(2).

NAME

times — get process and child process times

SYNOPSIS

#include <sys/types.h>
#include <sys/times.h>

long times (buffer)
struct tms *buffer;

DESCRIPTION

Times fills the structure pointed to by *buffer* with time-accounting information. The following are the contents of this structure:

```
struct  tms {
        time_t  tms_utime;
        time_t  tms_stime;
        time_t  tms_cutime;
        time_t  tms_cstime;
};
```

This information comes from the calling process and each of its terminated child processes for which it has executed a *wait*. All times are in 60ths of a second on DEC processors, 100ths of a second on AT&T processors.

Tms_utime is the CPU time used while executing instructions in the user space of the calling process.

Tms_stime is the CPU time used by the system on behalf of the calling process.

Tms_cutime is the sum of the *tms_utime*s and *tms_cutime*s of the child processes.

Tms_cstime is the sum of the *tms_stime*s and *tms_cstime*s of the child processes.

[EFAULT] *Times* will fail if *buffer* points to an illegal address.

RETURN VALUE

Upon successful completion, *times* returns the elapsed real time, in 60ths (100ths) of a second, since an arbitrary point in the past (e.g., system start-up time). This point does not change from one invocation of *times* to another. If *times* fails, a −1 is returned and *errno* is set to indicate the error.

SEE ALSO

exec(2), fork(2), time(2), wait(2).

NAME

ulimit − get and set user limits

SYNOPSIS

long ulimit (cmd, newlimit)
int cmd;
long newlimit;

DESCRIPTION

This function provides for control over process limits. The *cmd* values available are:

1 Get the file size limit of the process. The limit is in units of 512-byte blocks and is inherited by child processes. Files of any size can be read.

2 Set the file size limit of the process to the value of *newlimit*. Any process may decrease this limit, but only a process with an effective user ID of super-user may increase the limit. *Ulimit* will fail and the limit will be unchanged if a process with an effective user ID other than super-user attempts to increase its file size limit. [EPERM]

3 Get the maximum possible break value. See *brk*(2).

RETURN VALUE

Upon successful completion, a non-negative value is returned. Otherwise, a value of −1 is returned and *errno* is set to indicate the error.

SEE ALSO

brk(2), write(2).

NAME

umask − set and get file creation mask

SYNOPSIS

int umask (cmask)
int cmask;

DESCRIPTION

Umask sets the process's file mode creation mask to *cmask* and returns the previous value of the mask. Only the low-order 9 bits of *cmask* and the file mode creation mask are used.

RETURN VALUE

The previous value of the file mode creation mask is returned.

SEE ALSO

chmod(2), creat(2), mknod(2), open(2).
mkdir(1), sh(1) in the *UNIX Programmer's Manual—Volume 1: Commands and Utilities*.

NAME

umount − unmount a file system

SYNOPSIS

int umount (spec)
char *spec;

DESCRIPTION

Umount requests that a previously mounted file system contained on the block special device identified by *spec* be unmounted. *Spec* is a pointer to a path name. After unmounting the file system, the directory upon which the file system was mounted reverts to its ordinary interpretation.

Umount may be invoked only by the super-user.

Umount will fail if one or more of the following are true:

[EPERM] The process's effective user ID is not super-user.

[ENXIO] *Spec* does not exist.

[ENOTBLK] *Spec* is not a block special device.

[EINVAL] *Spec* is not mounted.

[EBUSY] A file on *spec* is busy.

[EFAULT] *Spec* points to an illegal address.

RETURN VALUE

Upon successful completion a value of 0 is returned. Otherwise, a value of −1 is returned and *errno* is set to indicate the error.

SEE ALSO

mount(2).

NAME

uname — get name of current UNIX system

SYNOPSIS

#include <sys/utsname.h>

int uname (name)
struct utsname *name;

DESCRIPTION

Uname stores information identifying the current UNIX system in the structure pointed to by *name*.

Uname uses the structure defined in **<sys/utsname.h>** whose members are:

```
char    sysname[9];
char    nodename[9];
char    release[9];
char    version[9];
char    machine[9];
```

Uname returns a null-terminated character string naming the current UNIX system in the character array *sysname*. Similarly, *nodename* contains the name that the system is known by on a communications network. *Release* and *version* further identify the operating system. *Machine* contains a standard name that identifies the hardware that the UNIX system is running on.

[EFAULT] *Uname* will fail if *name* points to an invalid address.

RETURN VALUE

Upon successful completion, a non-negative value is returned. Otherwise, −1 is returned and *errno* is set to indicate the error.

SEE ALSO

uname(1) in the *UNIX Programmer's Manual—Volume 1: Commands and Utilities.*

NAME

unlink – remove directory entry

SYNOPSIS

int unlink (path)
char *path;

DESCRIPTION

Unlink removes the directory entry named by the path name pointed to be *path*.

The named file is unlinked unless one or more of the following are true:

[ENOTDIR]	A component of the path prefix is not a directory.
[ENOENT]	The named file does not exist.
[EACCES]	Search permission is denied for a component of the path prefix.
[EACCES]	Write permission is denied on the directory containing the link to be removed.
[EPERM]	The named file is a directory and the effective user ID of the process is not super-user.
[EBUSY]	The entry to be unlinked is the mount point for a mounted file system.
[ETXTBSY]	The entry to be unlinked is the last link to a pure procedure (shared text) file that is being executed.
[EROFS]	The directory entry to be unlinked is part of a read-only file system.
[EFAULT]	*Path* points outside the process's allocated address space.

When all links to a file have been removed and no process has the file open, the space occupied by the file is freed and the file ceases to exist. If one or more processes have the file open when the last link is removed, the removal is postponed until all references to the file have been closed.

RETURN VALUE

Upon successful completion, a value of 0 is returned. Otherwise, a value of −1 is returned and *errno* is set to indicate the error.

SEE ALSO

close(2), link(2), open(2).

rm(1) in the *UNIX Programmer's Manual—Volume 1: Commands and Utilities.*

NAME

ustat − get file system statistics

SYNOPSIS

```
#include <sys/types.h>
#include <ustat.h>

int ustat (dev, buf)
int dev;
struct ustat *buf;
```

DESCRIPTION

Ustat returns information about a mounted file system. *Dev* is a device number identifying a device containing a mounted file system. *Buf* is a pointer to a *ustat* structure that includes to following elements:

```
daddr_t  f_tfree;        /* Total free blocks */
ino_t    f_tinode;       /* Number of free inodes */
char     f_fname[6];     /* Filsys name */
char     f_fpack[6];     /* Filsys pack name */
```

Ustat will fail if one or more of the following are true:

[EINVAL] *Dev* is not the device number of a device containing a mounted file system.

[EFAULT] *Buf* points outside the process's allocated address space.

RETURN VALUE

Upon successful completion, a value of 0 is returned. Otherwise, a value of −1 is returned and *errno* is set to indicate the error.

SEE ALSO

stat(2), fs(4).

NAME

utime – set file access and modification times

SYNOPSIS

#include <sys/types.h>
int utime (path, times)
char *path;
struct utimbuf *times;

DESCRIPTION

Path points to a path name naming a file. *Utime* sets the access and modification times of the named file.

If *times* is **NULL**, the access and modification times of the file are set to the current time. A process must be the owner of the file or have write permission to use *utime* in this manner.

If *times* is not **NULL**, *times* is interpreted as a pointer to a *utimbuf* structure and the access and modification times are set to the values contained in the designated structure. Only the owner of the file or the super-user may use *utime* this way.

The times in the following structure are measured in seconds since 00:00:00 GMT, Jan. 1, 1970.

```
struct  utimbuf {
        time_t  actime;     /* access time */
        time_t  modtime;    /* modification time */
};
```

Utime will fail if one or more of the following are true:

[ENOENT] The named file does not exist.

[ENOTDIR] A component of the path prefix is not a directory.

[EACCES] Search permission is denied by a component of the path prefix.

[EPERM] The effective user ID is not super-user and not the owner of the file and *times* is not **NULL**.

[EACCES] The effective user ID is not super-user and not the owner of the file and *times* is **NULL** and write access is denied.

[EROFS] The file system containing the file is mounted read-only.

[EFAULT] *Times* is not **NULL** and points outside the process's allocated address space.

[EFAULT] *Path* points outside the process's allocated address space.

RETURN VALUE

Upon successful completion, a value of 0 is returned. Otherwise, a value of −1 is returned and *errno* is set to indicate the error.

SEE ALSO

stat(2).

NAME

wait — wait for child process to stop or terminate

SYNOPSIS

int wait (stat_loc)
int *stat_loc;

int wait ((int *)0)

DESCRIPTION

Wait suspends the calling process until until one of the immediate children terminates or until a child that is being traced stops, because it has hit a break point. The *wait* system call will return prematurely if a signal is received and if a child process stopped or terminated prior to the call on *wait*, return is immediate.

If *stat_loc* (taken as an integer) is non-zero, 16 bits of information called status are stored in the low order 16 bits of the location pointed to by *stat_loc*. *Status* can be used to differentiate between stopped and terminated child processes and if the child process terminated, status identifies the cause of termination and passes useful information to the parent. This is accomplished in the following manner:

> If the child process stopped, the high order 8 bits of status will contain the number of the signal that caused the process to stop and the low order 8 bits will be set equal to 0177.
>
> If the child process terminated due to an *exit* call, the low order 8 bits of status will be zero and the high order 8 bits will contain the low order 8 bits of the argument that the child process passed to *exit*; see *exit*(2).
>
> If the child process terminated due to a signal, the high order 8 bits of status will be zero and the low order 8 bits will contain the number of the signal that caused the termination. In addition, if the low order seventh bit (i.e., bit 200) is set, a "core image" will have been produced; see *signal*(2).

If a parent process terminates without waiting for its child processes to terminate, the parent process ID of each child process is set to 1. This means the initialization process inherits the child processes; see *intro*(2).

Wait will fail and return immediately if one or more of the following are true:

[ECHILD] The calling process has no existing unwaited-for child processes.

[EFAULT] *Stat_loc* points to an illegal address.

RETURN VALUE

If *wait* returns due to the receipt of a signal, a value of −1 is returned to the calling process and *errno* is set to EINTR. If *wait* returns due to a stopped or terminated child process, the process ID of the child is returned to the calling process. Otherwise, a value of −1 is returned and *errno* is set to indicate the error.

SEE ALSO

exec(2), exit(2), fork(2), intro(2), pause(2), ptrace(2), signal(2).

WARNING

See *WARNING* in *signal*(2).

NAME

write — write on a file

SYNOPSIS

int write (fildes, buf, nbyte)
int fildes;
char *buf;
unsigned nbyte;

DESCRIPTION

Fildes is a file descriptor obtained from a *creat*, *open*, *dup*, *fcntl*, or *pipe* system call.

Write attempts to write *nbyte* bytes from the buffer pointed to by *buf* to the file associated with the *fildes*.

On devices capable of seeking, the actual writing of data proceeds from the position in the file indicated by the file pointer. Upon return from *write*, the file pointer is incremented by the number of bytes actually written.

On devices incapable of seeking, writing always takes place starting at the current position. The value of a file pointer associated with such a device is undefined.

If the O_APPEND flag of the file status flags is set, the file pointer will be set to the end of the file prior to each write.

Write will fail and the file pointer will remain unchanged if one or more of the following are true:

[EBADF] *Fildes* is not a valid file descriptor open for writing.

[EPIPE and SIGPIPE signal] An attempt is made to write to a pipe that is not open for reading by any process.

[EFBIG] An attempt was made to write a file that exceeds the process's file size limit or the maximum file size. See *ulimit*(2).

[EFAULT] *Buf* points outside the process's allocated address space.

[EINTR] A signal was caught during the *write* system call.

If a *write* requests that more bytes be written than there is room for (e.g., the *ulimit* (see *ulimit*(2)) or the physical end of a medium), only as many bytes as there is room for will be written.

For example, suppose there is space for 20 bytes more in a file before reaching a limit. A write of 512 bytes will return 20. The next write of a non-zero number of bytes will give a failure return (except as noted below).

If the file being written is a pipe (or FIFO) and the O_NDELAY flag of the file flag word is set, then write to a full pipe (or FIFO) will return a count of 0. Otherwise (O_NDELAY clear), writes to a full pipe (or FIFO) will block until space becomes available.

RETURN VALUE

Upon successful completion the number of bytes actually written is returned. Otherwise, −1 is returned and *errno* is set to indicate the error.

SEE ALSO

creat(2), dup(2), lseek(2), open(2), pipe(2), ulimit(2).

NAME

intro − introduction to subroutines and libraries

SYNOPSIS

#include <stdio.h>

#include <math.h>

DESCRIPTION

This section describes functions found in various libraries, other than those functions that directly invoke UNIX system primitives, which are described in Section 2 of this volume. Certain major collections are identified by a letter after the section number:

(3C) These functions, together with those of Section 2 and those marked (3S), constitute the Standard C Library *libc*, which is automatically loaded by the C compiler, *cc*(1). The link editor *ld*(1) searches this library under the **−lc** option. Declarations for some of these functions may be obtained from **#include** files indicated on the appropriate pages.

(3S) These functions constitute the "standard I/O package" [see *stdio*(3S)]. These functions are in the library *libc*, already mentioned. Declarations for these functions may be obtained from the **#include** file **<stdio.h>**.

(3M) These functions constitute the Math Library, *libm*. They are automatically accessed by the F77 compiler to implement the intrinsic math functions described in section 3F. They are not automatically loaded by the C compiler, *cc*(1); however, the link editor searches this library under the **−lm** option. Declarations for these functions may be obtained from the **#include** file **<math.h>**. Several generally useful mathematical constants are also defined there [see *math*(5)].

(3X) Various specialized libraries. The files in which these libraries are found are given on the appropriate pages.

(3F) These functions constitute the F77 intrinsic functions library, *libF77*, which includes the standard FORTRAN intrinsic functions as a subset. These functions are automatically available to the FORTRAN programmer and require no special invocation of the compiler.

DEFINITIONS

A *character* is any bit pattern able to fit into a byte on the machine. The *null character* is a character with value 0, represented in the C language as '\0'. A *character array* is a sequence of characters. A *null-terminated character array* is a sequence of characters, the last of which is the *null character*. A *string* is a designation for a *null-terminated character array*. The *null string* is a character array containing only the null character. A **NULL** pointer is the value that is obtained by casting **0** into a pointer. The C language guarantees that this value will not match that of any legitimate pointer, so many functions that return pointers return it to indicate an error. **NULL** is defined as **0** in **<stdio.h>**; the user can include an appropriate definition if not using **<stdio.h>**.

Many groups of FORTRAN intrinsic functions have *generic* function names that do not require explicit or implicit type declaration. The type of the function will be determined by the type of its argument(s). For example, the generic function *max* will return an integer value if given integer arguments (*max0*), a real value if given real arguments (*amax1*), or a double-precision value if given double-precision arguments (*dmax1*).

FILES

/lib/libc.a
/lib/libm.a
/usr/lib/libF77.a

SEE ALSO

intro(2), stdio(3S), math(5).
ar(1), cc(1), f77(1), ld(1), lint(1), nm(1) in the *UNIX Programmer's Manual—Volume 1: Commands and Utilities.*

DIAGNOSTICS

Functions in the C and Math Libraries (3C and 3M) may return the conventional values **0** or **±HUGE** (the largest-magnitude single-precision floating-point numbers; **HUGE** is defined in the *<math.h>* header file) when the function is undefined for the given arguments or when the value is not representable. In these cases, the external variable *errno* [see *intro*(2)] is set to the value EDOM or ERANGE. As many of the FORTRAN intrinsic functions use the routines found in the Math Library, the same conventions apply.

WARNING

Many of the functions in the libraries call and/or refer to other functions and external variables described in this section and in section 2 (*System Calls*). If a program inadvertantly defines a function or external variable with the same name, the presumed library version of the function or external variable may not be loaded. The *lint*(1) program checker reports name conflicts of this kind as "multiple declarations" of the names in question. Definitions for sections 2, 3C, and 3S are checked automatically. Other definitions can be included by using the **−l** option (for example, **−l***m* includes definitions for the Math Library, section 3M). Use of *lint* is highly recommended.

NAME

a64l, l64a − convert between long integer and base-64 ASCII string

SYNOPSIS

long a64l (s)
char *s;

char *l64a (l)
long l;

DESCRIPTION

These functions are used to maintain numbers stored in *base-64* ASCII characters. This is a notation by which long integers can be represented by up to six characters; each character represents a "digit" in a radix-64 notation.

The characters used to represent "digits" are **.** for 0, **/** for 1, **0** through **9** for 2−11, **A** through **Z** for 12−37, and **a** through **z** for 38−63.

A64l takes a pointer to a null-terminated base-64 representation and returns a corresponding **long** value. If the string pointed to by *s* contains more than six characters, *a64l* will use the first six.

L64a takes a **long** argument and returns a pointer to the corresponding base-64 representation. If the argument is 0, *l64a* returns a pointer to a null string.

BUGS

The value returned by *l64a* is a pointer into a static buffer, the contents of which are overwritten by each call.

NAME

abort − generate an IOT fault

SYNOPSIS

int abort ( )

DESCRIPTION

Abort first closes all open files if possible, then causes an IOT signal to be sent to the process. This usually results in termination with a core dump.

It is possible for *abort* to return control if **SIGIOT** is caught or ignored, in which case the value returned is that of the *kill*(2) system call.

SEE ALSO

exit(2), kill(2), signal(2).
sdb(1) in the *UNIX Programmer's Manual—Volume 1: Commands and Utilities.*

DIAGNOSTICS

If **SIGIOT** is neither caught nor ignored, and the current directory is writable, a core dump is produced and the message "abort − core dumped" is written by the shell.

NAME

abs − return integer absolute value

SYNOPSIS

```
int abs (i)
int i;
```

DESCRIPTION

Abs returns the absolute value of its integer operand.

BUGS

In two's-complement representation, the absolute value of the negative integer with largest magnitude is undefined. Some implementations trap this error, but others simply ignore it.

SEE ALSO

floor(3M).

NAME

bsearch — binary search a sorted table

SYNOPSIS

#include <search.h>

char *bsearch ((char *) key, (char *) base, nel, sizeof (*key), compar)
unsigned nel;
int (*compar)( );

DESCRIPTION

Bsearch is a binary search routine generalized from Knuth (6.2.1) Algorithm B. It returns a pointer into a table indicating where a datum may be found. The table must be previously sorted in increasing order according to a provided comparison function. *Key* points to a datum instance to be sought in the table. *Base* points to the element at the base of the table. *Nel* is the number of elements in the table. *Compar* is the name of the comparison function, which is called with two arguments that point to the elements being compared. The function must return an integer less than, equal to, or greater than zero as accordinly the first argument is to be considered less than, equal to, or greater than the second.

EXAMPLE

The example below searches a table containing pointers to nodes consisting of a string and its length. The table is ordered alphabetically on the string in the node pointed to by each entry.

This code fragment reads in strings and either finds the corresponding node and prints out the string and its length, or prints an error message.

```
#include <stdio.h>
#include <search.h>

#define TABSIZE         1000

struct node {                        /* stored in the table */
        char *string;
        int length;
};
struct node table[TABSIZE];          /* table to be searched */
        .
        .
        .
```

```
{
        struct node *node_ptr, node;
        int node_compare( );  /* compare 2 nodes */
        char str_space[20];   /* space to read string into */
        .
        .
        .
        node.string = str_space;
        while (scanf("%s", node.string) != EOF) {
                node_ptr = (struct node *)bsearch((char *)(&node),
                           (char *)table, TABSIZE,
                           sizeof(struct node), node_compare);
                if (node_ptr != NULL) {
                        (void)printf("string = %20s, length = %d\n",
                                node_ptr->string, node_ptr->length);
                } else {
                        (void)printf("not found: %s\n", node.string);
                }
        }
}
/*
        This routine compares two nodes based on an
        alphabetical ordering of the string field.
*/
int
node_compare(node1, node2)
struct node *node1, *node2;
{
        return strcmp(node1->string, node2->string);
}
```

NOTES

The pointers to the key and the element at the base of the table should be of type pointer-to-element, and cast to type pointer-to-character.

The comparison function need not compare every byte, so arbitrary data may be contained in the elements in addition to the values being compared.

Although declared as type pointer-to-character, the value returned should be cast into type pointer-to-element.

SEE ALSO

hsearch(3C), lsearch(3C), qsort(3C), tsearch(3C).

DIAGNOSTICS

A NULL pointer is returned if the key cannot be found in the table.

NAME

clock – report CPU time used

SYNOPSIS

long clock ( )

DESCRIPTION

Clock returns the amount of CPU time (in microseconds) used since the first call to *clock*. The time reported is the sum of the user and system times of the calling process and its terminated child processes for which it has executed *wait*(2) or *system*(3S).

The resolution of the clock is 10 milliseconds on AT&T 3B computer processors, 16.667 milliseconds on Digital Equipment Corporation processors.

SEE ALSO

times(2), wait(2), system(3S).

BUGS

The value returned by *clock* is defined in microseconds for compatibility with systems that have CPU clocks with much higher resolution. Because of this, the value returned will wrap around after accumulating only 2147 seconds of CPU time (about 36 minutes).

NAME

toupper, tolower, _toupper, _tolower, toascii — translate characters

SYNOPSIS

```
#include <ctype.h>

int toupper (c)
int c;

int tolower (c)
int c;

int _toupper (c)
int c;

int _tolower (c)
int c;

int toascii (c)
int c;
```

DESCRIPTION

Toupper and *tolower* have as domain the range of *getc*(3S): the integers from −1 through 255. If the argument of *toupper* represents a lower-case letter, the result is the corresponding upper-case letter. If the argument of *tolower* represents an upper-case letter, the result is the corresponding lower-case letter. All other arguments in the domain are returned unchanged.

The macros *_toupper* and *_tolower*, are macros that accomplish the same thing as *toupper* and *tolower* but have restricted domains and are faster. *_toupper* requires a lower-case letter as its argument; its result is the corresponding upper-case letter. The macro *_tolower* requires an upper-case letter as its argument; its result is the corresponding lower-case letter. Arguments outside the domain cause undefined results.

Toascii yields its argument with all bits turned off that are not part of a standard ASCII character; it is intended for compatibility with other systems.

SEE ALSO

ctype(3C), getc(3S).

NAME

crypt, setkey, encrypt – generate DES encryption

SYNOPSIS

char *crypt (key, salt)
char *key, *salt;

void setkey (key)
char *key;

void encrypt (block, edflag)
char *block;
int edflag;

DESCRIPTION

Crypt is the password encryption function. It is based on the NBS Data Encryption Standard (DES), with variations intended (among other things) to frustrate use of hardware implementations of the DES for key search.

Key is a user's typed password. *Salt* is a two-character string chosen from the set **[a-zA-Z0-9./]**; this string is used to perturb the DES algorithm in one of 4096 different ways, after which the password is used as the key to encrypt repeatedly a constant string. The returned value points to the encrypted password. The first two characters are the salt itself.

The *setkey* and *encrypt* entries provide (rather primitive) access to the actual DES algorithm. The argument of *setkey* is a character array of length 64 containing only the characters with numerical value 0 and 1. If this string is divided into groups of 8, the low-order bit in each group is ignored; this gives a 56-bit key which is set into the machine. This is the key that will be used with the above mentioned algorithm to encrypt or decrypt the string *block* with the function *encrypt*.

The argument to the *encrypt* entry is a character array of length 64 containing only the characters with numerical value 0 and 1. The argument array is modified in place to a similar array representing the bits of the argument after having been subjected to the DES algorithm using the key set by *setkey*. If *edflag* is zero, the argument is encrypted; if non-zero, it is decrypted.

SEE ALSO

getpass(3C), passwd(4).
login(1), passwd(1) in the *UNIX Programmer's Manual—Volume 1: Commands and Utilities.*

BUGS

The return value points to static data that are overwritten by each call.

NAME

ctime, localtime, gmtime, asctime, tzset — convert date and time to string

SYNOPSIS

#include <time.h>

char *ctime (clock)
long *clock;

struct tm *localtime (clock)
long *clock;

struct tm *gmtime (clock)
long *clock;

char *asctime (tm)
struct tm *tm;

extern long timezone;

extern int daylight;

extern char *tzname[2];

void tzset ( )

DESCRIPTION

Ctime converts a long integer, pointed to by *clock*, representing the time in seconds since 00:00:00 GMT, January 1, 1970, and returns a pointer to a 26-character string in the following form. All the fields have constant width.

Sun Sep 16 01:03:52 1973\n\0

Localtime and *gmtime* return pointers to "tm" structures, described below. *Localtime* corrects for the time zone and possible Daylight Savings Time; *gmtime* converts directly to Greenwich Mean Time (GMT), which is the time the UNIX system uses.

Asctime converts a "tm" structure to a 26-character string, as shown in the above example, and returns a pointer to the string.

Declarations of all the functions and externals, and the "tm" structure, are in the *<time.h>* header file. The structure declaration is:

```
struct tm {
        int tm_sec;         /* seconds (0 - 59) */
        int tm_min;         /* minutes (0 - 59) */
        int tm_hour;        /* hours (0 - 23) */
```

```
        int tm_mday;        /* day of month (1 - 31) */
        int tm_mon;         /* month of year (0 - 11) */
        int tm_year;        /* year − 1900 */
        int tm_wday;        /* day of week (Sunday = 0) */
        int tm_yday;        /* day of year (0 - 365) */
        int tm_isdst;
};
```

Tm_isdst is non-zero if Daylight Savings Time is in effect.

The external **long** variable *timezone* contains the difference, in seconds, between GMT and local standard time (in EST, *timezone* is 5*60*60); the external variable *daylight* is non-zero if and only if the standard U.S.A. Daylight Savings Time conversion should be applied. The program knows about the peculiarities of this conversion in 1974 and 1975; if necessary, a table for these years can be extended.

If an environment variable named **TZ** is present, *asctime* uses the contents of the variable to override the default time zone. The value of **TZ** must be a three-letter time zone name, followed by a number representing the difference between local time and Greenwich Mean Time in hours, followed by an optional three-letter name for a daylight time zone. For example, the setting for New Jersey would be **EST5EDT**. The effects of setting **TZ** are thus to change the values of the external variables *timezone* and *daylight*; in addition, the time zone names contained in the external variable

char *tzname[2] = { "EST", "EDT" };

are set from the environment variable **TZ**. The function *tzset* sets these external variables from **TZ**; *tzset* is called by *asctime* and may also be called explicitly by the user.

Note that in most installations, **TZ** is set by default when the user logs on, to a value in the local /etc/profile file (see *profile*(4)).

SEE ALSO

time(2), getenv(3C), profile(4), environ(5).

BUGS

The return values point to static data whose content is overwritten by each call.

NAME

isalpha, isupper, islower, isdigit, isxdigit, isalnum, isspace, ispunct, isprint, isgraph, iscntrl, isascii — classify characters

SYNOPSIS

#include <ctype.h>

int isalpha (c)
int c;

. . .

DESCRIPTION

These macros classify character-coded integer values by table lookup. Each is a predicate returning nonzero for true, zero for false. *Isascii* is defined on all integer values; the rest are defined only where *isascii* is true and on the single non-ASCII value **EOF** (−1 − see *stdio*(3S)).

isalpha	*c* is a letter.
isupper	*c* is an upper-case letter.
islower	*c* is a lower-case letter.
isdigit	*c* is a digit [0-9].
isxdigit	*c* is a hexadecimal digit [0-9], [A-F] or [a-f].
isalnum	*c* is an alphanumeric (letter or digit).
isspace	*c* is a space, tab, carriage return, new-line, vertical tab, or form-feed.
ispunct	*c* is a punctuation character (neither control nor alphanumeric).
isprint	*c* is a printing character, code 040 (space) through 0176 (tilde).
isgraph	*c* is a printing character, like *isprint* except false for space.
iscntrl	*c* is a delete character (0177) or an ordinary control character (less than 040).
isascii	*c* is an ASCII character, code less than 0200.

DIAGNOSTICS

If the argument to any of these macros is not in the domain of the function, the result is undefined.

SEE ALSO

stdio(3S), ascii(5).

NAME

dial – establish an out-going terminal line connection

SYNOPSIS

#include <dial.h>

int dial (call)
CALL call;

void undial (fd)
int fd;

DESCRIPTION

Dial returns a file-descriptor for a terminal line open for read/write. The argument to *dial* is a CALL structure (defined in the *<dial.h>* header file).

When finished with the terminal line, the calling program must invoke *undial* to release the semaphore that has been set during the allocation of the terminal device.

The definition of CALL in the *<dial.h>* header file is:

```
typedef struct {
        struct termio *attr;  /* pointer to termio attribute struct */
        int        baud;      /* transmission data rate */
        int        speed;     /* 212A modem: low=300, high=1200 */
        char       *line;     /* device name for out-going line */
        char       *telno;    /* pointer to tel-no digits string */
        int        modcm;     /* specify modem control for direct lines */
        char       *device;   /*Will hald the name of the device used
                                 to make a connection */
        int        dev_len;   /* The length of the device used
                                 to make connection */
} CALL;
```

The CALL element *speed* is intended only for use with an outgoing dialed call, in which case its value should be either 300 or 1200 to identify the 113A modem, or the high- or low-speed setting on the 212A modem. Note that the 113A modem or the low-speed setting of the 212A modem will transmit at any rate between 0 and 300 bits per second. However, the high-speed setting of the 212A modem transmits and receivers at 1200 bits per secound only. The CALL element *baud* is for the desired transmission baud rate. For example, one might set *baud* to 110 and *speed* to 300 (or 1200). However, if **speed** set to 1200 **baud** must be set to high (1200).

If the desired terminal line is a direct line, a string pointer to its device-name should be placed in the *line* element in the CALL structure. Legal values for such terminal device names are kept in the *L-devices* file. In this case, the value of the *baud* element need not be specified as it will be determined from the *L-devices* file.

The *telno* element is for a pointer to a character string representing the telephone number to be dialed. Such numbers may consist only of symbols described on the *acu*(7). The termination symbol will be supplied by the *dial* function, and should not be included in the *telno* string passed to *dial* in the CALL structure.

The CALL element *modem* is used to specify modem control for direct lines. This element should be non-zero if modem control is required. The CALL element *attr* is a pointer to a *termio* structure, as defined in the *termio.h* header file. A NULL value for this pointer element may be passed to the *dial* function, but if such a structure is included, the elements specified in it will be set for the outgoing terminal line before the connection is established. This is often important for certain attributes such as parity and baud-rate.

The CALL element *device* is used to hold the device name (cul..) that establishes the connection.

The CALL element *dev_len* is the length of the device name that is copied into the array device.

FILES

/usr/lib/uucp/L-devices
/usr/spool/uucp/LCK..*tty-device*

SEE ALSO

uucp(1C) in the *UNIX Programmer's Manual—Volume 1: Commands and Utilities*.
alarm(2), read(2), write(2).
acu(7), termio(7) in the *UNIX System Administrator Reference Manual*.

DIAGNOSTICS

On failure, a negative value indicating the reason for the failure will be returned. Mnemonics for these negative indices as listed here are defined in the <*dial.h*> header file.

```
INTRPT     -1     /* interrupt occurred */
D_HUNG     -2     /* dialer hung (no return from write) */
NO_ANS     -3     /* no answer within 10 seconds */
```

```
ILL_BD     -4    /* illegal baud-rate */
A_PROB     -5    /* acu problem (open() failure) */
L_PROB     -6    /* line problem (open() failure) */
NO_Ldv     -7    /* can't open LDEVS file */
DV_NT_A    -8    /* requested device not available */
DV_NT_K    -9    /* requested device not known */
NO_BD_A    -10   /* none available at requested baud */
NO_BD_K    -11   /* no device known at requested baud */
```

WARNINGS

Including the **<dial.h>** header file automatically includes the **<termio.h>** header file.

The above routine uses **<stdio.h>**, which causes it to increase the size of programs, not otherwise using standard I/O, more than might be expected.

BUGS

An *alarm*(2) system call for 3600 seconds is made (and caught) within the *dial* module for the purpose of "touching" the *LCK..* file and constitutes the device allocation semaphore for the terminal device. Otherwise, *uucp*(1C) may simply delete the *LCK..* entry on its 90-minute clean-up rounds. The alarm may go off while the user program is in a *read*(2) or *write*(2) system call, causing an apparent error return. If the user program expects to be around for an hour or more, error returns from *read*s should be checked for **(errno==EINTR)**, and the *read* possibly reissued.

NAME

drand48, erand48, lrand48, nrand48, mrand48, jrand48, srand48, seed48, lcong48 — generate uniformly distributed pseudo-random numbers

SYNOPSIS

double drand48 ( )

double erand48 (xsubi)
unsigned short xsubi[3];

long lrand48 ( )

long nrand48 (xsubi)
unsigned short xsubi[3];

long mrand48 ( )

long jrand48 (xsubi)
unsigned short xsubi[3];

void srand48 (seedval)
long seedval;

unsigned short *seed48 (seed16v)
unsigned short seed16v[3];

void lcong48 (param)
unsigned short param[7];

DESCRIPTION

This family of functions generates pseudo-random numbers using the well-known linear congruential algorithm and 48-bit integer arithmetic.

Functions *drand48* and *erand48* return non-negative double-precision floating-point values uniformly distributed over the interval [0.0, 1.0).

Functions *lrand48* and *nrand48* return non-negative long integers uniformly distributed over the interval $[0, 2^{31})$.

Functions *mrand48* and *jrand48* return signed long integers uniformly distributed over the interval $[-2^{31}, 2^{31})$.

Functions *srand48, seed48* and *lcong48* are initialization entry points, one of which should be invoked before either *drand48, lrand48* or *mrand48* is called. (Although it is not recommended practice, constant default initializer values will be supplied automatically if *drand48, lrand48* or *mrand48* is called without a prior call to an initialization entry point.) Functions *erand48, nrand48* and *jrand48* do not require an initialization entry point to be called first.

All the routines work by generating a sequence of 48-bit integer values, X_i, according to the linear congruential formula

$$X_{n+1} = (aX_n + c)_{\mathrm{mod}\ m} \qquad n \geqslant 0.$$

The parameter $m = 2^{48}$; hence 48-bit integer arithmetic is performed. Unless *lcong48* has been invoked, the multiplier value a and the addend value c are given by

$$a = \mathrm{5DEECE66D}_{16} = 273673163155_8$$
$$c = \mathrm{B}_{16} = 13_8.$$

The value returned by any of the functions *drand48, erand48, lrand48, nrand48, mrand48* or *jrand48* is computed by first generating the next 48-bit X_i in the sequence. Then the appropriate number of bits, according to the type of data item to be returned, are copied from the high-order (leftmost) bits of X_i and transformed into the returned value.

The functions *drand48, lrand48* and *mrand48* store the last 48-bit X_i generated in an internal buffer; that is why they must be initialized prior to being invoked. The functions *erand48, nrand48* and *jrand48* require the calling program to provide storage for the successive X_i values in the array specified as an argument when the functions are invoked. That is why these routines do not have to be initialized; the calling program merely has to place the desired initial value of X_i into the array and pass it as an argument. By using different arguments, functions *erand48, nrand48* and *jrand48* allow separate modules of a large program to generate several *independent* streams of pseudo-random numbers, i.e., the sequence of numbers in each stream will *not* depend upon how many times the routines have been called to generate numbers for the other streams.

The initializer function *srand48* sets the high-order 32 bits of X_i to the 32 bits contained in its argument. The low-order 16 bits of X_i are set to the arbitrary value $330\mathrm{E}_{16}$.

The initializer function *seed48* sets the value of X_i to the 48-bit value specified in the argument array. In addition, the previous value of X_i is copied into a 48-bit internal buffer, used only by *seed48,* and a pointer to this buffer is the value returned by *seed48*. This returned pointer, which can just be ignored if not needed, is useful if a program is to be restarted from a given point at some future time — use the pointer to get at and store the last X_i value, and then use this value to reinitialize via *seed48* when the program is restarted.

The initialization function *lcong48* allows the user to specify the initial X_i, the multiplier value a, and the addend value c. Argument array elements *param[0-2]* specify X_i, *param[3-5]* specify the multiplier a, and *param[6]* specifies the 16-bit addend c. After *lcong48* has been called, a subsequent call to either *srand48* or *seed48* will restore the "standard" multiplier and addend values, a and c, specified on the previous page.

NOTES

On most computers, the routines are coded in portable C. The source code for the portable version can even be used on computers which do not have floating-point arithmetic. In such a situation, functions *drand48* and *erand48* do not exist; instead, they are replaced by the two new functions below.

long irand48 (m)
unsigned short m;

long krand48 (xsubi, m)
unsigned short xsubi[3], m;

Functions *irand48* and *krand48* return non-negative long integers uniformly distributed over the interval [0, $m-1$].

SEE ALSO

rand(3C).

NAME

ecvt, fcvt, gcvt — convert floating-point number to string

SYNOPSIS

```
char *ecvt (value, ndigit, decpt, sign)
double value;
int ndigit, *decpt, *sign;

char *fcvt (value, ndigit, decpt, sign)
double value;
int ndigit, *decpt, *sign;

char *gcvt (value, ndigit, buf)
double value;
int ndigit;
char *buf;
```

DESCRIPTION

Ecvt converts *value* to a null-terminated string of *ndigit* digits and returns a pointer thereto. The high-order digit is non-zero, unless the value is zero. The low-order digit is rounded. The position of the decimal point relative to the beginning of the string is stored indirectly through *decpt* (negative means to the left of the returned digits). The decimal point is not included in the returned string. If the sign of the result is negative, the word pointed to by *sign* is non-zero, otherwise it is zero.

Fcvt is identical to *ecvt*, except that the correct digit has been rounded for printf "%f" (FORTRAN F-format) output of the number of digits specified by *ndigit*.

Gcvt converts the *value* to a null-terminated string in the array pointed to by *buf* and returns *buf*. It attempts to produce *ndigit* significant digits in FORTRAN F-format if possible, otherwise E-format, ready for printing. A minus sign, if there is one, or a decimal point will be included as part of the returned string. Trailing zeros are suppressed.

SEE ALSO

printf(3S).

BUGS

The values returned by *ecvt* and *fcvt* point to a single static data array whose content is overwritten by each call.

NAME

end, etext, edata − last locations in program

SYNOPSIS

extern end;
extern etext;
extern edata;

DESCRIPTION

These names refer neither to routines nor to locations with interesting contents. The address of *etext* is the first address above the program text, *edata* above the initialized data region, and *end* above the uninitialized data region.

When execution begins, the program break (the first location beyond the data) coincides with *end*, but the program break may be reset by the routines of *brk*(2), *malloc*(3C), standard input/output (*stdio*(3S)), the profile (**−p**) option of *cc*(1), and so on. Thus, the current value of the program break should be determined by **sbrk(0)** (see *brk*(2)).

SEE ALSO

brk(2), malloc(3C), stdio(3S).
cc(1) in the *UNIX Programmer's Manual—Volume 1: Commands and Utilities.*

NAME

frexp, ldexp, modf — manipulate parts of floating-point numbers

SYNOPSIS

double frexp (value, eptr)
double value;
int *eptr;

double ldexp (value, exp)
double value;
int exp;

double modf (value, iptr)
double value, *iptr;

DESCRIPTION

Every non-zero number can be written uniquely as $x * 2^n$, where the "mantissa" (fraction) x is in the range $0.5 \leqslant |x| < 1.0$, and the "exponent" n is an integer. *Frexp* returns the mantissa of a double *value*, and stores the exponent indirectly in the location pointed to by *eptr*. If *value* is zero, both results returned by *frexp* are zero.

Ldexp returns the quantity $value * 2^{exp}$.

Modf returns the signed fractional part of *value* and stores the integral part indirectly in the location pointed to by *iptr*.

DIAGNOSTICS

If *ldexp* would cause overflow, **±HUGE** is returned (according to the sign of *value*), and *errno* is set to **ERANGE**.
If *ldexp* would cause underflow, zero is returned and *errno* is set to **ERANGE**.

NAME

ftw − walk a file tree

SYNOPSIS

#include <ftw.h>

int ftw (path, fn, depth)
char *path;
int (*fn) ( );
int depth;

DESCRIPTION

Ftw recursively descends the directory hierarchy rooted in *path*. For each object in the hierarchy, *ftw* calls *fn*, passing it a pointer to a null-terminated character string containing the name of the object, a pointer to a **stat** structure (see *stat*(2)) containing information about the object, and an integer. Possible values of the integer, defined in the <ftw.h> header file, are FTW_F for a file, FTW_D for a directory, FTW_DNR for a directory that cannot be read, and FTW_NS for an object for which *stat* could not successfully be executed. If the integer is FTW_DNR, descendants of that directory will not be processed. If the integer is FTW_NS, the **stat** structure will contain garbage. An example of an object that would cause FTW_NS to be passed to *fn* would be a file in a directory with read but without execute (search) permission.

Ftw visits a directory before visiting any of its descendants.

The tree traversal continues until the tree is exhausted, an invocation of *fn* returns a nonzero value, or some error is detected within *ftw* (such as an I/O error). If the tree is exhausted, *ftw* returns zero. If *fn* returns a nonzero value, *ftw* stops its tree traversal and returns whatever value was returned by *fn*. If *ftw* detects an error, it returns −1, and sets the error type in *errno*.

Ftw uses one file descriptor for each level in the tree. The *depth* argument limits the number of file descriptors so used. If *depth* is zero or negative, the effect is the same as if it were 1. *Depth* must not be greater than the number of file descriptors currently available for use. *Ftw* will run more quickly if *depth* is at least as large as the number of levels in the tree.

SEE ALSO

stat(2), malloc(3C).

BUGS

Because *ftw* is recursive, it is possible for it to terminate with a memory fault when applied to very deep file structures.

It could be made to run faster and use less storage on deep structures at the cost of considerable complexity.

Ftw uses *malloc*(3C) to allocate dynamic storage during its operation. If *ftw* is forcibly terminated, such as by *longjmp* being executed by *fn* or an interrupt routine, *ftw* will not have a chance to free that storage, so it will remain permanently allocated. A safe way to handle interrupts is to store the fact that an interrupt has occurred, and arrange to have *fn* return a nonzero value at its next invocation.

NAME

getcwd − get path-name of current working directory

SYNOPSIS

char *getcwd (buf, size)
char *buf;
int size;

DESCRIPTION

Getcwd returns a pointer to the current directory path-name. The value of *size* must be at least two greater than the length of the path-name to be returned.

If *buf* is a NULL pointer, *getcwd* will obtain *size* bytes of space using *malloc*(3C). In this case, the pointer returned by *getcwd* may be used as the argument in a subsequent call to *free*.

The function is implemented by using *popen*(3S) to pipe the output of the *pwd*(1) command into the specified string space.

EXAMPLE

```
char *cwd, *getcwd();
.
.
.
if ((cwd = getcwd((char *)NULL, 64)) == NULL) {
        perror("pwd");
        exit(1);
}
printf("%s\n", cwd);
```

SEE ALSO

malloc(3C), popen(3S).
pwd(1) in the *UNIX Programmer's Manual—Volume 1: Commands and Utilities*.

DIAGNOSTICS

Returns **NULL** with *errno* set if *size* is not large enough, or if an error ocurrs in a lower-level function.

NAME

getenv – return value for environment name

SYNOPSIS

char *getenv (name)
char *name;

DESCRIPTION

Getenv searches the environment list (see *environ*(5)) for a string of the form *name*=*value*, and returns a pointer to the *value* in the current environment if such a string is present, otherwise a NULL pointer.

SEE ALSO

exec(2), putenv(3C), environ(5).

NAME

getgrent, getgrgid, getgrnam, setgrent, endgrent, fgetgrent — get group file entry

SYNOPSIS

#include <grp.h>

struct group *getgrent ( )

struct group *getgrgid (gid)
int gid;

struct group *getgrnam (name)
char *name;

void setgrent ( )

void endgrent ( )

struct group *fgetgrent (f)
FILE *f;

DESCRIPTION

Getgrent, *getgrgid* and *getgrnam* each return pointers to an object with the following structure containing the broken-out fields of a line in the **/etc/group** file. Each line contains a "group" structure, defined in the *<grp.h>* header file.

```
struct group {
        char    *gr_name;    /* the name of the group */
        char    *gr_passwd;  /* the encrypted group password */
        int     gr_gid;      /* the numerical group ID */
        char    **gr_mem;    /* vector of pointers to member names */
};
```

Getgrent when first called returns a pointer to the first group structure in the file; thereafter, it returns a pointer to the next group structure in the file; so, successive calls may be used to search the entire file. *Getgrgid* searches from the beginning of the file until a numerical group id matching *gid* is found and returns a pointer to the particular structure in which it was found. *Getgrnam* searches from the beginning of the file until a group name matching *name* is found and returns a pointer to the particular structure in which it was found. If an end-of-file or an error is encountered on reading, these functions return a NULL pointer.

A call to *setgrent* has the effect of rewinding the group file to allow repeated searches. *Endgrent* may be called to close the group file when processing is complete.

Fgetgrent returns a pointer to the next group structure in the stream *f*, which matches the format of **/etc/group**.

FILES

/etc/group

SEE ALSO

getlogin(3C), getpwent(3C), group(4).

DIAGNOSTICS

A **NULL** pointer is returned on **EOF** or error.

WARNING

The above routines use **<stdio.h>**, which causes them to increase the size of programs, not otherwise using standard I/O, more than might be expected.

BUGS

All information is contained in a static area, so it must be copied if it is to be saved.

NAME

getlogin — get login name

SYNOPSIS

char *getlogin ( );

DESCRIPTION

Getlogin returns a pointer to the login name as found in **/etc/utmp**. It may be used in conjunction with *getpwnam* to locate the correct password file entry when the same user ID is shared by several login names.

If *getlogin* is called within a process that is not attached to a terminal, it returns a **NULL** pointer. The correct procedure for determining the login name is to call *cuserid*, or to call *getlogin* and if it fails to call *getpwuid*.

FILES

/etc/utmp

SEE ALSO

cuserid(3S), getgrent(3C), getpwent(3C), utmp(4).

DIAGNOSTICS

Returns the **NULL** pointer if *name* is not found.

BUGS

The return values point to static data whose content is overwritten by each call.

NAME

getopt − get option letter from argument vector

SYNOPSIS

int getopt (argc, argv, optstring)
int argc;
char **argv;
char *optstring;

extern char *optarg;
extern int optind;

DESCRIPTION

Getopt retunrs the next option letter in *argv* that matches a letter in *optstring*. *Optstring* is a string of recognized option letters; if a letter is followed by a colon, the option is expected to have an argument that may or may not be separated from it by white space. *Optarg* is set to point to the start of the option argument.

Getopt places in *optind* the *argv* index of the next argument to be processed. Because *optind* is external, it is normally initialized to zero automatically before the first call to *getopt*.

When all options have been processed, getopt returns **EOF**. The special option −− may be used to delimit the end of the options; **EOF** will be returned, and −− will be skipped.

DIAGNOSTICS

Getopt prints an error message on *stderr* and returns a question mark (?) when it encounters an option letter not included in *optstring*.

WARNING

The above routine uses **<stdio.h>** which causes it to increase the size of programs, not otherwise using standard I/O, more than might be expected.

SEE ALSO

getopt(1).

NAME

getpass − read a password

SYNOPSIS

char *getpass (prompt)
char *prompt;

DESCRIPTION

Getpass reads up to a newline or **EOF** from the file **/dev/tty**, after prompting on the standard error output with the null-terminated string *prompt* and disabling echoing. A pointer is returned to a null-terminated string of at most 8 characters. If **/dev/tty** cannot be opened, a **NULL** pointer is returned. An interrupt will terminate input and send an interrupt signal to the calling program before returning.

FILES

/dev/tty

SEE ALSO

crypt(3C).

WARNING

The above routine uses **<stdio.h>**, which causes it to increase the size of programs not otherwise using standard I/O, more than might be expected.

BUGS

The return value points to static data whose content is overwritten by each call.

NAME

getpw − get name from UID

SYNOPSIS

```
int getpw (uid, buf)
int uid;
char *buf;
```

DESCRIPTION

Getpw searches the password file for a user id number that equals *uid*, copies the line of the password file in which *uid* was found into the array pointed to by *buf*, and returns 0. *Getpw* returns non-zero if *uid* cannot be found.

This routine is included only for compatibility with prior systems and should not be used; see *getpwent*(3C) for routines to use instead.

FILES

/etc/passwd

SEE ALSO

getpwent(3C), passwd(4).

DIAGNOSTICS

Getpw returns non-zero on error.

WARNING

The above routine uses **<stdio.h>**, which causes it to increase, more than might be expected, the size of programs not otherwise using standard I/O.

NAME

getpwent, getpwuid, getpwnam, setpwent, endpwent, fgetpwent − get password file entry

SYNOPSIS

#include <pwd.h>

struct passwd *getpwent ( )

struct passwd *getpwuid (uid)
int uid;

struct passwd *getpwnam (name)
char *name;

void setpwent ( )

void endpwent ( )

struct passwd *fgetpwent (f)
FILE *f;

DESCRIPTION

Getpwent, *getpwuid* and *getpwnam* each returns a pointer to an object with the following structure containing the broken-out fields of a line in the **/etc/passwd** file. Each line in the file contains a "passwd" structure, declared in the *<pwd.h>* header file:

```
struct passwd {
        char    *pw_name;
        char    *pw_passwd;
        int     pw_uid;
        int     pw_gid;
        char    *pw_age;
        char    *pw_comment;
        char    *pw_gecos;
        char    *pw_dir;
        char    *pw_shell;
};
```

This structure is declared in *<pwd.h>* so it is not necessary to redeclare it.

The *pw_comment* field is unused; the others have meanings described in *passwd*(4).

Getpwent when first called returns a pointer to the first passwd structure in the file; thereafter, it returns a pointer to the next passwd structure in the file; so successive calls can be used to search the entire file. *Getpwuid* searches from the beginning of the file until a numerical user id matching *uid* is found and returns a pointer to the particular structure in which it was found. *Getpwnam* searches from the beginning of the file until a login name matching *name* is found, and returns a pointer to the particular structure in which it was found. If an end-of-file or an error is encountered on reading, these functions return a NULL pointer.

A call to *setpwent* has the effect of rewinding the password file to allow repeated searches. *Endpwent* may be called to close the password file when processing is complete.

Fgetpwent returns a pointer to the next passwd structure in the stream *f*, which matches the format of **/etc/passwd**.

FILES

/etc/passwd

SEE ALSO

getlogin(3C), getgrent(3C), passwd(4).

DIAGNOSTICS

A **NULL** pointer is returned on **EOF** or error.

WARNING

The above routines use **<stdio.h>**, which causes them to increase the size of programs, not otherwise using standard I/O, more than might be expected.

BUGS

All information is contained in a static area, so it must be copied if it is to be saved.

NAME

getutent, getutid, getutline, pututline, setutent, endutent, utmpname — access utmp file entry

SYNOPSIS

#include <utmp.h>

struct utmp *getutent ( )

struct utmp *getutid (id)
struct utmp *id;

struct utmp *getutline (line)
struct utmp *line;

void pututline (utmp)
struct utmp *utmp;

void setutent ( )

void endutent ( )

void utmpname (file)
char *file;

DESCRIPTION

Getutent, *getutid* and *getutline* each return a pointer to a structure of the following type:

```
struct utmp {
        char        ut_user[8];          /* User login name */
        char        ut_id[4];            /* /etc/inittab id (usually line #) */
        char        ut_line[12];         /* device name (console, lnxx) */
        short       ut_pid;              /* process id */
        short       ut_type;             /* type of entry */
        struct      exit_status {
           short       e_termination;    /* Process termination status */
           short       e_exit;           /* Process exit status */
        } ut_exit;                       /* The exit status of a process
                                          * marked as DEAD_PROCESS. */
        time_t      ut_time;             /* time entry was made */
};
```

Getutent reads in the next entry from a *utmp*-like file. If the file is not already open, it opens it. If it reaches the end of the file, it fails.

Getutid searches forward from the current point in the *utmp* file until it finds an entry with a *ut_type* matching *id->ut_type* if the type specified is RUN_LVL, BOOT_TIME, OLD_TIME or NEW_TIME. If the type specified in *id* is INIT_PROCESS, LOGIN_PROCESS, USER_PROCESS or DEAD_PROCESS, then *getutid* will return a pointer to the first entry whose type is one of these four and whose *ut_id* field matches *id->ut_id*. If the end of file is reached without a match, it fails.

Getutline searches forward from the current point in the *utmp* file until it finds an entry of the type LOGIN_PROCESS or USER_PROCESS which also has a *ut_line* string matching the *line->ut_line* string. If the end of file is reached without a match, it fails.

Pututline writes out the supplied *utmp* structure into the *utmp* file. It uses *getutid* to search forward for the proper place if it finds that it is not already at the proper place. It is expected that normally the user of *pututline* will have searched for the proper entry using one of the *getut* routines. If so, *pututline* will not search. If *pututline* does not find a matching slot for the new entry, it will add a new entry to the end of the file.

Setutent resets the input stream to the beginning of the file. This should be done before each search for a new entry if it is desired that the entire file be examined.

Endutent closes the currently open file.

Utmpname allows the user to change the name of the file examined, from **/etc/utmp** to any other file. It is most often expected that this other file will be **/etc/wtmp**. If the file does not exist, this will not be apparent until the first attempt to reference the file is made. *Utmpname* does not open the file. It just closes the old file if it is currently open and saves the new file name.

FILES

/etc/utmp
/etc/wtmp

SEE ALSO

ttyslot(3C), utmp(4).

DIAGNOSTICS

A **NULL** pointer is returned upon failure to read, whether for permissions or having reached the end of file, or upon failure to write.

NAME

hsearch, hcreate, hdestroy — manage hash search tables

SYNOPSIS

#include <search.h>

ENTRY *hsearch (item, action)
ENTRY item;
ACTION action;

int hcreate (nel)
unsigned nel;

void hdestroy ( )

DESCRIPTION

Hsearch is a hash-table search routine generalized from Knuth (6.4) Algorithm D. It returns a pointer into a hash table indicating the location at which an entry can be found. *Item* is a structure of type ENTRY (defined in the *<search.h>* header file) containing two pointers: *item.key* points to the comparison key, and *item.data* points to any other data to be associated with that key. (Pointers to types other than character should be cast to pointer-to-character.) *Action* is a member of an enumeration type ACTION indicating the disposition of the entry if it cannot be found in the table. **ENTER** indicates that the item should be inserted in the table at an appropriate point. **FIND** indicates that no entry should be made. Unsuccessful resolution is indicated by the return of a NULL pointer.

Hcreate allocates sufficient space for the table, and must be called before *hsearch* is used. *Nel* is an estimate of the maximum number of entries that the table will contain. This number may be adjusted upward by the algorithm in order to obtain certain mathematically favorable circumstances.

Hdestroy destroys the search table, and may be followed by another call to *hcreate*.

NOTES

Hsearch uses *open addressing* with a *multiplicative* hash function. However, its source code has many other options available which the user may select by compiling the *hsearch* source with the following symbols defined to the preprocessor:

DIV Use the *remainder modulo table size* as the hash function instead of the multiplicative algorithm.

USCR Use a User Supplied Comparison Routine for ascertaining table membership. The routine should be named *hcompar* and should behave in a mannner similar to *strcmp* (see *string*(3C)).

CHAINED Use a linked list to resolve collisions. If this option is selected, the following other options become available.

START Place new entries at the beginning of the linked list (default is at the end).

SORTUP Keep the linked list sorted by key in ascending order.

SORTDOWN Keep the linked list sorted by key in descending order.

Additionally, there are preprocessor flags for obtaining debugging printout (**−DDEBUG**) and for including a test driver in the calling routine (**−DDRIVER**). The source code should be consulted for further details.

EXAMPLE

The following example will read in strings followed by two numbers and store them in a hash table, discarding duplicates. It will then read in strings and find the matching entry in the hash table and print it out.

```
#include <stdio.h>
#include <search.h>

struct info {                /* this is the info stored in the table */
        int age, room;       /* other than the key. */
};
#define NUM_EMPL      5000     /* # elements in search table */

main( )
{
        /* space to store strings */
        char string_space[NUM_EMPL*20];
        /* space to store employee info */
        struct info info_space[NUM_EMPL];
        /* next avail space in string_space */
```

```
        char *str_ptr = string_space;
        /* next avail space in info_space */
        struct info *info_ptr = info_space;
        ENTRY item, *found_item, *hsearch( );
        /* name to look for in table */
        char name_to_find[30];
        int i = 0;

        /* create table */
        (void) hcreate(NUM_EMPL);
        while (scanf("%s%d%d", str_ptr, &info_ptr->age,
                &info_ptr->room) != EOF && i++ < NUM_EMPL) {
                /* put info in structure, and structure in item */
                item.key = str_ptr;
                item.data = (char *)info_ptr;
                str_ptr += strlen(str_ptr) + 1;
                info_ptr++;
                /* put item into table */
                (void) hsearch(item, ENTER);
        }

        /* access table */
        item.key = name_to_find;
        while (scanf("%s", item.key) != EOF) {
            if ((found_item = hsearch(item, FIND)) != NULL) {
                /* if item is in the table */
                (void)printf("found %s, age = %d, room = %d\n",
                        found_item->key,
                        ((struct info *)found_item->data)->age,
                        ((struct info *)found_item->data)->room);
            } else {
                (void)printf("no such employee %s\n",
                        name_to_find)
            }
        }
}
```

SEE ALSO

bsearch(3C), lsearch(3C), malloc(3C), malloc(3X), string(3C), tsearch(3C).

DIAGNOSTICS

Hsearch returns a NULL pointer if either the action is **FIND** and the item could not be found or the action is **ENTER** and the table is full.

Hcreate returns zero if it cannot allocate sufficient space for the table.

WARNING

Hsearch and *hcreate* use *malloc*(3C) to allocate space.

BUGS

Only one hash search table may be active at any given time.

NAME

l3tol, ltol3 — convert between 3-byte integers and long integers

SYNOPSIS

```
void l3tol (lp, cp, n)
long *lp;
char *cp;
int n;

void ltol3 (cp, lp, n)
char *cp;
long *lp;
int n;
```

DESCRIPTION

L3tol converts a list of *n* three-byte integers packed into a character string pointed to by *cp* into a list of long integers pointed to by *lp*.

Ltol3 performs the reverse conversion from long integers (*lp*) to three-byte integers (*cp*).

These functions are useful for file-system maintenance where the block numbers are three bytes long.

SEE ALSO

fs(4).

BUGS

Because of possible differences in byte ordering, the numerical values of the long integers are machine-dependent.

NAME

lockf − record locking on files

SYNOPSIS

 # include <unistd.h>

lockf (fildes, function, size) long size; int fildes, function;

DESCRIPTION

The *lockf* call will allow sections of a file to be locked (advisory write locks). (Mandatory or enforcement mode record locks are not currently available.) Locking calls from other processes which attempt to lock the locked file section will either return an error value or be put to sleep until the resource becomes unlocked. All the locks for a process are removed when the process terminates. [See *fcntl*(2) for more information about record locking.]

Fildes is an open file descriptor. The file descriptor must have O_WRONLY or O_RDWR permission in order to establish a lock with this function call.

Function is a control value which specifies the action to be taken. The permissible values for *function* are defined in **<unistd.h>** as follows:

```
#define   F_ULOCK   0   /* Unlock previously locked section */
#define   F_LOCK    1   /* Lock section for exclusive use */
#define   F_TLOCK   2   /* Test/lock section for exclusive use */
#define   F_TEST    3   /* Test for other processes locks */
```

All other values of *function* are reserved for future extensions and will result in an error return if not implemented.

F_TEST is used to detect if a lock by another process is present on the specified section. F_LOCK and F_TLOCK both lock a section of a file if the section is available. F_UNLOCK removes locks from a section of the file.

Size is the number of contiguous bytes to be locked or unlocked. The resource to be locked starts at the current offset in the file and extends forward for positive size and backward for negative size. If *size* is zero, the section from current offset through the largest file offset is locked (i.e., from current offset through the present or any future end-of-file). An area need not be allocated to a file in order to be locked, as such locks may exist past end-of-file.

The sections locked with F_LOCK or F_TLOCK may, in whole or in part, contain or be contained by a previously locked section for the same process. When this occurs, or if adjacent sections occur, the sections are combined into a single section. If the request requires that a new element be added to the table of active locks and this table is already full, an error is returned, and the new section is not locked.

F_LOCK and F_TLOCK requests differ only by the action taken if the resource is not available. F_LOCK will cause the calling process to sleep until the resource is available. F_TLOCK will cause the function to return a −1 and set *errno* to [EACCESS] error if the section is already locked by another process.

F_ULOCK requests may, in whole or in part, release one or more locked sections controlled by the process. When sections are not fully released, the remaining sections are still locked by the process. Releasing the center section of a locked section requires an additional element in the table of active locks. If this table is full, an [EDEADLK] error is returned and the requested section is not released.

A potential for deadlock occurs if a process controlling a locked resource is put to sleep by accessing another process's locked resource. Thus calls to *lock* or *fcntl* scan for a deadlock prior to sleeping on a locked resource. An error return is made if sleeping on the locked resource would cause a deadlock.

Sleeping on a resource is interrupted with any signal. The *alarm*(2) command may be used to provide a timeout facility in applications which require this facility.

ERRORS

The *lockf* utility will fail if one or more of the following are true:

[EBADF]
: *Fildes* is not a valid open descriptor.

[EACCESS]
: *Cmd* is F_TLOCK or F_TEST and the section is already locked by another process.

[EDEADLK]
Cmd is F_LOCK or F_TLOCK and a deadlock would occur. Also the *cmd* is either of the above or F_ULOCK and the number of entries in the lock table would exceed the number allocated on the system.

RETURN VALUE

Upon successful completion, a value of 0 is returned. Otherwise, a value of −1 is returned and *errno* is set to indicate the error.

CAVEATS

Unexpected results may occur in processes that do buffering in the user address space. The process may later read/write data which is/was locked. The standard I/O package is the most common source of unexpected buffering.

SEE ALSO

close(2), creat(2), fcntl(2), intro(2), open(2), read(2), write(2).

NAME

lsearch, lfind — linear search and update

SYNOPSIS

#include <stdio.h>
#include <search.h>

char *lsearch ((char *)key, (char *)base, nelp, sizeof(*key), compar)
unsigned *nelp;
int (*compar)( );

char *lfind ((char *)key, (char *)base, nelp, sizeof(*key), compar)
unsigned *nelp;
int (*compar)( );

DESCRIPTION

Lsearch is a linear search routine generalized from Knuth (6.1) Algorithm S. It returns a pointer into a table indicating where a datum may be found. If the datum does not occur, it is added at the end of the table. **Key** points to the datum to be sought in the table. **Base** points to the first element in the table. **Nelp** points to an integer containing the current number of elements in the table. The integer is incremented if the datum is added to the table. **Compar** is the name of the comparison function which the user must supply (*strcmp*, for example). It is called with two arguments that point to the elements being compared. The function must return zero if the elements are equal and non-zero otherwise.

Lfind is the same as *lsearch* except that if the datum is not found, it is not added to the table. Instead, a NULL pointer is returned.

NOTES

The pointers to the key and the element at the base of the table should be of type pointer-to-element, and cast to type pointer-to-character.
The comparison function need not compare every byte, so arbitrary data may be contained in the elements in addition to the values being compared.
Although declared as type pointer-to-character, the value returned should be cast into type pointer-to-element.

EXAMPLE

This fragment will read in ≤ TABSIZE strings of length ≤ ELSIZE and store them in a table, eliminating duplicates.

```
#include <stdio.h>
#include <search.h>

#define TABSIZE 50
#define ELSIZE 120

        char line[ELSIZE], tab[TABSIZE][ELSIZE], *lsearch( );
        unsigned nel = 0;
        int strcmp( );
        . . .
        while (fgets(line, ELSIZE, stdin) != NULL &&
            nel < TABSIZE)
                (void) lsearch(line, (char *)tab, &nel,
                        ELSIZE, strcmp);
        . . .
```

SEE ALSO

bsearch(3C), hsearch(3C), tsearch(3C).

DIAGNOSTICS

If the searched for datum is found, both *lsearch* and *lfind* return a pointer to it. Otherwise, *lfind* returns NULL and *lsearch* returns a pointer to the newly added element.

BUGS

Undefined results can occur if there is not enough room in the table to add a new item.

NAME

malloc, free, realloc, calloc — main memory allocator

SYNOPSIS

char *malloc (size)
unsigned size;

void free (ptr)
char *ptr;

char *realloc (ptr, size)
char *ptr;
unsigned size;

char *calloc (nelem, elsize)
unsigned nelem, elsize;

DESCRIPTION

Malloc and *free* provide a simple general-purpose memory allocation package. *Malloc* returns a pointer to a block of at least *size* bytes suitably aligned for any use.

The argument to *free* is a pointer to a block previously allocated by *malloc*; after *free* is performed this space is made available for further allocation, but its contents are left undisturbed.

Undefined results will occur if the space assigned by *malloc* is overrun or if some random number is handed to *free*.

Malloc allocates the first big enough contiguous reach of free space found in a circular search from the last block allocated or freed, coalescing adjacent free blocks as it searches. It calls *sbrk* (see *brk*(2)) to get more memory from the system when there is no suitable space already free.

Realloc changes the size of the block pointed to by *ptr* to *size* bytes and returns a pointer to the (possibly moved) block. The contents will be unchanged up to the lesser of the new and old sizes. If no free block of *size* bytes is available in the storage arena, then *realloc* will ask *malloc* to enlarge the arena by *size* bytes and will then move the data to the new space.

Realloc also works if *ptr* points to a block freed since the last call of *malloc*, *realloc*, or *calloc*; thus sequences of *free*, *malloc* and *realloc* can exploit the search strategy of *malloc* to do storage compaction.

Calloc allocates space for an array of *nelem* elements of size *elsize*. The space is initialized to zeros.

Each of the allocation routines returns a pointer to space suitably aligned (after possible pointer coercion) for storage of any type of object.

SEE ALSO

brk(2), malloc(3X).

DIAGNOSTICS

Malloc, *realloc* and *calloc* return a NULL pointer if there is no available memory or if the arena has been detectably corrupted by storing outside the bounds of a block. When this happens the block pointed to by *ptr* may be destroyed.

NOTE

Search time increases when many objects have been allocated; that is, if a program allocates but never frees, then each successive allocation takes longer. For an alternate, more flexible implementation, see *malloc*(3X).

NAME

memccpy, memchr, memcmp, memcpy, memset — memory operations

SYNOPSIS

#include <memory.h>

char *memccpy (s1, s2, c, n)
char *s1, *s2;
int c, n;

char *memchr (s, c, n)
char *s;
int c, n;

int memcmp (s1, s2, n)
char *s1, *s2;
int n;

char *memcpy (s1, s2, n)
char *s1, *s2;
int n;

char *memset (s, c, n)
char *s;
int c, n;

DESCRIPTION

These functions operate as efficiently as possible on memory areas (arrays of characters bounded by a count, not terminated by a null character). They do not check for the overflow of any receiving memory area.

Memccpy copies characters from memory area **s2** into **s1**, stopping after the first occurrence of character **c** has been copied, or after **n** characters have been copied, whichever comes first. It returns a pointer to the character after the copy of **c** in **s1**, or a NULL pointer if **c** was not found in the first **n** characters of **s2**.

Memchr returns a pointer to the first occurrence of character **c** in the first **n** characters of memory area **s**, or a NULL pointer if **c** does not occur.

Memcmp compares its arguments, looking at the first **n** characters only, and returns an integer less than, equal to, or greater than 0, according as **s1** is lexicographically less than, equal to, or greater than **s2**.

Memcpy copies **n** characters from memory area **s2** to **s1**. It returns **s1**.

Memset sets the first **n** characters in memory area **s** to the value of character **c**. It returns **s**.

NOTE

For user convenience, all these functions are declared in the optional <*memory.h*> header file.

BUGS

Memcmp uses native character comparison, which is unsigned on on some machines. Thus the sign of the value returned when one of the characters has its high-order bit set is implementation-dependent.

Character movement is performed differently in different implementations. Thus overlapping moves may yield surprises.

NAME

mktemp − make a unique file name

SYNOPSIS

char *mktemp (template)
char *template;

DESCRIPTION

Mktemp replaces the contents of the string pointed to by *template* by a unique file name, and returns the address of *template*. The string in *template* should look like a file name with six trailing **X**s; *mktemp* will replace the **X**s with a letter and the current process ID. The letter will be chosen so that the resulting name does not duplicate an existing file.

SEE ALSO

getpid(2), tmpfile(3S), tmpnam(3S).

BUGS

It is possible to run out of letters.

NAME

monitor − prepare execution profile

SYNOPSIS

#include <mon.h>

void monitor (lowpc, highpc, buffer, bufsize, nfunc)
int (*lowpc)( ), (*highpc)( );
WORD *buffer;
int bufsize, nfunc;

DESCRIPTION

An executable program created by **cc −p** automatically includes calls for *monitor* with default parameters; *monitor* needn't be called explicitly except to gain fine control over profiling.

Monitor is an interface to *profil*(2). *Lowpc* and *highpc* are the addresses of two functions; *buffer* is the address of a (user supplied) array of *bufsize* WORDs (defined in the *<mon.h>* header file). *Monitor* arranges to record a histogram of periodically sampled values of the program counter, and of counts of calls of certain functions, in the buffer. The lowest address sampled is that of *lowpc* and the highest is just below *highpc*. *Lowpc* may not equal 0 for this use of *monitor*. At most *nfunc* call counts can be kept; only calls of functions compiled with the profiling option **−p** of *cc*(1) are recorded. (Except on the PDP-11, the C Library and Math Library supplied when **cc −p** is used also have call counts recorded.)

For the results to be significant, especially where there are small, heavily used routines, it is suggested that the buffer be no more than a few times smaller than the range of locations sampled.

To profile the entire program, it is sufficient to use

```
extern etext;
...
monitor ((int (*)())2, etext, buf, bufsize, nfunc);
```

Etext lies just above all the program text; see *end*(3C).

To stop execution monitoring and write the results on the file **mon.out**, use

```
monitor ((int (*)())0, 0, 0, 0, 0);
```

Prof(1) can then be used to examine the results.

FILES

mon.out
/lib/libp/libc.a
/lib/libp/libm.a

SEE ALSO

profil(2), end(3C).
cc(1), prof(1) in the *UNIX Programmer's Manual—Volume 1: Commands and Utilities.*

NAME

nlist − get entries from name list

SYNOPSIS

#include <nlist.h>

int nlist (file-name, nl)
char *file-name;
struct nlist *nl;

DESCRIPTION

Nlist examines the name list in the executable file whose name is pointed to by *file-name*, and selectively extracts a list of values and puts them in the array of nlist structures pointed to by *nl*. The name list *nl* consists of an array of structures containing names of variables, types and values. The list is terminated with a null name; that is, a null string is in the name position of the structure. Each variable name is looked up in the name list of the file. If the name is found, the type and value of the name are inserted in the next two fields. The type field will be set to 0 unless the file was compiled with the −g option. If the name is not found, both entries are set to 0. See *a.out*(4) for a discussion of the symbol table structure.

This function is useful for examining the system name list kept in the file **/unix**. In this way programs can obtain system addresses that are up to date.

NOTES

The *<nlist.h>* header file is automatically included by *<a.out.h>* for compatability. However, if the only information needed from *<a.out.h>* is for use of *nlist*, then including *<a.out.h>* is discouraged. If *<a.out.h>* is included, the line "#undef n_name" may need to follow it.

SEE ALSO

a.out(4).

DIAGNOSTICS

All value entries are set to 0 if the file cannot be read or if it does not contain a valid name list.

Nlist returns −1 upon error; otherwise it returns 0.

NAME

perror, errno, sys_errlist, sys_nerr — system error messages

SYNOPSIS

void perror (s)
char *s;

extern int errno;

extern char *sys_errlist[ ];

extern int sys_nerr;

DESCRIPTION

Perror produces a message on the standard error output, describing the last error encountered during a call to a system or library function. The argument string *s* is printed first, then a colon and a blank, then the message and a new-line. To be of most use, the argument string should include the name of the program that incurred the error. The error number is taken from the external variable *errno*, which is set when errors occur but not cleared when non-erroneous calls are made.

To simplify variant formatting of messages, the array of message strings *sys_errlist* is provided; *errno* can be used as an index in this table to get the message string without the new-line. *Sys_nerr* is the largest message number provided for in the table; it should be checked because new error codes may be added to the system before they are added to the table.

SEE ALSO

intro(2).

NAME

putenv – change or add value to environment

SYNOPSIS

int putenv (string)
char *string;

DESCRIPTION

String points to a string of the form *"name=value." Putenv* makes the value of the environment variable *name* equal to *value* by altering an existing variable or creating a new one. In either case, the string pointed to by *string* becomes part of the environment, so altering the string will change the environment. The space used by *string* is no longer used once a new string-defining *name* is passed to *putenv*.

DIAGNOSTICS

Putenv returns non-zero if it was unable to obtain enough space via *malloc* for an expanded environment, otherwise zero.

SEE ALSO

exec(2), getenv(3C), malloc(3C), environ(5).

WARNINGS

Putenv manipulates the environment pointed to by *environ*, and can be used in conjunction with *getenv*. However, *envp* (the third argument to *main*) is not changed.

This routine uses *malloc*(3C) to enlarge the environment.

After *putenv* is called, environmental variables are not in alphabetical order.

A potential error is to call *putenv* with an automatic variable as the argument, then exit the calling function while *string* is still part of the environment.

NAME

putpwent — write password file entry

SYNOPSIS

#include <pwd.h>

int putpwent (p, f)
struct passwd *p;
FILE *f;

DESCRIPTION

Putpwent is the inverse of *getpwent*(3C). Given a pointer to a passwd structure created by *getpwent* (or *getpwuid* or *getpwnam*), *putpwent* writes a line on the stream *f*, which matches the format of **/etc/passwd**.

DIAGNOSTICS

Putpwent returns non-zero if an error was detected during its operation, otherwise zero.

SEE ALSO

getpwent(3C).

WARNING

The above routine uses **<stdio.h>**, which causes it to increase the size of programs, not otherwise using standard I/O, more than might be expected.

NAME

qsort — quicker sort

SYNOPSIS

void qsort ((char *) base, nel, sizeof (*base), compar)
unsigned nel;
int (*compar)( );

DESCRIPTION

Qsort is an implementation of the quicker-sort algorithm. It sorts a table of data in place.

Base points to the element at the base of the table. *Nel* is the number of elements in the table. *Compar* is the name of the comparison function, which is called with two arguments that point to the elements being compared. As the function must return an integer less than, equal to, or greater than zero, so must the first argument to be considered be less than, equal to, or greater than the second.

NOTES

The pointer to the base of the table should be of type pointer-to-element, and cast to type pointer-to-character.
The comparison function need not compare every byte, so arbitrary data may be contained in the elements in addition to the values being compared.
The order in the output of two items which compare as equal is unpredictable.

SEE ALSO

bsearch(3C), lsearch(3C), string(3C).
sort(1) in the *UNIX Programmer's Manual—Volume 1: Commands and Utilities*.

NAME

rand, srand — simple random-number generator

SYNOPSIS

int rand ( )

void srand (seed)
unsigned seed;

DESCRIPTION

Rand uses a multiplicative congruential random-number generator with period 2^{32} that returns successive pseudo-random numbers in the range from 0 to $2^{15}-1$.

Srand can be called at any time to reset the random-number generator to a random starting point. The generator is initially seeded with a value of 1.

NOTE

The spectral properties of *rand* leave a great deal to be desired. *Drand48*(3C) provides a much better, though more elaborate, random-number generator.

SEE ALSO

drand48(3C).

NAME

setjmp, longjmp − non-local goto

SYNOPSIS

#include <setjmp.h>

int setjmp (env)
jmp_buf env;

void longjmp (env, val)
jmp_buf env;
int val;

DESCRIPTION

These functions are useful for dealing with errors and interrupts encountered in a low-level subroutine of a program.

Setjmp saves its stack environment in *env* (whose type, *jmp_buf*, is defined in the *<setjmp.h>* header file) for later use by *longjmp*. It returns the value 0.

Longjmp restores the environment saved by the last call of *setjmp* with the corresponding *env* argument. After *longjmp* is completed, program execution continues as if the corresponding call of *setjmp* (which must not itself have returned in the interim) had just returned the value *val*. *Longjmp* cannot cause *setjmp* to return the value 0. If *longjmp* is invoked with a second argument of 0, *setjmp* will return 1. All accessible data had values as of the time *longjmp* was called.

SEE ALSO

signal(2)

WARNING

If *longjmp* is called even though *env* was never primed by a call to *setjmp*, or when the last such call was in a function which has since returned, absolute chaos is guaranteed.

NAME

sleep – suspend execution for interval

SYNOPSIS

unsigned sleep (seconds)
unsigned seconds;

DESCRIPTION

The current process is suspended from execution for the number of *seconds* specified by the argument. The actual suspension time may be less than that requested for two reasons: (1) Because scheduled wakeups occur at fixed 1-second intervals, (on the second, according to an internal clock) and (2) because any caught signal will terminate the *sleep* following execution of that signal's catching routine. Also, the suspension time may be longer than requested by an arbitrary amount due to the scheduling of other activity in the system. The value returned by *sleep* will be the "unslept" amount (the requested time minus the time actually slept) in case the caller had an alarm set to go off earlier than the end of the requested *sleep* time, or premature arousal due to another caught signal.

The routine is implemented by setting an alarm signal and pausing until it (or some other signal) occurs. The previous state of the alarm signal is saved and restored. The calling program may have set up an alarm signal before calling *sleep*. If the *sleep* time exceeds the time till such alarm signal, the process sleeps only until the alarm signal would have occurred. The caller's alarm catch routine is executed just before the *sleep* routine returns. But if the *sleep* time is less than the time till such alarm, the prior alarm time is reset to go off at the same time it would have without the intervening *sleep*.

SEE ALSO

alarm(2), pause(2), signal(2).

NAME

ssignal, gsignal — software signals

SYNOPSIS

#include <signal.h>

int (*ssignal (sig, action))( )
int sig, (*action)( );

int gsignal (sig)
int sig;

DESCRIPTION

Ssignal and *gsignal* implement a software facility similar to *signal*(2). This facility is used by the Standard C Library to enable users to indicate the disposition of error conditions, and is also made available to users for their own purposes.

Software signals made available to users are associated with integers in the inclusive range 1 through 15. A call to *ssignal* associates a procedure, *action*, with the software signal *sig*; the software signal, *sig*, is raised by a call to *gsignal*. Raising a software signal causes the action established for that signal to be *taken*.

The first argument to *ssignal* is a number identifying the type of signal for which an action is to be established. The second argument defines the action; it is either the name of a (user-defined) *action function* or one of the manifest constants **SIG_DFL** (default) or **SIG_IGN** (ignore). *Ssignal* returns the action previously established for that signal type; if no action has been established or the signal number is illegal, *ssignal* returns **SIG_DFL**.

Gsignal raises the signal identified by its argument, *sig*:

> If an action function has been established for *sig*, then that action is reset to **SIG_DFL** and the action function is entered with argument *sig*. *Gsignal* returns the value returned to it by the action function.
>
> If the action for *sig* is **SIG_IGN**, *gsignal* returns the value 1 and takes no other action.
>
> If the action for *sig* is **SIG_DFL**, *gsignal* returns the value 0 and takes no other action.
>
> If *sig* has an illegal value or no action was ever specified for *sig*, *gsignal* returns the value 0 and takes no other action.

SEE ALSO

signal(2).

NOTES

There are some additional signals with numbers outside the range 1 through 15 which are used by the Standard C Library to indicate error conditions. Thus, some signal numbers outside the range 1 through 15 are legal, although their use may interfere with the operation of the Standard C Library.

NAME

ftok − standard interprocess communication package

SYNOPSIS

```
#include <sys/types.h>
#include <sys/ipc.h>

key_t ftok(path, id)
char *path;
char id;
```

DESCRIPTION

All interprocess communication facilities require the user to supply a key to be used by the *msgget*(2), *semget*(2), and *shmget*(2) system calls to obtain interprocess communication identifiers. One suggested method for forming a key is to use the *ftok* subroutine described below. Another way to compose keys is to include the project ID in the most significant byte and to use the remaining portion as a sequence number. There are many other ways to form keys, but it is necessary for each system to define standards for forming them. If some standard is not adhered to, it will be possible for unrelated processes to unintentionally interfere with each other's operation. Therefore, it is strongly suggested that the most significant byte of a key in some sense refer to a project so that keys do not conflict across a given system.

Ftok returns a key based on *path* and *id* that is usable in subsequent *msgget*, *semget*, and *shmget* system calls. *Path* must be the path name of an existing file that is accessible to the process. *Id* is a character which uniquely identifies a project. Note that *ftok* will return the same key for linked files when called with the same *id* and that it will return different keys when called with the same file name but different *ids*.

SEE ALSO

intro(2), msgget(2), semget(2), shmget(2).

DIAGNOSTICS

Ftok returns **(key_t) −1** if *path* does not exist or if it is not accessible to the process.

WARNING

If the file whose *path* is passed to *ftok* is removed when keys still refer to the file, future calls to *ftok* with the same *path* and *id* will return an error. If the same file is recreated, then *ftok* is likely to return a different key than it did the original time it was called.

NAME

strcat, strncat, strcmp, strncmp, strcpy, strncpy, strlen, strchr, strrchr, strpbrk, strspn, strcspn, strtok — string operations

SYNOPSIS

```
#include <string.h>

char *strcat (s1, s2)
char *s1, *s2;

char *strncat (s1, s2, n)
char *s1, *s2;
int n;

int strcmp (s1, s2)
char *s1, *s2;

int strncmp (s1, s2, n)
char *s1, *s2;
int n;

char *strcpy (s1, s2)
char *s1, *s2;

char *strncpy (s1, s2, n)
char *s1, *s2;
int n;

int strlen (s)
char *s;

char *strchr (s, c)
char *s;
int c;

char *strrchr (s, c)
char *s;
int c;

char *strpbrk (s1, s2)
char *s1, *s2;

int strspn (s1, s2)
char *s1, *s2;

int strcspn (s1, s2)
char *s1, *s2;

char *strtok (s1, s2)
char *s1, *s2;
```

DESCRIPTION

The arguments **s1, s2** and **s** point to strings (arrays of characters terminated by a null character). The functions *strcat*, *strncat*, *strcpy*, and *strncpy* all alter **s1**. These functions do not check for overflow of the array pointed to by **s1**.

Strcat appends a copy of string **s2** to the end of string **s1**. *Strncat* appends at most **n** characters. Each returns a pointer to the null-terminated result.

Strcmp compares its arguments and returns an integer less than, equal to, or greater than 0, according as **s1** is lexicographically less than, equal to, or greater than **s2**. *Strncmp* makes the same comparison but looks at at most **n** characters.

Strcpy copies string **s2** to **s1**, stopping after the null character has been copied. *Strncpy* copies exactly **n** characters, truncating **s2** or adding null characters to **s1** if necessary. The result will not be null-terminated if the length of **s2** is **n** or more. Each function returns **s1**.

Strlen returns the number of characters in **s**, not including the terminating null character.

Strchr (*strrchr*) returns a pointer to the first (last) occurrence of character **c** in string **s**, or a NULL pointer if **c** does not occur in the string. The null character terminating a string is considered to be part of the string.

Strpbrk returns a pointer to the first occurrence in string **s1** of any character from string **s2**, or a NULL pointer if no character from **s2** exists in **s1**.

Strspn (*strcspn*) returns the length of the initial segment of string **s1** which consists entirely of characters from (not from) string **s2**.

Strtok considers the string **s1** to consist of a sequence of zero or more text tokens separated by spans of one or more characters from the separator string **s2**. The first call (with pointer **s1** specified) returns a pointer to the first character of the first token, and will have written a null character into **s1** immediately following the returned token. The function keeps track of its position in the string between separate calls, so that subsequent calls (which must be made with the first argument a NULL pointer) will work through the string **s1** immediately following that token. In this way subsequent calls will work through the string **s1** until no tokens remain. The separator string **s2** may be different from call to call. When no token remains in **s1**, a NULL pointer is returned.

NOTE

For user convenience, all these functions are declared in the optional <*string.h*> header file.

BUGS

Strcmp and *strncmp* use native character comparison, which is signed on most machines and unsigned on other machines. Thus the sign of the value returned when one of the characters has its high-order bit set is implementation-dependent.

Character movement is performed differently in different implementations. Thus overlapping moves may yield surprises.

NAME

strtod, atof — convert string to double-precision number

SYNOPSIS

double strtod (str, ptr)
char *str, **ptr;

double atof (str)
char *str;

DESCRIPTION

Strtod returns as a double-precision floating-point number the value represented by the character string pointed to by *str*. The string is scanned up to the first unrecognized character.

Strtod recognizes an optional string of "white-space" characters (as defined by *isspace* in *ctype*(3C)), then an optional sign, then a string of digits optionally containing a decimal point, then an optional **e** or **E** followed by an optional sign or space, followed by an integer.

If the value of *ptr* is not (char **)NULL, a pointer to the character terminating the scan is returned in the location pointed to by *ptr*. If no number can be formed, **ptr* is set to *str*, and zero is returned.

Atof(str) is equivalent to *strtod(str, (char **)NULL)*.

SEE ALSO

ctype(3C), scanf(3S), strtol(3C).

DIAGNOSTICS

If the correct value would cause overflow, ±**HUGE** is returned (according to the sign of the value), and *errno* is set to **ERANGE**.
If the correct value would cause underflow, zero is returned and *errno* is set to **ERANGE**.

NAME

strtol, atol, atoi — convert string to integer

SYNOPSIS

long strtol (str, ptr, base)
char *str, **ptr;
int base;

long atol (str)
char *str;

int atoi (str)
char *str;

DESCRIPTION

Strtol returns as a long integer the value represented by the character string pointed to by *str*. The string is scanned up to the first character inconsistent with the base. Leading "white-space" characters (as defined by *isspace* in *ctype*(3C)) are ignored.

If the value of *ptr* is not (char **)NULL, a pointer to the character terminating the scan is returned in the location pointed to by *ptr*. If no integer can be formed, that location is set to *str*, and zero is returned.

If *base* is positive (and not greater than 36), it is used as the base for conversion. After an optional leading sign, leading zeros are ignored, and "0x" or "0X" is ignored if *base* is 16.

If *base* is zero, the string itself determines the base thusly: After an optional leading sign a leading zero indicates octal conversion, and a leading "0x" or "0X" hexadecimal conversion. Otherwise, decimal conversion is used.

Truncation from long to int can, of course, take place upon assignment or by an explicit cast.

Atol(str) is equivalent to *strtol(str, (char **)NULL, 10)*.

Atoi(str) is equivalent to *(int) strtol(str, (char **)NULL, 10)*.

SEE ALSO

ctype(3C), scanf(3S), strtod(3C).

BUGS

Overflow conditions are ignored.

NAME

swab — swap bytes

SYNOPSIS

void swab (from, to, nbytes)
char *from, *to;
int nbytes;

DESCRIPTION

Swab copies *nbytes* bytes pointed to by *from* to the array pointed to by *to*, exchanging adjacent even and odd bytes. It is useful for carrying binary data between PDP-11s and other machines. *Nbytes* should be even and non-negative. If *nbytes* is odd and positive *swab* uses *nbytes*−1 instead. If *nbytes* is negative, *swab* does nothing.

NAME

tsearch, tfind, tdelete, twalk − manage binary search trees

SYNOPSIS

#include <search.h>

char *tsearch ((char *) key, (char **) rootp, compar)
int (*compar)( );

char *tfind ((char *) key, (char **) rootp, compar)
int (*compar)( );

char *tdelete ((char *) key, (char **) rootp, compar)
int (*compar)( );

void twalk ((char *) root, action)
void (*action)( );

DESCRIPTION

Tsearch, tfind, tdelete, and *twalk* are routines for manipulating binary search trees. They are generalized from Knuth (6.2.2) Algorithms T and D. All comparisons are done with a user-supplied routine. This routine is called with two arguments, the pointers to the elements being compared. It returns an integer less than, equal to, or greater than 0, according to whether the first argument is to be considered less than, equal to or greater than the second argument. The comparison function need not compare every byte, so arbitrary data may be contained in the elements in addition to the values being compared.

Tsearch is used to build and access the tree. **Key** is a pointer to a datum to be accessed or stored. If there is a datum in the tree equal to *key (the value pointed to by key), a pointer to this found datum is returned. Otherwise, *key is inserted, and a pointer to it returned. Only pointers are copied, so the calling routine must store the data. **Rootp** points to a variable that points to the root of the tree. A NULL value for the variable pointed to by **rootp** denotes an empty tree; in this case, the variable will be set to point to the datum which will be at the root of the new tree.

Like *tsearch*, *tfind* will search for a datum in the tree, returning a pointer to it if found. However, if it is not found, *tfind* will return a NULL pointer. The arguments for *tfind* are the same as for *tsearch*.

Tdelete deletes a node from a binary search tree. The arguments are the same as for *tsearch*. The variable pointed to by **rootp** will be changed if the deleted node was the root of the tree. *Tdelete* returns a pointer to the parent of the deleted node, or a NULL pointer if the node is not found.

Twalk traverses a binary search tree. **Root** is the root of the tree to be traversed. (Any node in a tree may be used as the root for a walk below that node.) *Action* is the name of a routine to be invoked at each node. This routine is, in turn, called with three arguments. The first argument is the address of the node being visited. The second argument is a value from an enumeration data type *typedef enum* { *preorder, postorder, endorder, leaf* } *VISIT;* (defined in the *<search.h>* header file), depending on whether this is the first, second or third time that the node has been visited (during a depth-first, left-to-right traversal of the tree), or whether the node is a leaf. The third argument is the level of the node in the tree, with the root being level zero.

The pointers to the key and the root of the tree should be of type pointer-to-element, and cast to type pointer-to-character. Similarly, although declared as type pointer-to-character, the value returned should be cast into type pointer-to-element.

EXAMPLE

The following code reads in strings and stores structures containing a pointer to each string and a count of its length. It then walks the tree, printing out the stored strings and their lengths in alphabetical order.

```
#include <search.h>
#include <stdio.h>

struct node {                   /* pointers to these are stored in the tree */
        char *string;
        int length;
};
char string_space[10000]; /* space to store strings */
struct node nodes[500];         /* nodes to store */
struct node *root = NULL;       /* this points to the root */

main( )
{
        char *strptr = string_space;
        struct node *nodeptr = nodes;
        void print_node( ), twalk( );
        int i = 0, node_compare( );
```

```
		while (gets(strptr) != NULL && i++ < 500)  {
			/* set node */
			nodeptr->string = strptr;
			nodeptr->length = strlen(strptr);
			/* put node into the tree */
			(void) tsearch((char *)nodeptr, &root,
				node_compare);
			/* adjust pointers, so we don't overwrite tree */
			strptr += nodeptr->length + 1;
			nodeptr++;
		}
		twalk(root, print_node);
	}
	/*
		This routine compares two nodes, based on an
		alphabetical ordering of the string field.
	*/
	int
	node_compare(node1, node2)
	struct node *node1, *node2;
	{
		return strcmp(node1->string, node2->string);
	}
	/*
		This routine prints out a node, the first time
		twalk encounters it.
	*/
	void
	print_node(node, order, level)
	struct node **node;
	VISIT order;
	int level;
	{
		if (order == preorder || order == leaf)  {
			(void)printf("string = %20s,  length = %d\n",
				(*node)->string, (*node)->length);
		}
	}
```

SEE ALSO

bsearch(3C), hsearch(3C), lsearch(3C).

DIAGNOSTICS

A NULL pointer is returned by *tsearch* if there is not enough space available to create a new node.

A NULL pointer is returned by *tsearch, tfind* and *tdelete* if **rootp** is NULL on entry.

If the datum is found, both *tsearch* and *tfind* return a pointer to it. If not, *tfind* returns NULL, and *tsearch* returns a pointer to the inserted item.

WARNINGS

The **root** argument to *twalk* is one level of indirection less than the **rootp** arguments to *tsearch* and *tdelete*.

There are two nomenclatures used to refer to the order in which tree nodes are visited. *Tsearch* uses preorder, postorder and endorder to respectively refer to visting a node before any of its children, after its left child and before its right, and after both its children. The alternate nomenclature uses preorder, inorder and postorder to refer to the same visits, which could result in some confusion over the meaning of postorder.

BUGS

If the calling function alters the pointer to the root, results are unpredictable.

NAME

ttyname, isatty — find name of a terminal

SYNOPSIS

char *ttyname (fildes)
int fildes;

int isatty (fildes)
int fildes;

DESCRIPTION

Ttyname returns a pointer to a string containing the null-terminated path name of the terminal device associated with file descriptor *fildes*.

Isatty returns 1 if *fildes* is associated with a terminal device, 0 otherwise.

FILES

/dev/*

DIAGNOSTICS

Ttyname returns a NULL pointer if *fildes* does not describe a terminal device in directory **/dev**.

BUGS

The return value points to static data whose content is overwritten by each call.

NAME

ttyslot − find the slot in the utmp file of the current user

SYNOPSIS

int ttyslot ( )

DESCRIPTION

Ttyslot returns the index of the current user's entry in the **/etc/utmp** file. This is accomplished by actually scanning the file **/etc/inittab** for the name of the terminal associated with the standard input, the standard output, or the error output (0, 1 or 2).

FILES

/etc/inittab
/etc/utmp

SEE ALSO

getut(3C), ttyname(3C).

DIAGNOSTICS

A value of 0 is returned if an error was encountered while searching for the terminal name or if none of the above file descriptors is associated with a terminal device.

NAME

ctermid − generate file name for terminal

SYNOPSIS

#include <stdio.h>
char *ctermid (s)
char *s;

DESCRIPTION

Ctermid generates the path name of the controlling terminal for the current process, and stores it in a string.

If *s* is a NULL pointer, the string is stored in an internal static area, the contents of which are overwritten at the next call to *ctermid*, and the address of which is returned. Otherwise, *s* is assumed to point to a character array of at least **L_ctermid** elements; the path name is placed in this array and the value of *s* is returned. The constant **L_ctermid** is defined in the *<stdio.h>* header file.

NOTES

The difference between *ctermid* and *ttyname*(3C) is that *ttyname* must be handed a file descriptor and returns the actual name of the terminal associated with that file descriptor, while *ctermid* returns a string (**/dev/tty**) that will refer to the terminal if used as a file name. Thus *ttyname* is useful only if the process already has at least one file open to a terminal.

SEE ALSO

ttyname(3C).

NAME

cuserid — get character login name of the user

SYNOPSIS

#include <stdio.h>

char *cuserid (s)
char *s;

DESCRIPTION

Cuserid generates a character-string representation of the login name that the owner of the current process is logged in under. If *s* is a NULL pointer, this representation is generated in an internal static area, the address of which is returned. Otherwise, *s* is assumed to point to an array of at least **L_cuserid** characters; the representation is left in this array. The constant **L_cuserid** is defined in the **<stdio.h>** header file.

DIAGNOSTICS

If the login name cannot be found, *cuserid* returns a NULL pointer; if *s* is not a NULL pointer, a null character (**\0**) will be placed at *s[0]*.

SEE ALSO

getlogin(3C), getpwent(3C).

NAME

fclose, fflush − close or flush a stream

SYNOPSIS

```
#include <stdio.h>

int fclose (stream)
FILE *stream;

int fflush (stream)
FILE *stream;
```

DESCRIPTION

Fclose causes any buffered data for the named *stream* to be written out, and the *stream* to be closed.

Fclose is performed automatically for all open files upon calling *exit*(2).

Fflush causes any buffered data for the named *stream* to be written to that file. The *stream* remains open.

DIAGNOSTICS

These functions return 0 for success, and **EOF** if any error (such as trying to write to a file that has not been opened for writing) was detected.

SEE ALSO

close(2), exit(2), fopen(3S), setbuf(3S).

NAME

ferror, feof, clearerr, fileno — stream status inquiries

SYNOPSIS

#include <stdio.h>

int ferror (stream)
FILE *stream;

int feof (stream)
FILE *stream;

void clearerr (stream)
FILE *stream;

int fileno (stream)
FILE *stream;

DESCRIPTION

Ferror returns non-zero when an I/O error has previously occurred reading from or writing to the named *stream*, otherwise zero.

Feof returns non-zero when **EOF** has previously been detected reading the named input *stream*, otherwise zero.

Clearerr resets the error indicator and **EOF** indicator to zero on the named *stream*.

Fileno returns the integer file descriptor associated with the named *stream*; see *open* (2).

NOTE

All these functions are implemented as macros; they cannot be declared or redeclared.

SEE ALSO

open(2), fopen(3S).

NAME

fopen, freopen, fdopen – open a stream

SYNOPSIS

#include <stdio.h>

FILE *fopen (file-name, type)
char *file-name, *type;

FILE *freopen (file-name, type, stream)
char *file-name, *type;
FILE *stream;

FILE *fdopen (fildes, type)
int fildes;
char *type;

DESCRIPTION

Fopen opens the file named by *file-name* and associates a *stream* with it. *Fopen* returns a pointer to the FILE structure associated with the *stream*.

File-name points to a character string that contains the name of the filc to be opened.

Type is a character string having one of the following values:

"r"	open for reading
"w"	truncate or create for writing
"a"	append; open for writing at end of file, or create for writing
"r+"	open for update (reading and writing)
"w+"	truncate or create for update
"a+"	append; open or create for update at end-of-file

Freopen substitutes the named file in place of the open *stream*. The original *stream* is closed, regardless of whether the open ultimately succeeds. *Freopen* returns a pointer to the FILE structure associated with *stream*.

Freopen is typically used to attach the preopened *streams* associated with **stdin, stdout** and **stderr** to other files.

Fdopen associates a *stream* with a file descriptor. File descriptors are obtained from *open*, *dup*, *creat*, or *pipe*(2), which open files but do not return pointers to a FILE structure *stream*. Streams are necessary input for many of the Section 3S library routines. The *type* of *stream* must agree with the mode of the open file.

When a file is opened for update, both input and output may be done on the resulting *stream*. However, output may not be directly followed by input without an intervening *fseek* or *rewind*, and input may not be directly followed by output without an intervening *fseek*, *rewind*, or an input operation which encounters end-of-file.

When a file is opened for append (i.e., when *type* is "a" or "a+"), it is impossible to overwrite information already in the file. *Fseek* may be used to reposition the file pointer to any position in the file, but when output is written to the file, the current file pointer is disregarded. All output is written at the end of the file and causes the file pointer to be repositioned at the end of the output. If two separate processes open the same file for append, each process may write freely to the file without fear of destroying output being written by the other. The output from the two processes will be intermixed in the file in the order in which it is written.

SEE ALSO

creat(2), dup(2), open(2), pipe(2), fclose(3S), fseek(3S).

DIAGNOSTICS

Fopen and *freopen* return a NULL pointer on failure.

NAME

fread, fwrite − binary input/output

SYNOPSIS

```
#include <stdio.h>

int fread (ptr, size, nitems, stream)
char *ptr;
int size, nitems;
FILE *stream;

int fwrite (ptr, size, nitems, stream)
char *ptr;
int size, nitems;
FILE *stream;
```

DESCRIPTION

Fread copies, into an array pointed to by *ptr*, *nitems* items of data from the named input *stream*, where an item of data is a sequence of bytes (not necessarily terminated by a null byte) of length *size*. *Fread* stops appending bytes if an end-of-file or error condition is encountered while reading *stream,* or if *nitems* items have been read. *Fread* leaves the file pointer in *stream*, if defined, pointing to the byte following the last byte read if there is one. *Fread* does not change the contents of *stream*.

Fwrite appends at most *nitems* items of data from the array pointed to by *ptr* to the named output *stream*. *Fwrite* stops appending when it has appended *nitems* items of data or if an error condition is encountered on *stream*. *Fwrite* does not change the contents of the array pointed to by *ptr*.

The argument *size* is typically *sizeof(*ptr)* where the pseudo-function *sizeof* specifies the length of an item pointed to by *ptr*. If *ptr* points to a data type other than *char* it should be cast into a pointer to *char*.

SEE ALSO

read(2), write(2), fopen(3S), getc(3S), gets(3S), printf(3S), putc(3S), puts(3S), scanf(3S).

DIAGNOSTICS

Fread and *fwrite* return the number of items read or written. If *size* or *nitems* is non-positive, no characters are read or written and 0 is returned by both *fread* and *fwrite*.

NAME

fseek, rewind, ftell − reposition a file pointer in a stream

SYNOPSIS

```
#include <stdio.h>

int fseek (stream, offset, ptrname)
FILE *stream;
long offset;
int ptrname;

void rewind (stream)
FILE *stream;

long ftell (stream)
FILE *stream;
```

DESCRIPTION

Fseek sets the position of the next input or output operation on the *stream*. The new position is at the signed distance *offset* bytes from the beginning, from the current position, or from the end of the file, according as *ptrname* has the value 0, 1, or 2.

Rewind(*stream*) is equivalent to *fseek*(*stream*, 0L, 0), except that no value is returned.

Fseek and *rewind* undo any effects of *ungetc*(3S).

After *fseek* or *rewind*, the next operation on a file opened for update may be either input or output.

Ftell returns the offset of the current byte relative to the beginning of the file associated with the named *stream*.

SEE ALSO

lseek(2), fopen(3S), popen(3S), ungetc(3S).

DIAGNOSTICS

Fseek returns non-zero for improper seeks, otherwise zero. An improper seek can be, for example, an *fseek* done on a file that has not been opened via *fopen*; in particular, *fseek* may not be used on a terminal, or on a file opened via *popen*(3S).

WARNING

Although on the UNIX system an offset returned by *ftell* is measured in bytes, and it is permissible to seek to positions relative to that offset, portability to non-UNIX systems requires that an offset be used by *fseek* directly. Arithmetic may not meaningfully be performed on such an offset.

NAME

getc, getchar, fgetc, getw — get character or word from a stream

SYNOPSIS

#include <stdio.h>

int getc (stream)
FILE *stream;

int getchar ()

int fgetc (stream)
FILE *stream;

int getw (stream)
FILE *stream;

DESCRIPTION

Getc returns the next character (i.e., byte) from the named input *stream*, as an integer. It also moves the file pointer, if defined, ahead one character in *stream*. *Getchar* is defined as *getc(stdin)*. *Getc* and *getchar* are macros.

Fgetc behaves like *getc*, but is a function rather than a macro. *Fgetc* runs more slowly than *getc*, but it takes less space per invocation and its name can be passed as an argument to a function.

Getw returns the next word (i.e., integer) from the named input *stream*. *Getw* increments the associated file pointer, if defined, to point to the next word. The size of a word is the size of an integer and varies from machine to machine. *Getw* assumes no special alignment in the file.

SEE ALSO

fclose(3S), ferror(3S), fopen(3S), fread(3S), gets(3S), putc(3S), scanf(3S).

DIAGNOSTICS

These functions return the constant **EOF** at end-of-file or upon an error. Because **EOF** is a valid integer, *ferror*(3S) should be used to detect *getw* errors.

WARNING

If the integer value returned by *getc*, *getchar*, or *fgetc* is stored into a character variable and then compared against the integer constant **EOF**, the comparison may never succeed, because sign-extension of a character on widening to integer is machine-dependent.

BUGS

Because it is implemented as a macro, *getc* treats incorrectly a *stream* argument with side effects. In particular, **getc(*f++)** does not work sensibly. *Fgetc* should be used instead.
Because of possible differences in word length and byte ordering, files written using *putw* are machine-dependent, and may not be read using *getw* on a different processor.

NAME

gets, fgets — get a string from a stream

SYNOPSIS

```
#include <stdio.h>

char *gets (s)
char *s;

char *fgets (s, n, stream)
char *s;
int n;
FILE *stream;
```

DESCRIPTION

Gets reads characters from the standard input stream, *stdin,* into the array pointed to by *s*, until a new-line character is read or an end-of-file condition is encountered. The new-line character is discarded and the string is terminated with a null character.

Fgets reads characters from the *stream* into the array pointed to by *s*, until *n*−1 characters are read, or a new-line character is read and transferred to *s*, or an end-of-file condition is encountered. The string is then terminated with a null character.

SEE ALSO

ferror(3S), fopen(3S), fread(3S), getc(3S), scanf(3S).

DIAGNOSTICS

If end-of-file is encountered and no characters have been read, no characters are transferred to *s* and a NULL pointer is returned. If a read error occurs, such as trying to use these functions on a file that has not been opened for reading, a NULL pointer is returned. Otherwise *s* is returned.

NAME

popen, pclose — initiate pipe to/from a process

SYNOPSIS

#include <stdio.h>

FILE *popen (command, type)
char *command, *type;

int pclose (stream)
FILE *stream;

DESCRIPTION

The arguments to *popen* are pointers to null-terminated strings containing, respectively, a shell command line and an I/O mode, either **r** for reading or **w** for writing. *Popen* creates a pipe between the calling program and the command to be executed. The value returned is a stream pointer such that one can write to the standard input of the command, if the I/O mode is **w**, by writing to the file *stream*; and one can read from the standard output of the command, if the I/O mode is **r**, by reading from the file *stream*.

A stream opened by *popen* should be closed by *pclose*, which waits for the associated process to terminate and returns the exit status of the command.

Because open files are shared, a type **r** command may be used as an input filter and a type **w** as an output filter.

SEE ALSO

pipe(2), wait(2), fclose(3S), fopen(3S), system(3S).

DIAGNOSTICS

Popen returns a NULL pointer if files or processes cannot be created, or if the shell cannot be accessed.

Pclose returns −1 if *stream* is not associated with a "*popen*ed" command.

BUGS

If the original and "*popen*ed" processes concurrently read or write a common file, neither should use buffered I/O, because the buffering gets all mixed up. Problems with an output filter may be forestalled by careful buffer flushing, e.g. with *fflush*; see *fclose*(3S).

NAME

printf, fprintf, sprintf — print formatted output

SYNOPSIS

#include <stdio.h>

int printf (format [, arg] ... **)**
char *format;

int fprintf (stream, format [, arg] ... **)**
FILE *stream;
char *format;

int sprintf (s, format [, arg] ... **)**
char *s, format;

DESCRIPTION

Printf places output on the standard output stream *stdout*. *Fprintf* places output on the named output *stream*. *Sprintf* places "output," followed by the null character (**\0**), in consecutive bytes starting at **s*; it is the user's responsibility to ensure that enough storage is available. Each function returns the number of characters transmitted (not including the **\0** in the case of *sprintf*), or a negative value if an output error was encountered.

Each of these functions converts, formats, and prints its *args* under control of the *format*. The *format* is a character string that contains two types of objects: plain characters, which are simply copied to the output stream, and conversion specifications, each of which results in fetching of zero or more *args*. The results are undefined if there are insufficient *args* for the format. If the format is exhausted while *args* remain, the excess *args* are simply ignored.

Each conversion specification is introduced by the character %. After the %, the following appear in sequence:

> Zero or more *flags*, which modify the meaning of the conversion specification.
>
> An optional decimal digit string specifying a minimum *field width*. If the converted value has fewer characters than the field width, it will be padded on the left (or right, if the left-adjustment flag '—', described below, has been given) to the field width. If the field width for an s conversion is preceded by a 0, the string is right adjusted with zero-padding on the left.

A *precision* that gives the minimum number of digits to appear for the **d**, **o**, **u**, **x**, or **X** conversions, the number of digits to appear after the decimal point for the **e** and **f** conversions, the maximum number of significant digits for the **g** conversion, or the maximum number of characters to be printed from a string in **s** conversion. The precision takes the form of a period (**.**) followed by a decimal digit string; a null digit string is treated as zero.

An optional **l** (ell) specifying that a following **d**, **o**, **u**, **x**, or **X** conversion character applies to a long integer *arg*. A **l** before any other conversion character is ignored.

A character that indicates the type of conversion to be applied.

A field width or precision may be indicated by an asterisk (*) instead of a digit string. In this case, an integer *arg* supplies the field width or precision. The *arg* that is actually converted is not fetched until the conversion letter is seen, so the *arg*s specifying field width or precision must appear *before* the *arg* (if any) to be converted.

The flag characters and their meanings are:

− The result of the conversion will be left-justified within the field.

+ The result of a signed conversion will always begin with a sign (**+** or **−**).

blank If the first character of a signed conversion is not a sign, a blank will be prefixed to the result. This implies that if the blank and **+** flags both appear, the blank flag will be ignored.

This flag specifies that the value is to be converted to an "alternate form." For **c**, **d**, **s**, and **u** conversions, the flag has no effect. For **o** conversion, it increases the precision to force the first digit of the result to be a zero. For **x or X** conversion, a non-zero result will have **0x or 0X** prefixed to it. For **e**, **E**, **f**, **g**, and **G** conversions, the result will always contain a decimal point, even if no digits follow the point (normally, a decimal point appears in the result of these conversions only if a digit follows it). For **g** and **G** conversions, trailing zeroes will *not* be removed from the result (which they normally are).

The conversion characters and their meanings are:

d,o,u,x,x The integer *arg* is converted to signed decimal, unsigned octal, decimal, or hexadecimal notation (**x** and **X**), respectively; the letters **abcdef** are used for **x** conversion and the letters **ABCDEF** for **X** conversion. The precision specifies the minimum number of digits to appear; if the value being converted can be represented in fewer digits, it will be expanded with leading zeroes. (For compatibility with older versions, padding with leading zeroes may alternatively be specified by prepending a zero to the field width. This does not imply an octal value for the field width.) The default precision is 1. The result of converting a zero value with a precision of zero is a null string.

f The float or double *arg* is converted to decimal notation in the style "[−]ddd.ddd," where the number of digits after the decimal point is equal to the precision specification. If the precision is missing, six digits are output; if the precision is explicitly 0, no decimal point appears.

e,E The float or double *arg* is converted in the style "[−]d.ddde±dd," where there is one digit before the decimal point and the number of digits after it is equal to the precision; when the precision is missing, six digits are produced; if the precision is zero, no decimal point appears. The **E** format code will produce a number with **E** instead of **e** introducing the exponent. The exponent always contains at least two digits.

g,G The float or double *arg* is printed in style **f** or **e** (or in style **E** in the case of a **G** format code), with the precision specifying the number of significant digits. The style used depends on the value converted: style **e** will be used only if the exponent resulting from the conversion is less than −4 or greater than the precision. Trailing zeroes are removed from the result; a decimal point appears only if it is followed by a digit.

c The character *arg* is printed.

s The *arg* is taken to be a string (character pointer) and characters from the string are printed until a null character (**\0**) is encountered or the number of characters indicated by the precision specification is reached. If the precision is missing, it is taken to be infinite, so all characters up to the first null character are printed. A NULL value for *arg* will yield undefined results.

% Print a %; no argument is converted.

In no case does a non-existent or small field width cause truncation of a field; if the result of a conversion is wider than the field width, the field is simply expanded to contain the conversion result. Characters generated by *printf* and *fprintf* are printed as if *putc*(3S) had been called.

EXAMPLES

To print a date and time in the form "Sunday, July 3, 10:02," where *weekday* and *month* are pointers to null-terminated strings:

```
printf("%s, %s %d, %d:%.2d", weekday, month, day, hour, min);
```

To print π to 5 decimal places:

```
printf("pi = %.5f", 4 * atan(1.0));
```

SEE ALSO

ecvt(3C), putc(3S), scanf(3S), stdio(3S).

NAME

putc, putchar, fputc, putw — put character or word on a stream

SYNOPSIS

```
#include <stdio.h>

int putc (c, stream)
int c;
FILE *stream;

int putchar (c)
int c;

int fputc (c, stream)
int c;
FILE *stream;

int putw (w, stream)
int w;
FILE *stream;
```

DESCRIPTION

Putc writes the character *c* onto the output *stream* (at the position where the file pointer, if defined, is pointing). *Putchar*(*c*) is defined as *putc*(*c, stdout*). *Putc* and *putchar* are macros.

Fputc behaves like *putc*, but is a function rather than a macro. *Fputc* runs more slowly than *putc*, but it takes less space per invocation and its name can be passed as an argument to a function.

Putw writes the word (i.e. integer) *w* to the output *stream* (at the position at which the file pointer, if defined, is pointing). The size of a word is the size of an integer and varies from machine to machine. *Putw* neither assumes nor causes special alignment in the file.

Output streams, with the exception of the standard error stream *stderr*, are by default buffered if the output refers to a file and line-buffered if the output refers to a terminal. The standard error output stream *stderr* is by default unbuffered, but use of *freopen* (see *fopen*(3S)) will cause it to become buffered or line-buffered.

When an output stream is unbuffered, information is queued for writing on the destination file or terminal as soon as written; when it is buffered, many characters are saved up and written as a block. When it is line-buffered, each line of output is queued for writing on the destination terminal as soon as the line is completed (that is, as soon as a new-line character is written or terminal input is requested). *Setbuf*(3S) or *Setbuf*(3S) may be used to change the stream's buffering strategy.

SEE ALSO

fclose(3S), ferror(3S), fopen(3S), fread(3S), printf(3S), puts(3S), setbuf(3S).

DIAGNOSTICS

On success, these functions each return the value they have written. On failure, they return the constant **EOF**. This will occur if the file *stream* is not open for writing or if the output file cannot be grown. Because **EOF** is a valid integer, *ferror*(3S) should be used to detect *putw* errors.

BUGS

Because it is implemented as a macro, *putc* treats incorrectly a *stream* argument with side effects. In particular, **putc(c, *f++);** doesn't work sensibly. *Fputc* should be used instead.
Because of possible differences in word length and byte ordering, files written using *putw* are machine-dependent, and may not be read using *getw* on a different processor.

NAME

puts, fputs — put a string on a stream

SYNOPSIS

#include <stdio.h>

int puts (s)
char *s;

int fputs (s, stream)
char *s;
FILE *stream;

DESCRIPTION

Puts writes the null-terminated string pointed to by *s*, followed by a new-line character, to the standard output stream *stdout*.

Fputs writes the null-terminated string pointed to by *s* to the named output *stream*.

Neither function writes the terminating null character.

DIAGNOSTICS

Both routines return **EOF** on error. This will happen if the routines try to write on a file that has not been opened for writing.

SEE ALSO

ferror(3S), fopen(3S), fread(3S), printf(3S), putc(3S).

NOTES

Puts appends a new-line character while *fputs* does not.

NAME

scanf, fscanf, sscanf — convert formatted input

SYNOPSIS

#include <stdio.h>

int scanf (format [, pointer] ... **)**
char *format;

int fscanf (stream, format [, pointer] ... **)**
FILE *stream;
char *format;

int sscanf (s, format [, pointer] ... **)**
char *s, *format;

DESCRIPTION

Scanf reads from the standard input stream *stdin*. *Fscanf* reads from the named input *stream*. *Sscanf* reads from the character string *s*. Each function reads characters, interprets them according to a format, and stores the results in its arguments. Each expects, as arguments, a control string *format* described below, and a set of *pointer* arguments indicating where the converted input should be stored.

The control string usually contains conversion specifications, which are used to direct interpretation of input sequences. The control string may contain:

1. White-space characters (blanks, tabs, new-lines, or form-feeds) which, except in two cases described below, cause input to be read up to the next non-white-space character.
2. An ordinary character (not %), which must match the next character of the input stream.
3. Conversion specifications, consisting of the character %, an optional assignment suppressing character *, an optional numerical maximum field width, an optional **l** (ell) or **h** indicating the size of the receiving variable, and a conversion code.

A conversion specification directs the conversion of the next input field; the result is placed in the variable pointed to by the corresponding argument, unless assignment suppression was indicated by *. The suppression of assignment provides a way of describing an input field which is to be skipped.

An input field is defined as a string of non-space characters; it extends to the next inappropriate character or until the field width, if specified, is exhausted. For all descriptors except "[" and "c", white space leading an input field is ignored.

The conversion code indicates the interpretation of the input field; the corresponding pointer argument must usually be of a restricted type. For a suppressed field, no pointer argument is given. The following conversion codes are legal:

% a single % is expected in the input at this point; no assignment is done.

d a decimal integer is expected; the corresponding argument should be an integer pointer.

u an unsigned decimal integer is expected; the corresponding argument should be an unsigned integer pointer.

o an octal integer is expected; the corresponding argument should be an integer pointer.

x a hexadecimal integer is expected; the corresponding argument should be an integer pointer.

e,f,g a floating point number is expected; the next field is converted accordingly and stored through the corresponding argument, which should be a pointer to a *float*. The input format for floating point numbers is an optionally signed string of digits, possibly containing a decimal point, followed by an optional exponent field consisting of an **E** or an **e**, followed by an optional +, −, or space, followed by an integer.

s a character string is expected; the corresponding argument should be a character pointer pointing to an array of characters large enough to accept the string and a terminating **\0**, which will be added automatically. The input field is terminated by a white-space character.

c a character is expected; the corresponding argument should be a character pointer. The normal skip over white space is suppressed in this case; to read the next non-space character, use **%1s**. If a field width is given, the corresponding argument should refer to a character array; the indicated number of characters is read.

[indicates string data and the normal skip over leading white space is suppressed. The left bracket is followed by a set of characters, which we will call the *scanset,* and a right bracket; the input field is the maximal sequence of input characters consisting entirely of characters in the scanset. The circumflex (^), when it appears as the first character in the scanset, serves as a complement operator and redefines the scanset as the set of all characters *not* contained in the remainder of the scanset string. There are some conventions used in the construction of the scanset. A range of characters may be represented by the construct *first*−*last*, thus [0123456789] may be expressed [0−9]. Using this convention, *first* must be lexically less than or equal to *last*, or else the dash will stand for itself. The dash will also stand for itself whenever it is the first or the last character in the scanset. To include the right square bracket as an element of the scanset, it must appear as the first character (possibly preceded by a circumflex) of the scanset, and in this case it will not be syntactically interpreted as the closing bracket. The corresponding argument must point to a character array large enough to hold the data field and the terminating **\0**, which will be added automatically. At least one character must match for this conversion to be considered successful.

The conversion characters **d**, **u**, **o**, and **x** may be preceded by **l** or **h** to indicate that a pointer to **long** or to **short** rather than to **int** is in the argument list. Similarly, the conversion characters **e**, **f**, and **g** may be preceded by **l** to indicate that a pointer to **double** rather than to **float** is in the argument list. The **l** or **h** modifier is ignored for other conversion characters.

Scanf conversion terminates at **EOF**, at the end of the control string, or when an input character conflicts with the control string. In the latter case, the offending character is left unread in the input stream.

Scanf returns the number of successfully matched and assigned input items; this number can be zero in the event of an early conflict between an input character and the control string. If the input ends before the first conflict or conversion, **EOF** is returned.

EXAMPLES

The call:

```
int i, n; float x; char name[50];
n = scanf ("%d%f%s", &i, &x, name);
```

with the input line:

```
25 54.32E−1 thompson
```

will assign to *n* the value **3**, to *i* the value **25**, to *x* the value **5.432**, and *name* will contain **thompson\0**. Or:

```
int i; float x; char name[50];
(void) scanf("%2d%f%*d %[0-9]", &i, &x, name);
```

with input:

```
56789 0123 56a72
```

will assign **56** to *i*, **789.0** to *x*, skip **0123**, and place the string **56\0** in *name*. The next call to *getchar* (see *getc*(3S)) will return **a**.

SEE ALSO

getc(3S), printf(3S), strtod(3C), strtol(3C).

NOTE

Trailing white space (including a new-line) is left unread unless matched in the control string.

DIAGNOSTICS

These functions return **EOF** on end of input and a short count for missing or illegal data items.

BUGS

The success of literal matches and suppressed assignments is not directly determinable.

NAME

setbuf, setvbuf — assign buffering to a stream

SYNOPSIS

```
#include <stdio.h>

void setbuf (stream, buf)
FILE *stream;
char *buf;

int setvbuf (stream, buf, type, size)
FILE *stream;
char *buf;
int type, size;
```

DESCRIPTION

Setbuf may be used after a stream has been opened but before it is read or written. It causes the array pointed to by *buf* to be used instead of an automatically allocated buffer. If *buf* is the NULL pointer input/output will be completely unbuffered.

A constant **BUFSIZ,** defined in the **<stdio.h>** header file, tells how big an array is needed:

```
char buf[BUFSIZ];
```

Setvbuf may be used after a stream has been opened but before it is read or written. *Type* determines how *stream* will be buffered. Legal values for *type* (defined in stdio.h) are:

_IOFBF causes input/output to be fully buffered.

_IOLBF causes output to be line buffered; the buffer will be flushed when a newline is written, the buffer is full, or input is requested.

_IONBF causes input/output to be completely unbuffered.

If *buf* is not the **NULL** pointer, the array it points to will be used for buffering, instead of an automatically allocated buffer. *Size* specifies the size of the buffer to be used. The constant **BUFSIZ** in **<stdio.h>** is suggested as a good buffer size. If input/output is unbuffered, *buf* and *size* are ignored.

By default, output to a terminal is line buffered and all other input/output is fully buffered.

SEE ALSO

fopen(3S), getc(3S), malloc(3C), putc(3S), stdio(3S).

DIAGNOSTICS

If an illegal value for *type* or *size* is provided, *setvbuf* returns a non-zero value. Otherwise, the value returned will be zero.

NOTE

A common source of error is allocating buffer space as an "automatic" variable in a code block, and then failing to close the stream in the same block.

NAME

stdio − standard buffered input/output package

SYNOPSIS

#include <stdio.h>

FILE *stdin, *stdout, *stderr;

DESCRIPTION

The functions described in the entries of sub-class 3S of this manual constitute an efficient, user-level I/O buffering scheme. The in-line macros *getc*(3S) and *putc*(3S) handle characters quickly. The macros *getchar* and *putchar*, and the higher-level routines *fgetc*, *fgets*, *fprintf*, *fputc*, *fputs*, *fread*, *fscanf*, *fwrite*, *gets*, *getw*, *printf*, *puts*, *putw*, and *scanf* all use or act as if they use *getc* and *putc*; they can be freely intermixed.

A file with associated buffering is called a *stream* and is declared to be a pointer to a defined type **FILE**. *Fopen*(3S) creates certain descriptive data for a stream and returns a pointer to designate the stream in all further transactions. Normally, there are three open streams with constant pointers declared in the <stdio.h> header file and associated with the standard open files:

stdin	standard input file
stdout	standard output file
stderr	standard error file

A constant **NULL** (0) designates a nonexistent pointer.

An integer-constant **EOF** (−1) is returned upon end-of-file or error by most integer functions that deal with streams (see the individual descriptions for details).

An integer constant **BUFSIZ** specifies the size of the buffers used by the particular implementation.

Any program that uses this package must include the header file of pertinent macro definitions, as follows:

```
#include <stdio.h>
```

The functions and constants mentioned in the entries of sub-class 3S of this manual are declared in that header file and need no further declaration. The constants and the following "functions" are implemented as macros (redeclaration of these names is perilous): *getc*, *getchar*, *putc*, *putchar*, *ferror*, *feof*, *clearerr*, and *fileno*.

SEE ALSO

open(2), close(2), lseek(2), pipe(2), read(2), write(2), ctermid(3S), cuserid(3S), fclose(3S), ferror(3S), fopen(3S), fread(3S), fseek(3S), getc(3S), gets(3S), popen(3S), printf(3S), putc(3S), puts(3S), scanf(3S), setbuf(3S), system(3S), tmpfile(3S), tmpnam(3S), ungetc(3S).

DIAGNOSTICS

Invalid *stream* pointers will usually cause grave disorder, possibly including program termination. Individual function descriptions describe the possible error conditions.

NAME

system — issue a shell command

SYNOPSIS

#include <stdio.h>

int system (string)
char *string;

DESCRIPTION

System causes the *string* to be given to *sh*(1) as input, as if the string had been typed as a command at a terminal. The current process waits until the shell has completed, then returns the exit status of the shell.

FILES

/bin/sh

SEE ALSO

exec(2).
sh(1) in the *UNIX Programmer's Manual—Volume 1: Commands and Utilities.*

DIAGNOSTICS

System forks to create a child process that in turn exec's **/bin/sh** in order to execute *string*. If the fork or exec fails, *system* returns a negative value and sets *errno*.

NAME

tmpfile − create a temporary file

SYNOPSIS

#include <stdio.h>

FILE *tmpfile ( )

DESCRIPTION

Tmpfile creates a temporary file using a name generated by *tmpnam*(3S), and returns a corresponding FILE pointer. If the file cannot be opened, an error message is printed using *perror*(3C), and a NULL pointer is returned. The file will automatically be deleted when the process using it terminates. The file is opened for update ("w+").

SEE ALSO

creat(2), unlink(2), fopen(3S), mktemp(3C), perror(3C), tmpnam(3S).

NAME

tmpnam, tempnam — create a name for a temporary file

SYNOPSIS

#include <stdio.h>

char *tmpnam (s)
char *s;

char *tempnam (dir, pfx)
char *dir, *pfx;

DESCRIPTION

These functions generate file names that can safely be used for a temporary file.

Tmpnam always generates a file name using the path-prefix defined as **P_tmpdir** in the *<stdio.h>* header file. If *s* is NULL, *tmpnam* leaves its result in an internal static area and returns a pointer to that area. The next call to *tmpnam* will destroy the contents of the area. If *s* is not NULL, it is assumed to be the address of an array of at least **L_tmpnam** bytes, where **L_tmpnam** is a constant defined in *<stdio.h>*; *tmpnam* places its result in that array and returns *s*.

Tempnam allows the user to control the choice of a directory. The argument *dir* points to the name of the directory in which the file is to be created. If *dir* is NULL or points to a string which is not a name for an appropriate directory, the path-prefix defined as **P_tmpdir** in the *<stdio.h>* header file is used. If that directory is not accessible, **/tmp** will be used as a last resort. This entire sequence can be up-staged by providing an environment variable **TMPDIR** in the user's environment, whose value is the name of the desired temporary-file directory.

Many applications prefer their temporary files to have certain favorite initial letter sequences in their names. Use the *pfx* argument for this. This argument may be NULL or point to a string of up to five characters to be used as the first few characters of the temporary-file name.

Tempnam uses *malloc*(3C) to get space for the constructed file name, and returns a pointer to this area. Thus, any pointer value returned from *tempnam* may serve as an argument to *free* (see *malloc*(3C)).

If *tempnam* cannot return the expected result for any reason, i.e. *malloc*(3C) failed, or none of the above mentioned attempts to find an appropriate directory was successful, a NULL pointer will be returned.

NOTES

These functions generate a different file name each time they are called.

Files created using these functions and either *fopen*(3S) or *creat*(2) are temporary only in the sense that they reside in a directory intended for temporary use, and their names are unique. It is the user's responsibility to use *unlink* (2) to remove the file when its use is ended.

SEE ALSO

creat(2), unlink(2), fopen(3S), malloc(3C), mktemp(3C), tmpfile(3S).

BUGS

If called more than 17,576 times in a single process, these functions will start recycling previously used names.
Between the time a file name is created and the file is opened, it is possible for some other process to create a file with the same name. This can never happen if that other process is using these functions or *mktemp*, and the file names are chosen so as to render duplication by other means unlikely.

NAME

ungetc — push character back into input stream

SYNOPSIS

#include <stdio.h>

int ungetc (c, stream)
int c;
FILE *stream;

DESCRIPTION

Ungetc inserts the character *c* into the buffer associated with an input *stream*. That character, *c*, will be returned by the next *getc(3S)* call on that *stream*. *Ungetc* returns *c*, and leaves the file *stream* unchanged.

One character of pushback is guaranteed, provided something has already been read from the stream and the stream is actually buffered. In the case that *stream* is *stdin*, one character may be pushed back onto the buffer without a previous read statement.

If *c* equals **EOF**, *ungetc* does nothing to the buffer and returns **EOF**.

Fseek (3S) erases all memory of inserted characters.

SEE ALSO

fseek(3S), getc(3S), setbuf(3S).

DIAGNOSTICS

Ungetc returns **EOF** if it cannot insert the character.

NAME

vprintf, vfprintf, vsprintf — print formatted output of a varargs argument list

SYNOPSIS

#include <stdio.h>
#include <varargs.h>

int vprintf (format, ap)
char *format;
va_list ap;

int vfprintf (stream, format, ap)
FILE *stream;
char *format;
va_list ap;

int vsprintf (s, format, ap)
char *s, *format;
va_list ap;

DESCRIPTION

vprintf, *vfprintf*, and *vsprintf* are the same as *printf*, *fprintf*, and *sprintf* respectively, except that instead of being called with a variable number of arguments, they are called with an argument list as defined by *varargs*(5).

EXAMPLE

The following demonstrates how *vfprintf* could be used to write an error routine.

```
#include <stdio.h>
#include <varargs.h>
        .
        .
        .
/*
 *      error should be called like
 *              error(function_name, format, arg1, arg2...);
 */
/*VARARGS0*/
void
error(va_alist)
/* Note the function_name and format arguments cannot be
 *      separately declared because of the definition of varargs.
 */
```

```
va_dcl
{
        va_list args;
        char *fmt;

        va_start(args);
        /* print out name of function causing error */
        (void)fprintf(stderr, "ERROR in %s: ", va_arg(args, char *));
        fmt = va_arg(args, char *);
        /* print out remainder of message */
        (void)vfprintf(fmt, args);
        va_end(args);
        (void)abort( );
}
```

SEE ALSO

vprintf(3X), varargs(5).

NAME

j0, j1, jn, y0, y1, yn − Bessel functions

SYNOPSIS

```
#include <math.h>

double j0 (x)
double x;

double j1 (x)
double x;

double jn (n, x)
int n;
double x;

double y0 (x)
double x;

double y1 (x)
double x;

double yn (n, x)
int n;
double x;
```

DESCRIPTION

J0 and *j1* return Bessel functions of *x* of the first kind of orders 0 and 1 respectively. *Jn* returns the Bessel function of *x* of the first kind of order *n*.

Y0 and *y1* return Bessel functions of *x* of the second kind of orders 0 and 1 respectively. *Yn* returns the Bessel function of *x* of the second kind of order *n*. The value of *x* must be positive.

DIAGNOSTICS

Non-positive arguments cause *y0*, *y1* and *yn* to return the value **−HUGE** and to set *errno* to **EDOM**. In addition, a message indicating DOMAIN error is printed on the standard error output.

Arguments too large in magnitude cause *j0*, *j1*, *y0* and *y1* to return zero and to set *errno* to **ERANGE**. In addition, a message indicating TLOSS error is printed on the standard error output.

These error-handling procedures may be changed with the function *matherr*(3M).

SEE ALSO

matherr(3M).

NAME

erf, erfc — error function and complementary error function

SYNOPSIS

```
#include <math.h>

double erf (x)
double x;

double erfc (x)
double x;
```

DESCRIPTION

Erf returns the error function of x, defined as $\frac{2}{\sqrt{\pi}}\int_0^x e^{-t^2}\,dt$.

Erfc, which returns 1.0 − *erf(x)*, is provided because of the extreme loss of relative accuracy if *erf(x)* is called for large x and the result subtracted from 1.0 (e.g., for $x = 5$, 12 places are lost).

SEE ALSO

exp(3M).

NAME

exp, log, log10, pow, sqrt — exponential, logarithm, power, square root functions

SYNOPSIS

```
#include <math.h>

double exp (x)
double x;

double log (x)
double x;

double log10 (x)
double x;

double pow (x, y)
double x, y;

double sqrt (x)
double x;
```

DESCRIPTION

Exp returns e^x.

Log returns the natural logarithm of x. The value of x must be positive.

Log10 returns the logarithm base ten of x. The value of x must be positive.

Pow returns x^y. If x is zero, y must be positive. If x is negative, y must be an integer.

Sqrt returns the non-negative square root of x. The value of x may not be negative.

DIAGNOSTICS

Exp returns **HUGE** when the correct value would overflow, or 0 when the correct value would underflow, and sets *errno* to **ERANGE**.

Log and *log10* return **−HUGE** and set *errno* to **EDOM** when x is non-positive. A message indicating DOMAIN error (or SING error when x is 0) is printed on the standard error output.

Pow returns 0 and sets *errno* to **EDOM** when x is 0 and y is non-positive, or when x is negative and y is not an integer. In these cases a message indicating DOMAIN error is printed on the standard error output.

When the correct value for *pow* would overflow or underflow, *pow* returns **±HUGE** or 0 respectively, and sets *errno* to **ERANGE.**

Sqrt returns 0 and sets *errno* to **EDOM** when *x* is negative. A message indicating DOMAIN error is printed on the standard error output.

These error-handling procedures may be changed with the function *matherr*(3M).

SEE ALSO

hypot(3M), matherr(3M), sinh(3M).

NAME

floor, ceil, fmod, fabs — floor, ceiling, remainder, absolute value functions

SYNOPSIS

#include <math.h>

double floor (x)
double x;

double ceil (x)
double x;

double fmod (x, y)
double x, y;

double fabs (x)
double x;

DESCRIPTION

Floor returns the largest integer (as a double-precision number) not greater than x.

Ceil returns the smallest integer not less than x.

Fmod returns the floating-point remainder of the division of x by y: zero if y is zero or if x/y would overflow; otherwise the number f with the same sign as x, such that $x = iy + f$ for some integer i, and $|f| < |y|$.

Fabs returns the absolute value of x, $|x|$.

SEE ALSO

abs(3C).

NAME

gamma – log gamma function

SYNOPSIS

```
#include <math.h>

double gamma (x)
double x;

extern int signgam;
```

DESCRIPTION

Gamma returns $\ln(|\Gamma(x)|)$, where $\Gamma(x)$ is defined as $\int_0^\infty e^{-t} t^{x-1} dt$.

The sign of $\Gamma(x)$ is returned in the external integer *signgam*. The argument x may not be a non-positive integer.

The following C program fragment might be used to calculate Γ:

```
if ((y = gamma(x)) > LN_MAXDOUBLE)
        error();
y = signgam * exp(y);
```

where LN_MAXDOUBLE is the least value that causes *exp*(3M) to return a range error, and is defined in the *<values.h>* header file.

DIAGNOSTICS

For non-negative integer arguments **HUGE** is returned, and *errno* is set to **EDOM**. A message indicating SING error is printed on the standard error output.

If the correct value would overflow, *gamma* returns **HUGE** and sets *errno* to **ERANGE**.

These error-handling procedures may be changed with the function *matherr*(3M).

SEE ALSO

exp(3M), matherr(3M), values(5).

NAME

hypot − Euclidean distance function

SYNOPSIS

#include <math.h>

double hypot (x, y)
double x, y;

DESCRIPTION

Hypot returns

sqrt(x * x + y * y),

taking precautions against unwarranted overflows.

DIAGNOSTICS

When the correct value would overflow, *hypot* returns **HUGE** and sets *errno* to **ERANGE.**

These error-handling procedures may be changed with the function *matherr*(3M).

SEE ALSO

matherr(3M).

NAME

matherr — error-handling function

SYNOPSIS

#include <math.h>

int matherr (x)
struct exception *x;

DESCRIPTION

Matherr is invoked by functions in the Math Library when errors are detected. Users may define their own procedures for handling errors, by including a function named *matherr* in their programs. *Matherr* must be of the form described above. When an error occurs, a pointer to the exception structure *x* will be passed to the user-supplied *matherr* function. This structure, which is defined in the *<math.h>* header file, is as follows:

```
struct exception {
        int type;
        char *name;
        double arg1, arg2, retval;
};
```

The element *type* is an integer describing the type of error that has occurred, from the following list of constants (defined in the header file):

DOMAIN	argument domain error
SING	argument singularity
OVERFLOW	overflow range error
UNDERFLOW	underflow range error
PLOSS	partial loss of significance

The element *name* points to a string containing the name of the function that incurred the error. The variables *arg1* and *arg2* are the arguments with which the function was invoked. *Retval* is set to the default value that will be returned by the function unless the user's *matherr* sets it to a different value.

If the user's *matherr* function returns non-zero, no error message will be printed, and *errno* will not be set. If *matherr* is not supplied by the user, the default error-handling procedures, described with the math functions involved, will be invoked upon error (summarized in the table below). In every case, *errno* is set to EDOM or ERANGE and the program continues.

EXAMPLE

```
#include <math.h>

int
matherr(x)
register struct exception *x;
{
	switch (x->type) {
	case DOMAIN:
		/* change sqrt to return sqrt(-arg1), not 0 */
		if (!strcmp(x->name, "sqrt")) {
			x->retval = sqrt(-x->arg1);
			return (0); /* print message and set errno */
		}
	case SING:
		/* all other domain/sing errors, print message & abort */
		fprintf(stderr, "domain error in %s\n", x->name);
		abort( );
	case PLOSS:
		/* print detailed error message */
		fprintf(stderr, "loss of significance in %s(%g) = %g\n",
			x->name, x->arg1, x->retval);
		return (1); /* take no other action */
	}
	return (0); /* all other errors, execute default procedure */
}
```

DEFAULT ERROR HANDLING PROCEDURES				
	Types of Errors			
type	DOMAIN	SING	OVERFLOW	UNDERFLOW
errno	EDOM	EDOM	ERANGE	ERANGE
BESSEL:	−	−	−	−
y0, y1, yn (arg ⩽ 0)	M, −H	−	−	−
EXP:	−	−	H	0
LOG, LOG10:				
(arg < 0)	M, −H	−	−	−
(arg = 0)	−	M, −H	−	−
POW:	−	−	±H	0
neg ** non-int	M, 0	−	−	−
0 ** non-pos				
SQRT:	M, 0	−	−	−
GAMMA:	−	M, H	H	−
HYPOT:	−	−	H	−
SINH:	−	−	±H	−
COSH:	−	−	H	−
SIN, COS, TAN: −	−	−	−	M, 0
ASIN, ACOS, ATAN3: M	, 0 −	−	−	−

ABBREVIATIONS	
*	As much as possible of the value is returned.
M	Message is printed (EDOM error).
H	HUGE is returned.
−H	−HUGE is returned.
±H	HUGE or −HUGE is returned.
0	0 is returned.

NAME

sinh, cosh, tanh — hyperbolic functions

SYNOPSIS

```
#include <math.h>

double sinh (x)
double x;

double cosh (x)
double x;

double tanh (x)
double x;
```

DESCRIPTION

Sinh, *cosh*, and *tanh* return, respectively, the hyberbolic sine, cosine and tangent of their argument.

DIAGNOSTICS

Sinh and *cosh* return **HUGE** (and *sinh* may return **−HUGE** for negative *x*) when the correct value would overflow and set *errno* to **ERANGE.**

These error-handling procedures may be changed with thc function *matherr*(3M).

SEE ALSO

matherr(3M).

NAME

sin, cos, tan, asin, acos, atan, atan2 — trigonometric functions

SYNOPSIS

```
#include <math.h>

double sin (x)
double x;

double cos (x)
double x;

double tan (x)
double x;

double asin (x)
double x;

double acos (x)
double x;

double atan (x)
double x;

double atan2 (y, x)
double y, x;
```

DESCRIPTION

Sin, *cos* and *tan* return respectively the sine, cosine and tangent of their argument, *x*, measured in radians.

Asin returns the arcsine of *x*, in the range $-\pi/2$ to $\pi/2$.

Acos returns the arccosine of *x*, in the range 0 to π.

Atan returns the arctangent of *x*, in the range $-\pi/2$ to $\pi/2$.

Atan2 returns the arctangent of y/x, in the range $-\pi$ to π, using the signs of both arguments to determine the quadrant of the return value.

DIAGNOSTICS

Sin, *cos*, and *tan* lose accuracy when their argument is far from zero. For arguments sufficiently large, these functions return zero when there would otherwise be a complete loss of significance. In this case a message indicating TLOSS error is printed on the standard error output. For less extreme arguments causing partial loss of significance, a PLOSS error is generated but no message is printed. In both cases, *errno* is set to **ERANGE.**

If the magnitude of the argument of *asin* or *acos* is greater than one, or if both arguments of *atan2* are zero, zero is returned and *errno* is set to **EDOM**. In addition, a message indicating DOMAIN error is printed on the standard error output.

These error-handling procedures may be changed with the function *matherr*(3M).

SEE ALSO

matherr(3M).

NAME

assert − verify program assertion

SYNOPSIS

#include <assert.h>

assert (expression)
int expression;

DESCRIPTION

This macro is useful for putting diagnostics into programs. When it is executed, if *expression* is false (zero), *assert* prints

"Assertion failed: *expression*, file *xyz*, line *nnn*"

on the standard error output and aborts. In the error message, *xyz* is the name of the source file and *nnn* the source line number of the *assert* statement.

Compiling with the preprocessor option **−DNDEBUG** (see *cpp* (1)), or with the preprocessor control statement **"#define** NDEBUG" ahead of the **"#include** <assert.h>" statement, will stop assertions from being compiled into the program.

SEE ALSO

abort(3C).
cpp(1) in the *UNIX Programmer's Manual—Volume 1: Commands and Utilities.*

NAME

curses – CRT screen handling and optimization package

SYNOPSIS

#include <curses.h>

cc [flags] files **-lcurses** [libraries]

DESCRIPTION

These routines give the user a method of updating screens with reasonable optimization. In order to initialize the routines, the routine *initscr()* must be called before any of the other routines that deal with windows and screens are used. The routine *endwin()* should be called before exiting. To get character-at-a-time input without echoing, (most interactive, screen oriented-programs want this) after calling *initscr()* you should call *"nonl(); cbreak(); noecho();"*

The full curses interface permits manipulation of data structures called *windows* which can be thought of as two dimensional arrays of characters representing all or part of a CRT screen. A default window called **stdscr** is supplied, and others can be created with **newwin**. Windows are referred to by variables declared "WINDOW *", the type WINDOW is defined in curses.h to be a C structure. These data structures are manipulated with functions described below, among which the most basic are **move**, and **addch**. (More general versions of these functions are included with names beginning with 'w', allowing you to specify a window. The routines not beginning with 'w' affect **stdscr**.) Then *refresh()* is called, telling the routines to make the users CRT screen look like **stdscr**.

Mini-Curses is a subset of curses which does not allow manipulation of more than one window. To invoke this subset, use -DMINICURSES as a **cc** option. This level is smaller and faster than full curses.

If the environment variable TERMINFO is defined, any program using curses will check for a local terminal definition before checking in the standard place. For example, if the standard place is **/usr/lib/terminfo**, and TERM is set to "vt100", then normally the compiled file is found in **/usr/lib/terminfo/v/vt100**. (The "v" is copied from the first letter of "vt100" to avoid creation of huge directories.) However, if TERMINFO is set to **/usr/mark/myterms,** curses will first check **/opusr/mark/myterms/v/vt100**, and if that fails, will then check

/usr/lib/terminfo/v/vt100. This is useful for developing experimental definitions or when write permission in **/usr/lib/terminfo** is not available.

SEE ALSO

terminfo(4).

FUNCTIONS

Routines listed here may be called when using the full curses. Those marked with an asterisk may be called when using Mini-Curses.

addch(ch)*	add a character to *stdscr* (like putchar) (wraps to next line at end of line)
addstr(str)*	calls addch with each character in *str*
attroff(attrs)*	turn off attributes named
attron(attrs)*	turn on attributes named
attrset(attrs)*	set current attributes to *attrs*
baudrate()*	current terminal speed
beep()*	sound beep on terminal
box(win, vert, hor)	draw a box around edges of *win* *vert* and *hor* are chars to use for vert. and hor. edges of box
clear()	clear *stdscr*
clearok(win, bf)	clear screen before next redraw of *win*
clrtobot()	clear to bottom of *stdscr*
clrtoeol()	clear to end of line on *stdscr*
cbreak()*	set cbreak mode
delay_output(ms)*	insert ms millisecond pause in output
delch()	delete a character
deleteln()	delete a line
delwin(win)	delete *win*
doupdate()	update screen from all wnooutrefresh
echo()*	set echo mode
endwin()*	end window modes
erase()	erase *stdscr*
erasechar()	return user's erase character
fixterm()	restore tty to "in curses" state
flash()	flash screen or beep
flushinp()*	throw away any typeahead
getch()*	get a char from tty
getstr(str)	get a string through *stdscr*
gettmode()	establish current tty modes
getyx(win, y, x)	get (y, x) co-ordinates

has_ic()	true if terminal can do insert character
has_il()	true if terminal can do insert line
idlok(win, bf)*	use terminal's insert/delete line if bf != 0
inch()	get char at current (y, x) co-ordinates
initscr()*	initialize screens
insch(c)	insert a char
insertln()	insert a line
intrflush(win, bf)	interrupts flush output if bf is TRUE
keypad(win, bf)	enable keypad input
killchar()	return current user's kill character
leaveok(win, flag)	OK to leave cursor anywhere after refresh if flag!=0 for *win*, otherwise cursor must be left at current position.
longname()	return verbose name of terminal
meta(win, flag)*	allow meta characters on input if flag != 0
move(y, x)*	move to (y, x) on *stdscr*
mvaddch(y, x, ch)	move(y, x) then addch(ch)
mvaddstr(y, x, str)	similar...
mvcur(oldrow, oldcol, newrow, newcol)	low level cursor motion
mvdelch(y, x)	like delch, but move(y, x) first
mvgetch(y, x)	etc.
mvgetstr(y, x)	
mvinch(y, x)	
mvinsch(y, x, c)	
mvprintw(y, x, fmt, args)	
mvscanw(y, x, fmt, args)	
mvwaddch(win, y, x, ch)	
mvwaddstr(win, y, x, str)	
mvwdelch(win, y, x)	
mvwgetch(win, y, x)	
mvwgetstr(win, y, x)	
mvwin(win, by, bx)	
mvwinch(win, y, x)	
mvwinsch(win, y, x, c)	
mvwprintw(win, y, x, fmt, args)	
mvwscanw(win, y, x, fmt, args)	
newpad(nlines, ncols)	create a new pad with given dimensions
newterm(type, fd)	set up new terminal of given type to output on fd
newwin(lines, cols, begin_y, begin_x)	create a new window
nl()*	set newline mapping
nocbreak()*	unset cbreak mode
nodelay(win, bf)	enable nodelay input mode through getch

noecho()*	unset echo mode
nonl()*	unset newline mapping
noraw()*	unset raw mode
overlay(win1, win2)	overlay win1 on win2
overwrite(win1, win2)	overwrite win1 on top of win2
pnoutrefresh(pad, pminrow, pmincol, sminrow, smincol, smaxrow, smaxcol)	like prefresh but with no output until doupdate called
prefresh(pad, pminrow, pmincol, sminrow, smincol, smaxrow, smaxcol)	refresh from pad starting with given upper left corner with output to given portion of screen
printw(fmt, arg1, arg2, ...)	printf on *stdscr*
raw()*	set raw mode
refresh()*	make current screen look like *stdscr*
resetterm()*	set tty modes to "out of curses" state
resetty()*	reset tty flags to stored value
saveterm()*	save current modes as "in curses" state
savetty()*	store current tty flags
scanw(fmt, arg1, arg2, ...)	scanf through *stdscr*
scroll(win)	scroll *win* one line
scrollok(win, flag)	allow terminal to scroll if flag != 0
set_term(new)	now talk to terminal new
setscrreg(t, b)	set user scrolling region to lines t through b
setterm(type)	establish terminal with given type
setupterm(term, filenum, errret)	
standend()*	clear standout mode attribute
standout()*	set standout mode attribute
subwin(win, lines, cols, begin_y, begin_x)	create a subwindow
touchwin(win)	change all of *win*
traceoff()	turn off debugging trace output
traceon()	turn on debugging trace output
typeahead(fd)	use file descriptor fd to check typeahead
unctrl(ch)*	printable version of *ch*
waddch(win, ch)	add char to *win*
waddstr(win, str)	add string to *win*
wattroff(win, attrs)	turn off *attrs* in *win*
wattron(win, attrs)	turn on *attrs* in *win*
wattrset(win, attrs)	set attrs in *win* to *attrs*
wclear(win)	clear *win*
wclrtobot(win)	clear to bottom of *win*
wclrtoeol(win)	clear to end of line on *win*
wdelch(win, c)	delete char from *win*
wdeleteln(win)	delete line from *win*

werase(win)	erase *win*
wgetch(win)	get a char through *win*
wgetstr(win, str)	get a string through *win*
winch(win)	get char at current (y, x) in *win*
winsch(win, c)	insert char into *win*
winsertln(win)	insert line into *win*
wmove(win, y, x)	set current (y, x) co-ordinates on *win*
wnoutrefresh(win)	refresh but no screen output
wprintw(win, fmt, arg1, arg2, ...)	printf on *win*
wrefresh(win)	make screen look like *win*
wscanw(win, fmt, arg1, arg2, ...)	scanf through *win*
wsetscrreg(win, t, b)	set scrolling region of *win*
wstandend(win)	clear standout attribute in *win*
wstandout(win)	set standout attribute in *win*

TERMINFO LEVEL ROUTINES

These routines should be called by programs wishing to deal directly with the terminfo database. Due to the low level of this interface, it is discouraged. Initially, *setupterm* should be called. This will define the set of terminal dependent variables defined in terminfo(4). The include files <curses.h> and <term.h> should be included to get the definitions for these strings, numbers, and flags. Parmeterized strings should be passed through *tparm* to instantiate them. All terminfo strings (including the output of tparm) should be printed with *tputs* or *putp* . Before exiting, *resetterm* should be called to restore the tty modes. (Programs desiring shell escapes or suspending with control Z can call *resetterm* before the shell is called and *fixterm* after returning from the shell.)

fixterm()	restore tty modes for terminfo use (called by setupterm)
resetterm()	reset tty modes to state before program entry
setupterm(term, fd, rc)	read in database. Terminal type is the character string *term*, all output is to UNIX System file descriptor *fd*. A status value is returned in the integer pointed to by *rc*: 1 is normal. The simplest call would be *setupterm(0, 1, 0)* which uses all the defaults.
tparm(str, p1, p2, ..., p9)	instantiate string str with parms p_i
tputs(str, affcnt, putc)	apply padding info to string *str*. *affcnt* is the number of lines affected, or 1 if not applicable. *Putc* is a putchar-like function to which the characters are passed, one at a time.
putp(str)	handy function that calls tputs(str, 1, putchar).

vidputs(attrs, putc)	output the string to put terminal in video attribute mode *attrs*, which is any combination of the attributes listed below. Chars are passed to putchar-like function *putc*.
vidattr(attrs)	Like vidputs but outputs through putchar

TERMCAP COMPATIBILITY ROUTINES

These routines were included as a conversion aid for programs that use termcap. Their parameters are the same as for termcap. They are emulated using the *terminfo* database. They may go away at a later date.

tgetent(bp, name)	look up termcap entry for name
tgetflag(id)	get boolean entry for id
tgetnum(id)	get numeric entry for id
tgetstr(id, area)	get string entry for id
tgoto(cap, col, row)	apply parms to given cap
tputs(cap, affcnt, fn)	apply padding to cap calling fn as putchar

ATTRIBUTES

The following video attributes can be passed to the functions *attron*,*attroff*,*attrset*.

A_STANDOUT	Terminal's best highlighting mode
A_UNDERLINE	Underlining
A_REVERSE	Reverse video
A_BLINK	Blinking
A_DIM	Half bright
A_BOLD	Extra bright or bold
A_BLANK	Blanking (invisible)
A_PROTECT	Protected
A_ALTCHARSET	Alternate character set

FUNCTION KEYS

The following function keys might be returned by *getch* if *keypad* has been enabled. Note that not all of these are currently supported, due to lack of definitions in *terminfo* or the terminal not transmitting a unique code when the key is pressed.

Name	*Value*	*Key name*
KEY_BREAK	0401	break key (unreliable)
KEY_DOWN	0402	The four arrow keys ...
KEY_UP	0403	
KEY_LEFT	0404	
KEY_RIGHT	0405	...
KEY_HOME	0406	Home key (upward+left arrow)
KEY_BACKSPACE	0407	backspace (unreliable)
KEY_F0	0410	Function keys. Space for 64 is reserved.

KEY_F(n)	(KEY_F0+(n))	Formula for fn.
KEY_DL	0510	Delete line
KEY_IL	0511	Insert line
KEY_DC	0512	Delete character
KEY_IC	0513	Insert char or enter insert mode
KEY_EIC	0514	Exit insert char mode
KEY_CLEAR	0515	Clear screen
KEY_EOS	0516	Clear to end of screen
KEY_EOL	0517	Clear to end of line
KEY_SF	0520	Scroll 1 line forward
KEY_SR	0521	Scroll 1 line backwards (reverse)
KEY_NPAGE	0522	Next page
KEY_PPAGE	0523	Previous page
KEY_STAB	0524	Set tab
KEY_CTAB	0525	Clear tab
KEY_CATAB	0526	Clear all tabs
KEY_ENTER	0527	Enter or send (unreliable)
KEY_SRESET	0530	soft (partial) reset (unreliable)
KEY_RESET	0531	reset or hard reset (unreliable)
KEY_PRINT	0532	print or copy
KEY_LL	0533	home down or bottom (lower left)

WARNING

The plotting library *plot*(3X) and the curses library *curses*(3X) both use the names erase() and move(). The curses versions are macros. If you need both libraries, put the *plot*(3X) code in a different source file than the *curses*(3X) code, and/or #undef move() and erase() in the *plot*(3X) code.

NAME

ldahread – read the archive header of a member of an archive file

SYNOPSIS

```
#include <stdio.h>
#include <ar.h>
#include <filehdr.h>
#include <ldfcn.h>

int ldahread (ldptr, arhead)
LDFILE *ldptr;
ARCHDR *arhead;
```

DESCRIPTION

If **TYPE**(*ldptr*) is the archive file magic number, *ldahread* reads the archive header of the common object file currently associated with *ldptr* into the area of memory beginning at *arhead*.

Ldahread returns **SUCCESS** or **FAILURE**. *Ldahread* will fail if **TYPE**(*ldptr*) does not represent an archive file, or if it cannot read the archive header.

The program must be loaded with the object file access routine library **libld.a**.

SEE ALSO

ldclose(3X), ldopen(3X), ldfcn(4), ar(4).

NAME

ldclose, ldaclose — close a common object file

SYNOPSIS

#include <stdio.h>
#include <filehdr.h>
#include <ldfcn.h>

int ldclose (ldptr)
LDFILE *ldptr;

int ldaclose (ldptr)
LDFILE *ldptr;

DESCRIPTION

Ldopen(3X) and *ldclose* are designed to provide uniform access to both simple object files and object files that are members of archive files. Thus an archive of common object files can be processed as if it were a series of simple common object files.

If **TYPE(***ldptr***)** does not represent an archive file, *ldclose* will close the file and free the memory allocated to the **LDFILE** structure associated with *ldptr*. If **TYPE(***ldptr***)** is the magic number of an archive file, and if there are any more files in the archive, *ldclose* will reinitialize **OFFSET(***ldptr***)** to the file address of the next archive member and return **FAILURE**. The **LDFILE** structure is prepared for a subsequent *ldopen*(3X). In all other cases, *ldclose* returns **SUCCESS**.

Ldaclose closes the file and frees the memory allocated to the **LDFILE** structure associated with *ldptr* regardless of the value of **TYPE***(ldptr)*. *Ldaclose* always returns **SUCCESS**. The function is often used in conjunction with *ldaopen*.

The program must be loaded with the object file access routine library **libld.a**.

SEE ALSO

fclose(3S), ldopen(3X), ldfcn(4).

NAME

ldfhread — read the file header of a common object file

SYNOPSIS

#include <stdio.h>
#include <filehdr.h>
#include <ldfcn.h>

int ldfhread (ldptr, filehead)
LDFILE *ldptr;
FILHDR *filehead;

DESCRIPTION

Ldfhread reads the file header of the common object file currently associated with *ldptr* into the area of memory beginning at *filehead*.

Ldfhread returns **SUCCESS** or **FAILURE**. *Ldfhread* will fail if it cannot read the file header.

In most cases the use of *ldfhread* can be avoided by using the macro **HEADER(***ldptr***)** defined in **ldfcn.h** (see ldfcn (4)). The information in any field, *fieldname*, of the file header may be accessed using **HEADER(ldptr).fieldname**.

The program must be loaded with the object file access routine library **libld.a**.

SEE ALSO

ldclose(3X), ldopen(3X), ldfcn(4).

NAME

ldgetname − retrieve symbol name for common object file symbol table entry

SYNOPSIS

#include <stdio.h>
#include <filehdr.h>
#include <syms.h>
#include <ldfcn.h>

char *ldgetname (ldptr, symbol)
LDFILE *ldptr;
SYMENT *symbol;

DESCRIPTION

Ldgetname returns a pointer to the name associated with **symbol** as a string. The string is contained in a static buffer local to *ldgetname* that is overwritten by each call to *ldgetname*, and therefore must be copied by the caller if the name is to be saved.

As of UNIX System V Release 2.0, the common object file format has been extended to handle arbitrary length symbol names with the addition of a "string table". *Ldgetname* will return the symbol name associated with a symbol table entry for either a pre-UNIX System V Release 2.0 object file or a UNIX System V Release 2.0 object file. Thus, *ldgetname* can be used to retrieve names from object files without any backward compatibility problems. *Ldgetname* will return NULL (defined in **stdio.h**) for an object file if the name cannot be retrieved. This situation can occur:

- if the "string table" cannot be found,
- if not enough memory can be allocated for the string table,
- if the string table appears not to be a string table (for example, if an auxiliary entry is handed to *ldgetname* that looks like a reference to a name in a non-existent string table), or
- if the name's offset into the string table is past the end of the string table.

Typically, *ldgetname* will be called immediately after a successful call to *ldtbread* to retrieve the name associated with the symbol table entry filled by *ldtbread*.

The program must be loaded with the object file access routine library **libld.a**.

SEE ALSO

ldclose(3X), ldopen(3X), ldtbread(3X), ldtbseek(3X), ldfcn(4).

NAME

ldlread, ldlinit, ldlitem − manipulate line number entries of a common object file function

SYNOPSIS

```
#include <stdio.h>
#include <filehdr.h>
#include <linenum.h>
#include <ldfcn.h>

int ldlread(ldptr, fcnindx, linenum, linent)
LDFILE *ldptr;
long fcnindx;
unsigned short linenum;
LINENO linent;

int ldlinit(ldptr, fcnindx)
LDFILE *ldptr;
long fcnindx;

int ldlitem(ldptr, linenum, linent)
LDFILE *ldptr;
unsigned short linenum;
LINENO linent;
```

DESCRIPTION

Ldlread searches the line number entries of the common object file currently associated with *ldptr*. *Ldlread* begins its search with the line number entry for the beginning of a function and confines its search to the line numbers associated with a single function. The function is identified by *fcnindx*, the index of its entry in the object file symbol table. *Ldlread* reads the entry with the smallest line number equal to or greater than *linenum* into *linent*.

Ldlinit and *ldlitem* together perform exactly the same function as *ldlread.* After an initial call to *ldlread* or *ldlinit, ldlitem* may be used to retrieve a series of line number entries associated with a single function. *Ldlinit* simply locates the line number entries for the function identified by *fcnindx. Ldlitem* finds and reads the entry with the smallest line number equal to or greater than *linenum* into *linent*.

Ldlread, *ldlinit*, and *ldlitem* each return either **SUCCESS** or **FAILURE**. *Ldlread* will fail if there are no line number entries in the object file, if *fcnindx* does not index a function entry in the symbol table, or if it finds no line number equal to or greater than *linenum*. *Ldlinit* will fail if there are no line number entries in the object file or if *fcnindx* does not index a function entry in the symbol table. *Ldlitem* will fail if it finds no line number equal to or greater than *linenum*.

The programs must be loaded with the object file access routine library **libld.a**.

SEE ALSO
ldclose(3X), ldopen(3X), ldtbindex(3X), ldfcn(4).

NAME

ldlseek, ldnlseek — seek to line number entries of a section of a common object file

SYNOPSIS

#include <stdio.h>
#include <filehdr.h>
#include <ldfcn.h>

int ldlseek (ldptr, sectindx)
LDFILE *ldptr;
unsigned short sectindx;

int ldnlseek (ldptr, sectname)
LDFILE *ldptr;
char *sectname;

DESCRIPTION

Ldlseek seeks to the line number entries of the section specified by *sectindx* of the common object file currently associated with *ldptr*.

Ldnlseek seeks to the line number entries of the section specified by *sectname*.

Ldlseek and *ldnlseek* return **SUCCESS** or **FAILURE**. *Ldlseek* will fail if *sectindx* is greater than the number of sections in the object file; *ldnlseek* will fail if there is no section name corresponding with **sectname*. Either function will fail if the specified section has no line number entries or if it cannot seek to the specified line number entries.

Note that the first section has an index of *one*.

The program must be loaded with the object file access routine library **libld.a**.

SEE ALSO

ldclose(3X), ldopen(3X), ldshread(3X), ldfcn(4).

NAME

ldohseek − seek to the optional file header of a common object file

SYNOPSIS

```
#include <stdio.h>
#include <filehdr.h>
#include <ldfcn.h>

int ldohseek (ldptr)
LDFILE *ldptr;
```

DESCRIPTION

Ldohseek seeks to the optional file header of the common object file currently associated with *ldptr*.

Ldohseek returns **SUCCESS** or **FAILURE**. *Ldohseek* will fail if the object file has no optional header or if it cannot seek to the optional header.

The program must be loaded with the object file access routine library **libld.a**.

SEE ALSO

ldclose(3X), ldopen(3X), ldfhread(3X), ldfcn(4).

NAME

ldopen, ldaopen — open a common object file for reading

SYNOPSIS

#include <stdio.h>
#include <filehdr.h>
#include <ldfcn.h>

LDFILE *ldopen (filename, ldptr)
char *filename;
LDFILE *ldptr;

LDFILE *ldaopen (filename, oldptr)
char *filename;
LDFILE *oldptr;

DESCRIPTION

Ldopen and *ldclose*(3X) are designed to provide uniform access to both simple object files and object files that are members of archive files. Thus an archive of common object files can be processed as if it were a series of simple common object files.

If *ldptr* has the value **NULL**, then *ldopen* will open *filename* and allocate and initialize the **LDFILE** structure, and return a pointer to the structure to the calling program.

If *ldptr* is valid and if **TYPE(***ldptr***)** is the archive magic number, *ldopen* will reinitialize the **LDFILE** structure for the next archive member of *filename*.

Ldopen and *ldclose*(3X) are designed to work in concert. *Ldclose* will return **FAILURE** only when **TYPE(***ldptr***)** is the archive magic number and there is another file in the archive to be processed. Only then should *ldopen* be called with the current value of *ldptr*. In all other cases, in particular whenever a new *filename* is opened, *ldopen* should be called with a **NULL** *ldptr* argument.

The following is a prototype for the use of *ldopen* and *ldclose*(3X).

```
/* for each filename to be processed */

ldptr = NULL;
do
{
        if ( (ldptr = ldopen(filename, ldptr)) != NULL )
        {
                /* check magic number */
                /* process the file */
        }
} while (ldclose(ldptr) == FAILURE );
```

If the value of *oldptr* is not **NULL**, *ldaopen* will open *filename* anew and allocate and initialize a new **LDFILE** structure, copying the **TYPE**, **OFFSET**, and **HEADER** fields from *oldptr*. *Ldaopen* returns a pointer to the new **LDFILE** structure. This new pointer is independent of the old pointer, *oldptr*. The two pointers may be used concurrently to read separate parts of the object file. For example, one pointer may be used to step sequentially through the relocation information, while the other is used to read indexed symbol table entries.

Both *ldopen* and *ldaopen* open *filename* for reading. Both functions return **NULL** if *filename* cannot be opened, or if memory for the **LDFILE** structure cannot be allocated. A successful open does not insure that the given file is a common object file or an archived object file.

The program must be loaded with the object file access routine library **libld.a**.

SEE ALSO

fopen(3S), ldclose(3X), ldfcn(4).

NAME

ldrseek, ldnrseek — seek to relocation entries of a section of a common object file

SYNOPSIS

```
#include <stdio.h>
#include <filehdr.h>
#include <ldfcn.h>

int ldrseek (ldptr, sectindx)
LDFILE *ldptr;
unsigned short sectindx;

int ldnrseek (ldptr, sectname)
LDFILE *ldptr;
char *sectname;
```

DESCRIPTION

Ldrseek seeks to the relocation entries of the section specified by *sectindx* of the common object file currently associated with *ldptr*.

Ldnrseek seeks to the relocation entries of the section specified by *sectname*.

Ldrseek and *ldnrseek* return **SUCCESS** or **FAILURE**. *Ldrseek* will fail if *sectindx* is greater than the number of sections in the object file; *ldnrseek* will fail if there is no section name corresponding with *sectname*. Either function will fail if the specified section has no relocation entries or if it cannot seek to the specified relocation entries.

Note that the first section has an index of *one*.

The program must be loaded with the object file access routine library **libld.a**.

SEE ALSO

ldclose(3X), ldopen(3X), ldshread(3X), ldfcn(4).

NAME

ldshread, ldnshread − read an indexed/named section header of a common object file

SYNOPSIS

```
#include <stdio.h>
#include <filehdr.h>
#include <scnhdr.h>
#include <ldfcn.h>

int ldshread (ldptr, sectindx, secthead)
LDFILE *ldptr;
unsigned short sectindx;
SCNHDR *secthead;

int ldnshread (ldptr, sectname, secthead)
LDFILE *ldptr;
char *sectname;
SCNHDR *secthead;
```

DESCRIPTION

Ldshread reads the section header specified by *sectindx* of the common object file currently associated with *ldptr* into the area of memory beginning at *secthead*.

Ldnshread reads the section header specified by *sectname* into the area of memory beginning at *secthead*.

Ldshread and *ldnshread* return **SUCCESS** or **FAILURE**. *Ldshread* will fail if *sectindx* is greater than the number of sections in the object file; *ldnshread* will fail if there is no section name corresponding with *sectname*. Either function will fail if it cannot read the specified section header.

Note that the first section header has an index of *one*.

The program must be loaded with the object file access routine library **libld.a**.

SEE ALSO

ldclose(3X), ldopen(3X), ldfcn(4).

NAME

ldsseek, ldnsseek — seek to an indexed/named section of a common object file

SYNOPSIS

#include <stdio.h>
#include <filehdr.h>
#include <ldfcn.h>

int ldsseek (ldptr, sectindx)
LDFILE *ldptr;
unsigned short sectindx;

int ldnsseek (ldptr, sectname)
LDFILE *ldptr;
char *sectname;

DESCRIPTION

Ldsseek seeks to the section specified by *sectindx* of the common object file currently associated with *ldptr*.

Ldnsseek seeks to the section specified by *sectname*.

Ldsseek and *ldnsseek* return **SUCCESS** or **FAILURE**. *Ldsseek* will fail if *sectindx* is greater than the number of sections in the object file; *ldnsseek* will fail if there is no section name corresponding with *sectname*. Either function will fail if there is no section data for the specified section or if it cannot seek to the specified section.

Note that the first section has an index of *one*.

The program must be loaded with the object file access routine library **libld.a**.

SEE ALSO

ldclose(3X), ldopen(3X), ldshread(3X), ldfcn(4).

NAME

ldtbindex − compute the index of a symbol table entry of a common object file

SYNOPSIS

#include <stdio.h>
#include <filehdr.h>
#include <syms.h>
#include <ldfcn.h>

long ldtbindex (ldptr)
LDFILE *ldptr;

DESCRIPTION

Ldtbindex returns the (**long**) index of the symbol table entry at the current position of the common object file associated with *ldptr*.

The index returned by *ldtbindex* may be used in subsequent calls to *ldtbread*(3X). However, since *ldtbindex* returns the index of the symbol table entry that begins at the current position of the object file, if *ldtbindex* is called immediately after a particular symbol table entry has been read, it will return the index of the next entry.

Ldtbindex will fail if there are no symbols in the object file, or if the object file is not positioned at the beginning of a symbol table entry.

Note that the first symbol in the symbol table has an index of *zero*.

The program must be loaded with the object file access routine library **libld.a**.

SEE ALSO

ldclose(3X), ldopen(3X), ldtbread(3X), ldtbseek(3X), ldfcn(4).

NAME

ldtbread − read an indexed symbol table entry of a common object file

SYNOPSIS

```
#include <stdio.h>
#include <filehdr.h>
#include <syms.h>
#include <ldfcn.h>

int ldtbread (ldptr, symindex, symbol)
LDFILE *ldptr;
long symindex;
SYMENT *symbol;
```

DESCRIPTION

Ldtbread reads the symbol table entry specified by **symindex** of the common object file currently associated with **ldptr** into the area of memory beginning at **symbol**.

Ldtbread returns **SUCCESS** or **FAILURE**. *Ldtbread* will fail if **symindex** is greater than the number of symbols in the object file, or if it cannot read the specified symbol table entry.

Note that the first symbol in the symbol table has an index of *zero*.

The program must be loaded with the object file access routine library **libld.a**.

SEE ALSO

ldclose(3X), ldopen(3X), ldtbseek(3X), ldgetname(3X), ldfcn(4).

NAME

ldtbseek – seek to the symbol table of a common object file

SYNOPSIS

```
#include <stdio.h>
#include <filehdr.h>
#include <ldfcn.h>

int ldtbseek (ldptr)
LDFILE *ldptr;
```

DESCRIPTION

Ldtbseek seeks to the symbol table of the object file currently associated with *ldptr*.

Ldtbseek returns **SUCCESS** or **FAILURE**. *Ldtbseek* will fail if the symbol table has been stripped from the object file, or if it cannot seek to the symbol table.

The program must be loaded with the object file access routine library **libld.a**.

SEE ALSO

ldclose(3X), ldopen(3X), ldtbread(3X), ldfcn(4).

NAME

logname − return login name of user

SYNOPSIS

char *logname( )

DESCRIPTION

Logname returns a pointer to the null-terminated login name; it extracts the **$LOGNAME** variable from the user's environment.

This routine is kept in **/lib/libPW.a**.

FILES

/etc/profile

SEE ALSO

profile(4), environ(5).
env(1), login(1) in the *UNIX Programmer's Manual—Volume 1: Commands and Utilities*.

BUGS

The return values point to static data whose content is overwritten by each call.

This method of determining a login name is subject to forgery.

NAME

malloc, free, realloc, calloc, mallopt, mallinfo — fast main memory allocator

SYNOPSIS

```
#include <malloc.h>

char *malloc (size)
unsigned size;

void free (ptr)
char *ptr;

char *realloc (ptr, size)
char *ptr;
unsigned size;

char *calloc (nelem, elsize)
unsigned nelem, elsize;

int mallopt (cmd, value)
int cmd, value;

struct mallinfo mallinfo (max)
int max;
```

DESCRIPTION

Malloc and *free* provide a simple general-purpose memory allocation package, which runs considerably faster than the *malloc*(3C) package. It is found in the library "malloc", and is loaded if the option "−lmalloc" is used with *cc*(1) or *ld*(1).

Malloc returns a pointer to a block of at least *size* bytes suitably aligned for any use.

The argument to *free* is a pointer to a block previously allocated by *malloc*; after *free* is performed this space is made available for further allocation, and its contents have been destroyed (but see *mallopt* below for a way to change this behavior).

Undefined results will occur if the space assigned by *malloc* is overrun or if some random number is handed to *free*.

Realloc changes the size of the block pointed to by *ptr* to *size* bytes and returns a pointer to the (possibly moved) block. The contents will be unchanged up to the lesser of the new and old sizes.

Calloc allocates space for an array of *nelem* elements of size *elsize*. The space is initialized to zeros.

Mallopt provides for control over the allocation algorithm. The available values for *cmd* are:

M_MXFAST Set *maxfast* to *value*. The algorithm allocates all blocks below the size of *maxfast* in large groups and then doles them out very quickly. The default value for *maxfast* is 0.

M_NLBLKS Set *numlblks* to *value*. The above mentioned "large groups" each contain *numlblks* blocks. *Numlblks* must be greater than 0. The default value for *numlblks* is 100.

M_GRAIN Set *grain* to *value*. The sizes of all blocks smaller than *maxfast* are considered to be rounded up to the nearest multiple of *grain*. *Grain* must be greater than 0. The default value of *grain* is the smallest number of bytes which will allow alignment of any data type. Value will be rounded up to a multiple of the default when *grain* is set.

M_KEEP Preserve data in a freed block until the next *malloc*, *realloc*, or *calloc*. This option is provided only for compatibility with the old version of *malloc* and is not recommended.

These values are defined in the <*malloc.h*> header file.

Mallopt may be called repeatedly, but may not be called after the first small block is allocated.

Mallinfo provides instrumentation describing space usage. It returns the structure:

```
struct mallinfo {
        int arena;          /* total space in arena */
        int ordblks;        /* number of ordinary blocks */
        int smblks;         /* number of small blocks */
        int hblkhd;         /* space in holding block headers */
        int hblks;          /* number of holding blocks */
        int usmblks;        /* space in small blocks in use */
        int fsmblks;        /* space in free small blocks */
        int uordblks;       /* space in ordinary blocks in use */
        int fordblks;       /* space in free ordinary blocks */
        int keepcost;       /* space penalty if keep option */
                            /* is used */
}
```

This structure is defined in the <*malloc.h*> header file.

Each of the allocation routines returns a pointer to space suitably aligned (after possible pointer coercion) for storage of any type of object.

SEE ALSO

brk(2), malloc(3C).

DIAGNOSTICS

Malloc, realloc and *calloc* return a NULL pointer if there is not enough available memory. When *realloc* returns NULL, the block pointed to by *ptr* is left intact. If *mallopt* is called after any allocation or if *cmd* or *value* are invalid, non-zero is returned. Otherwise, it returns zero.

WARNINGS

This package usually uses more data space than *malloc*(3C).
The code size is also bigger than *malloc*(3C).
Note that unlike *malloc*(3C), this package does not preserve the contents of a block when it is freed, unless the M_KEEP option of *mallopt* is used.
Undocumented features of *malloc*(3C) have not been duplicated.

NAME

plot − graphics interface subroutines

SYNOPSIS

openpl ()

erase ()

label (s)
char *s;

line (x1, y1, x2, y2)
int x1, y1, x2, y2;

circle (x, y, r)
int x, y, r;

arc (x, y, x0, y0, x1, y1)
int x, y, x0, y0, x1, y1;

move (x, y)
int x, y;

cont (x, y)
int x, y;

point (x, y)
int x, y;

linemod (s)
char *s;

space (x0, y0, x1, y1)
int x0, y0, x1, y1;

closepl ()

DESCRIPTION

These subroutines generate graphic output in a relatively device-independent manner. *Space* must be used before any of these functions to declare the amount of space necessary. See *plot*(4). *Openpl* must be used before any of the others to open the device for writing. *Closepl* flushes the output.

Circle draws a circle of radius *r* with center at the point *(x, y)*.

Arc draws an arc of a circle with center at the point *(x, y)* between the points *(x0, y0)* and *(x1, y1)*.

String arguments to *label* and *linemod* are terminated by nulls and do not contain new-lines.

See *plot*(4) for a description of the effect of the remaining functions.

The library files listed below provide several flavors of these routines.

FILES

/usr/lib/libplot.a	produces output for *tplot*(1G) filters
/usr/lib/lib300.a	for DASI 300
/usr/lib/lib300s.a	for DASI 300s
/usr/lib/lib450.a	for DASI 450
/usr/lib/lib4014.a	for TEKTRONIX 4014

WARNINGS

In order to compile a program containing these functions in *file.c* it is necessary to use "cc *file.c* −lplot".

In order to execute it, it is necessary to use "a.out | tplot".

The above routines use **<stdio.h>**, which causes them to increase the size of programs, not otherwise using standard I/O, more than might be expected.

SEE ALSO

plot(4).
graph(1G), stat(1G), tplot(1G) in the *UNIX Programmer's Manual—Volume 1: Commands and Utilities.*

NAME

regcmp, regex — compile and execute regular expression

SYNOPSIS

char *regcmp (string1 [, string2, ...], (char *)0)
char *string1, *string2, ...;

char *regex (re, subject[, ret0, ...])
char *re, *subject, *ret0, ...;

extern char *__loc1;

DESCRIPTION

Regcmp compiles a regular expression and returns a pointer to the compiled form. *Malloc*(3C) is used to create space for the vector. It is the user's responsibility to free unneeded space so allocated. A NULL return from *regcmp* indicates an incorrect argument. *Regcmp*(1) has been written to generally preclude the need for this routine at execution time.

Regex executes a compiled pattern against the subject string. Additional arguments are passed to receive values back. *Regex* returns NULL on failure or a pointer to the next unmatched character on success. A global character pointer *__loc1* points to where the match began. *Regcmp* and *regex* were mostly borrowed from the editor, *ed*(1); however, the syntax and semantics have been changed slightly. The following are the valid symbols and their associated meanings.

[ ] * . ^ These symbols retain their current meaning.

$ Matches the end of the string; **\n** matches a new-line.

− Within brackets the minus means *through*. For example, **[a−z]** is equivalent to **[abcd...xyz]**. The − can appear as itself only if used as the first or last character. For example, the character class expression **[]−]** matches the characters **]** and −.

\+ A regular expression followed by + means *one or more times*. For example, **[0−9]+** is equivalent to **[0−9][0−9]***.

{m} {m,} {m,u}
Integer values enclosed in {} indicate the number of times the preceding regular expression is to be applied. The value *m* is the minimum number and *u* is a number, less than 256, which is the maximum. If only *m* is

present (e.g., {m}), it indicates the exact number of times the regular expression is to be applied. The value {m,} is analogous to {m,infinity}. The plus (+) and star (*) operations are equivalent to {1,} and {0,} respectively.

(...)$n The value of the enclosed regular expression is to be returned. The value will be stored in the *(n+1)*th argument following the subject argument. At most ten enclosed regular expressions are allowed. *Regex* makes its assignments unconditionally.

(...) Parentheses are used for grouping. An operator, e.g., *, +, {}, can work on a single character or a regular expression enclosed in parentheses. For example, (a*(cb+)*)$0.

By necessity, all the above defined symbols are special. They must, therefore, be escaped to be used as themselves.

EXAMPLES

Example 1:

```
char *cursor, *newcursor, *ptr;
        ...
newcursor = regex((ptr = regcmp("^\n", 0)), cursor);
free(ptr);
```

This example will match a leading new-line in the subject string pointed at by cursor.

Example 2:

```
char ret0[9];
char *newcursor, *name;
        ...
name = regcmp("([A−Za−z][A−za−z0−9_]{0,7})$0", 0);
newcursor = regex(name, "123Testing321", ret0);
```

This example will match through the string "Testing3" and will return the address of the character after the last matched character (cursor+11). The string "Testing3" will be copied to the character array *ret0*.

Example 3:

```
#include "file.i"
char *string, *newcursor;
        ...
newcursor = regex(name, string);
```

This example applies a precompiled regular expression in **file.i** (see *regcmp*(1)) against *string*.

This routine is kept in **/lib/libPW.a**.

SEE ALSO

malloc(3C).
ed(1), regcmp(1) in the *UNIX Programmer's Manual—Volume 1: Commands and Utilities*.

BUGS

The user program may run out of memory if *regcmp* is called iteratively without freeing the vectors no longer required. The following user-supplied replacement for *malloc*(3C) reuses the same vector saving time and space:

```
/* user's program */
        ...
char *
malloc(n)
unsigned n;
{
        static char rebuf[512];
        return (n <= sizeof rebuf) ? rebuf : NULL;
}
```

NAME

sputl, sgetl − access long integer data in a machine-independent fashion.

SYNOPSIS

void sputl (value, buffer)
long value;
char *buffer;

long sgetl (buffer)
char *buffer;

DESCRIPTION

Sputl takes the four bytes of the long integer *value* and places them in memory starting at the address pointed to by *buffer*. The ordering of the bytes is the same across all machines.

Sgetl retrieves the four bytes in memory starting at the address pointed to by *buffer* and returns the long integer value in the byte ordering of the host machine.

The combination of *sputl* and *sgetl* provides a machine-independent way of storing long numeric data in a file in binary form without conversion to characters.

A program which uses these functions must be loaded with the object-file access routine library **libld.a**.

NAME

vprintf, vfprintf, vsprintf − print formatted output of a varargs argument list

SYNOPSIS

```
#include <stdio.h>
#include <varargs.h>

int vprintf (format, ap)
char *format;
va_list ap;

int vfprintf (stream, format, ap)
FILE *stream;
char *format;
va_list ap;

int vsprintf (s, format, ap)
char *s, *format;
va_list ap;
```

DESCRIPTION

vprintf, *vfprintf*, and *vsprintf* are the same as *printf*, *fprintf*, and *sprintf* respectively, except that instead of being called with a variable number of arguments, they are called with an argument list as defined by *varargs*(5).

EXAMPLE

The following demonstrates how *vfprintf* could be used to write an error routine.

```
#include <stdio.h>
#include <varargs.h>
        .
        .
        .
/*
 *      error should be called like
 *              error(function_name, format, arg1, arg2...);
 */
/*VARARGS0*/
void
error(va_alist)
/* Note the function_name and format arguments cannot be
 *      separately declared because of the definition of varargs.
 */
```

```
va_dcl
{
        va_list args;
        char *fmt;

        va_start(args);
        /* print out name of function causing error */
        (void)fprintf(stderr, "ERROR in %s: ", va_arg(args, char *));
        fmt = va_arg(args, char *);
        /* print out remainder of message */
        (void)vfprintf(fmt, args);
        va_end(args);
        (void)abort( );
}
```

SEE ALSO

printf(3S), varargs(5).

NAME

abort — terminate Fortran program

SYNOPSIS

call abort ( )

DESCRIPTION

Abort terminates the program which calls it, closing all open files truncated to the current position of the file pointer. The abort usually results in a core dump.

DIAGNOSTICS

When invoked, *abort* prints "Fortran abort routine called" on the standard error output. The message "abort - core dumped" is sent to the terminal.

SEE ALSO

abort(3C).

NAME

abs, iabs, dabs, cabs, zabs — Fortran absolute value

SYNOPSIS

integer i1, i2
real r1, r2
double precision dp1, dp2
complex cx1, cx2
double complex dx1, dx2

r2 = abs(r1)

i2 = iabs(i1)
i2 = abs(i1)

dp2 = dabs(dp1)
dp2 = abs(dp1)

cx2 = cabs(cx1)
cx2 = abs(cx1)

dx2 = zabs(dx1)
dx2 = abs(dx1)

DESCRIPTION

Abs is the family of absolute value functions. *Iabs* returns the integer absolute value of its integer argument. *Dabs* returns the double-precision absolute value of its double-precision argument. *Cabs* returns the complex absolute value of its complex argument. *Zabs* returns the double-complex absolute value of its double-complex argument. The generic form *abs* returns the type of its argument.

SEE ALSO

floor(3M).

NAME

acos, dacos — Fortran arccosine intrinsic function

SYNOPSIS

real r1, r2
double precision dp1, dp2

r2 = acos(r1)

dp2 = dacos(dp1)
dp2 = acos(dp1)

DESCRIPTION

Acos returns the real arccosine of its real argument. *Dacos* returns the double-precision arccosine of its double-precision argument. The generic form *acos* may be used with impunity as its argument will determine the type of the returned value.

SEE ALSO

trig(3M).

NAME

aimag, dimag − Fortran imaginary part of complex argument

SYNOPSIS

```
real r
complex cxr
double precision dp
double complex cxd

r = aimag(cxr)

dp = dimag(cxd)
```

DESCRIPTION

Aimag returns the imaginary part of its single-precision complex argument. *Dimag* returns the double-precision imaginary part of its double-complex argument.

NAME

aint, dint − Fortran integer part intrinsic function

SYNOPSIS

real r1, r2
double precision dp1, dp2

r2 = aint(r1)

dp2 = dint(dp1)
dp2 = aint(dp1)

DESCRIPTION

Aint returns the truncated value of its real argument in a real. *Dint* returns the truncated value of its double-precision argument as a double-precision value. *Aint* may be used as a generic function name, returning either a real or double-precision value depending on the type of its argument.

NAME

asin, dasin — Fortran arcsine intrinsic function

SYNOPSIS

real r1, r2
double precision dp1, dp2

r2 = asin(r1)

dp2 = dasin(dp1)
dp2 = asin(dp1)

DESCRIPTION

Asin returns the real arcsine of its real argument. *Dasin* returns the double-precision arcsine of its double-precision argument. The generic form *asin* may be used with impunity as it derives its type from that of its argument.

SEE ALSO

trig(3M).

NAME

atan, datan – Fortran arctangent intrinsic function

SYNOPSIS

real r1, r2
double precision dp1, dp2

r2 = atan(r1)

dp2 = datan(dp1)
dp2 = atan(dp1)

DESCRIPTION

Atan returns the real arctangent of its real argument. *Datan* returns the double-precision arctangent of its double-precision argument. The generic form *atan* may be used with a double-precision argument returning a double-precision value.

SEE ALSO

trig(3M).

NAME

atan2, datan2 − Fortran arctangent intrinsic function

SYNOPSIS

real r1, r2, r3
double precision dp1, dp2, dp3

r3 = atan2(r1, r2)

dp3 = datan2(dp1, dp2)
dp3 = atan2(dp1, dp2)

DESCRIPTION

Atan2 returns the arctangent of *arg1/arg2* as a real value. *Datan2* returns the double-precision arctangent of its double-precision arguments. The generic form *atan2* may be used with impunity with double-precision arguments.

SEE ALSO

trig(3M).

NAME

and, or, xor, not, lshift, rshift − Fortran Bitwise Boolean functions

SYNOPSIS

integer i, j, k
real a, b, c

k = and(i, j)
c = or(a, b)
j = xor(i, a)
j = not(i)
k = lshift(i, j)
k = rshift(i, j)

DESCRIPTION

The generic intrinsic Boolean functions *and*, *or* and *xor* return the value of the binary operations on their arguments. *Not* is a unary operator returning the one's complement of its argument. *Lshift* and *rshift* return the value of the first argument shifted left or right, respectively, the number of times specified by the second (integer) argument.

The Boolean functions are generic; that is, they are defined for all data types as arguments and return values. Where required, the compiler will generate appropriate type conversions.

NOTE

Although defined for all data types, use of Boolean functions on any but integer data is bizarre and will probably result in unexpected consequences.

BUGS

The implementation of the shift functions may cause large shift values to deliver weird results.

SEE ALSO

mil(3F).

NAME

conjg, dconjg — Fortran complex conjugate intrinsic function

SYNOPSIS

complex cx1, cx2
double complex dx1, dx2

cx2 = conjg(cx1)

dx2 = dconjg(dx1)

DESCRIPTION

Conjg returns the complex conjugate of its complex argument. *Dconjg* returns the double-complex conjugate of its double-complex argument.

NAME

cos, dcos, ccos — Fortran cosine intrinsic function

SYNOPSIS

real r1, r2
double precision dp1, dp2
complex cx1, cx2

r2 = cos(r1)

dp2 = dcos(dp1)
dp2 = cos(dp1)

cx2 = ccos(cx1)
cx2 = cos(cx1)

DESCRIPTION

Cos returns the real cosine of its real argument. *Dcos* returns the double-precision cosine of its double-precision argument. *Ccos* returns the complex cosine of its complex argument. The generic form *cos* may be used with impunity as its returned type is determined by that of its argument.

SEE ALSO

trig(3M).

NAME

cosh, dcosh – Fortran hyperbolic cosine intrinsic function

SYNOPSIS

real r1, r2
double precision dp1, dp2

r2 = cosh(r1)

dp2 = dcosh(dp1)
dp2 = cosh(dp1)

DESCRIPTION

Cosh returns the real hyperbolic cosine of its real argument. *Dcosh* returns the double-precision hyperbolic cosine of its double-precision argument. The generic form *cosh* may be used to return the hyperbolic cosine in the type of its argument.

SEE ALSO

sinh(3M).

NAME

dim, ddim, idim − positive difference intrinsic functions

SYNOPSIS

```
integer a1, a2, a3
a3 = idim(a1, a2)

real a1, a2, a3
a3 = dim(a1, a2)

double precision a1, a2, a3
a3 = ddim(a1, a2)
```

DESCRIPTION

These functions return:

a1−a2	if a1 > a2
0	if a1 <= a2

NAME

dprod − double precision product intrinsic function

SYNOPSIS

real a1, a2

double precision a3

a3 = dprod(a1, a2)

DESCRIPTION

Dprod returns the double precision product of its real arguments.

NAME

exp, dexp, cexp — Fortran exponential intrinsic function

SYNOPSIS

real r1, r2
double precision dp1, dp2
complex cx1, cx2

r2 = exp(r1)

dp2 = dexp(dp1)
dp2 = exp(dp1)

cx2 = cexp(cx1)
cx2 = exp(cx1)

DESCRIPTION

Exp returns the real exponential function e^x of its real argument. *Dexp* returns the double-precision exponential function of its double-precision argument. *Cexp* returns the complex exponential function of its complex argument. The generic function *exp* becomes a call to *dexp* or *cexp* as required, depending on the type of its argument.

SEE ALSO

exp(3M).

NAME

int, ifix, idint, real, float, sngl, dble, cmplx, dcmplx, ichar, char — explicit Fortran type conversion

SYNOPSIS

integer i, j
real r, s
double precision dp, dq
complex cx
double complex dcx
character*1 ch

i = int(r)
i = int(dp)
i = int(cx)
i = int(dcx)
i = ifix(r)
i = idint(dp)

r = real(i)
r = real(dp)
r = real(cx)
r = real(dcx)
r = float(i)
r = sngl(dp)

dp = dble(i)
dp = dble(r)
dp = dble(cx)
dp = dble(dcx)

cx = cmplx(i)
cx = cmplx(i, j)
cx = cmplx(r)
cx = cmplx(r, s)
cx = cmplx(dp)
cx = cmplx(dp, dq)
cx = cmplx(dcx)

dcx = dcmplx(i)
dcx = dcmplx(i, j)
dcx = dcmplx(r)
dcx = dcmplx(r, s)
dcx = dcmplx(dp)
dcx = dcmplx(dp, dq)
dcx = dcmplx(cx)

i = ichar(ch)
ch = char(i)

DESCRIPTION

These functions perform conversion from one data type to another.

The function **int** converts to *integer* form its *real*, *double precision*, *complex*, or *double complex* argument. If the argument is *real* or *double precision*, **int** returns the integer whose magnitude is the largest integer that does not exceed the magnitude of the argument and whose sign is the same as the sign of the argument (i.e. truncation). For complex types, the above rule is applied to the real part. **ifix** and **idint** convert only *real* and *double precision* arguments respectively.

The function **real** converts to *real* form an *integer*, *double precision*, *complex*, or *double complex* argument. If the argument is *double precision* or *double complex*, as much precision is kept as is possible. If the argument is one of the complex types, the real part is returned. **float** and **sngl** convert only *integer* and *double precision* arguments respectively.

The function **dble** converts any *integer*, *real*, *complex*, or *double complex* argument to *double precision* form. If the argument is of a complex type, the real part is returned.

The function **cmplx** converts its *integer*, *real*, *double precision*, or *double complex* argument(s) to *complex* form.

The function **dcmplx** converts to *double complex* form its *integer*, *real*, *double precision*, or *complex* argument(s).

Either one or two arguments may be supplied to **cmplx** and **dcmplx** . If there is only one argument, it is taken as the real part of the complex type and an imaginary part of zero is supplied. If two arguments are supplied, the first is taken as the real part and the second as the imaginary part.

The function **ichar** converts from a character to an integer depending on the character's position in the collating sequence.

The function **char** returns the character in the *i*th position in the processor collating sequence where *i* is the supplied argument.

For a processor capable of representing *n* characters,

ichar(**char**(i)) = i for $0 \leq i < n$, and

char(**ichar**(ch)) = ch for any representable character *ch*.

NAME

getarg − return Fortran command-line argument

SYNOPSIS

character*N c
integer i

call getarg(i, c)

DESCRIPTION

Getarg returns the *i*-th command-line argument of the current process. Thus, if a program were invoked via

foo arg1 arg2 arg3

getarg(2, c) would return the string "arg2" in the character variable *c*.

SEE ALSO

getopt(3C).

NAME

getenv − return Fortran environment variable

SYNOPSIS

character*N c

call getenv("VARIABLE_NAME", c)

DESCRIPTION

Getenv returns the character-string value of the environment variable represented by its first argument into the character variable of its second argument. If no such environment variable exists, all blanks will be returned.

SEE ALSO

getenv(3C), environ(5).

NAME

iargc − return the number of command line arguments

SYNOPSIS

integer i

i = iargc( )

DESCRIPTION

The *iargc* function returns the number of command line arguments passed to the program. Thus, if a program were invoked via

```
foo arg1 arg2 arg3
```

iargc( ) would return 3.

SEE ALSO

getarg(3F).

NAME

index – return location of Fortran substring

SYNOPSIS

character*N1 ch1
character*N2 ch2
integer i

i = index(ch1, ch2)

DESCRIPTION

Index returns the location of substring *ch2* in string *ch1*. The value returned is the position at which substring *ch2* starts, or 0 if it is not present in string *ch1*. If N2 is greater than N1, a zero is returned.

NAME

len − return length of Fortran string

SYNOPSIS

character*N ch
integer i

i = len(ch)

DESCRIPTION

Len returns the length of string *ch*.

NAME

log, alog, dlog, clog — Fortran natural logarithm intrinsic function

SYNOPSIS

real r1, r2
double precision dp1, dp2
complex cx1, cx2

r2 = alog(r1)
r2 = log(r1)

dp2 = dlog(dp1)
dp2 = log(dp1)

cx2 = clog(cx1)
cx2 = log(cx1)

DESCRIPTION

Alog returns the real natural logarithm of its real argument. *Dlog* returns the double-precision natural logarithm of its double-precision argument. *Clog* returns the complex logarithm of its complex argument. The generic function *log* becomes a call to *alog*, *dlog*, or *clog* depending on the type of its argument.

SEE ALSO

exp(3M).

NAME

log10, alog10, dlog10 − Fortran common logarithm intrinsic function

SYNOPSIS

real r1, r2
double precision dp1, dp2

r2 = alog10(r1)
r2 = log10(r1)

dp2 = dlog10(dp1)
dp2 = log10(dp1)

DESCRIPTION

Alog10 returns the real common logarithm of its real argument. *Dlog10* returns the double-precision common logarithm of its double-precision argument. The generic function *log10* becomes a call to *alog10* or *dlog10* depending on the type of its argument.

SEE ALSO

exp(3M).

NAME

max, max0, amax0, max1, amax1, dmax1 − Fortran maximum-value functions

SYNOPSIS

integer i, j, k, l
real a, b, c, d
double precision dp1, dp2, dp3

l = max(i, j, k)
c = max(a, b)
dp = max(a, b, c)
k = max0(i, j)
a = amax0(i, j, k)
i = max1(a, b)
d = amax1(a, b, c)
dp3 = dmax1(dp1, dp2)

DESCRIPTION

The maximum-value functions return the largest of their arguments (of which there may be any number). *Max* is the generic form which can be used for all data types and takes its return type from that of its arguments (which must all be of the same type). *Max0* returns the integer form of the maximum value of its integer arguments; *amax0*, the real form of its integer arguments; *max1*, the integer form of its real arguments; *amax1*, the real form of its real arguments; and *dmax1*, the double-precision form of its double-precision arguments.

SEE ALSO

min(3F).

NAME

mclock − return Fortran time accounting

SYNOPSIS

integer i

i = mclock( )

DESCRIPTION

Mclock returns time accounting information about the current process and its child processes. The value returned is the sum of the current process's user time and the user and system times of all child processes.

SEE ALSO

times(2), clock(3C), system(3F).

NAME

ior, iand, not, ieor, ishft, ishftc, ibits, btest, ibset, ibclr, mvbits — bit field manipulation intrinsic functions and subroutines from the Fortran Military Standard (MIL-STD-1753).

SYNOPSIS

integer i, k, l, m, n, len
logical b

i = ior(m, n)
i = iand(m, n)
i = not(m)
i = ieor(m, n)
i = ishft(m, k)
i = ishftc(m, k, len)
i = ibits(m, k, len)
b = btest(n, k)
i = ibset(n, k)
i = ibclr(n, k)
call mvbits(m, k, len, n, l)

DESCRIPTION

ior, iand, not, ieor — return the same results as *and, or, not, xor* as defined in *bool*(3F).

ishft, ishftc — **m** specifies the integer to be shifted. **k** specifies the shift count. **k** > 0 indicates a left shift. **k** = 0 indicates no shift. **k** < 0 indicates a right shift. In *ishft*, zeros are shifted in. In *ishftc*, the rightmost **len** bits are shifted circularly **k** bits. If **k** is greater than the machine word-size, *ishftc* will not shift.

Bit fields are numbered from right to left and the rightmost bit position is zero. The length of the **len** field must be greater than zero.

ibits — extract a subfield of **len** bits from **m** starting with bit position **k** and extending left for **len** bits. The result field is right justified and the remaining bits are set to zero.

btest — The **k**th bit of argument **n** is tested. The value of the function is **.TRUE.** if the bit is 1 and **.FALSE.** if the bit is 0.

ibset — the result is the value of **n** with the **k**th bit set to 1.

ibclr — the result is the value of **n** with the **k**th bit set to 0.

mvbits — **len** bits are moved beginning at position **k** of argument **m** to position **l** of argument **n**.

SEE ALSO

bool(3f).

NAME

min, min0, amin0, min1, amin1, dmin1 — Fortran minimum-value functions

SYNOPSIS

integer i, j, k, l
real a, b, c, d
double precision dp1, dp2, dp3

l = min(i, j, k)
c = min(a, b)
dp = min(a, b, c)
k = min0(i, j)
a = amin0(i, j, k)
i = min1(a, b)
d = amin1(a, b, c)
dp3 = dmin1(dp1, dp2)

DESCRIPTION

The minimum-value functions return the minimum of their arguments (of which there may be any number). *Min* is the generic form which can be used for all data types and takes its return type from that of its arguments (which must all be of the same type). *Min0* returns the integer form of the minimum value of its integer arguments; *amin0*, the real form of its integer arguments; *min1*, the integer form of its real arguments; *amin1*, the real form of its real arguments; and *dmin1*, the double-precision form of its double-precision arguments.

SEE ALSO

max(3F).

NAME

mod, amod, dmod — Fortran remaindering intrinsic functions

SYNOPSIS

integer i, j, k
real r1, r2, r3
double precision dp1, dp2, dp3

k = mod(i, j)

r3 = amod(r1, r2)
r3 = mod(r1, r2)

dp3 = dmod(dp1, dp2)
dp3 = mod(dp1, dp2)

DESCRIPTION

Mod returns the integer remainder of its first argument divided by its second argument. *Amod* and *dmod* return, respectively, the real and double-precision whole number remainder of the integer division of their two arguments. The generic version *mod* will return the data type of its arguments.

NAME

irand, rand, srand — random number generator

SYNOPSIS

integer iseed, i, irand
double precision x, rand

call srand(iseed)

i = irand( )

x = rand( )

DESCRIPTION

Irand generates successive pseudo-random integers in the range from 0 to 2**15−1. *Rand* generates pseudo-random numbers distributed in [0, 1.0]. *Srand* uses its integer argument to re-initialize the seed for successive invocations of *irand* and *rand*.

SEE ALSO

rand(3C).

NAME

anint, dnint, nint, idnint − Fortran nearest integer functions

SYNOPSIS

integer i
real r1, r2
double precision dp1, dp2

r2 = anint(r1)
i = nint(r1)

dp2 = anint(dp1)
dp2 = dnint(dp1)

i = nint(dp1)
i = idnint(dp1)

DESCRIPTION

Anint returns the nearest whole real number to its real argument (i.e., int(a+0.5) if a ⩾ 0, int(a−0.5) otherwise). *Dnint* does the same for its double-precision argument. *Nint* returns the nearest integer to its real argument. *Idnint* is the double-precision version. *Anint* is the generic form of *anint* and *dnint* , performing the same operation and returning the data type of its argument. *Nint* is also the generic form of *idnint.*

NAME

sign, isign, dsign — Fortran transfer-of-sign intrinsic function

SYNOPSIS

integer i, j, k
real r1, r2, r3
double precision dp1, dp2, dp3

k = isign(i, j)
k = sign(i, j)

r3 = sign(r1, r2)

dp3 = dsign(dp1, dp2)
dp3 = sign(dp1, dp2)

DESCRIPTION

Isign returns the magnitude of its first argument with the sign of its second argument. *Sign* and *dsign* are its real and double-precision counterparts, respectively. The generic version is *sign* and will devolve to the appropriate type depending on its arguments.

NAME

signal – specify Fortran action on receipt of a system signal

SYNOPSIS

integer i, intfc
external intfc

call signal(i, intfc)

DESCRIPTION

The argument **i** specifies the signal to be caught. *Signal* allows a process to specify a function to be invoked upon receipt of a specific signal. The first argument specifies which fault or exception. The second argument specifies the function to be invoked.

NOTE: The interrupt processing function, *intfc*, does not take an argument.

SEE ALSO

kill(2), signal(2).

NAME

sin, dsin, csin — Fortran sine intrinsic function

SYNOPSIS

real r1, r2
double precision dp1, dp2
complex cx1, cx2

r2 = sin(r1)

dp2 = dsin(dp1)
dp2 = sin(dp1)

cx2 = csin(cx1)
cx2 = sin(cx1)

DESCRIPTION

Sin returns the real sine of its real argument. *Dsin* returns the double-precision sine of its double-precision argument. *Csin* returns the complex sine of its complex argument. The generic *sin* function becomes *dsin* or *csin* as required by argument type.

SEE ALSO

trig(3M).

NAME

sinh, dsinh − Fortran hyperbolic sine intrinsic function

SYNOPSIS

real r1, r2
double precision dp1, dp2

r2 = sinh(r1)

dp2 = dsinh(dp1)
dp2 = sinh(dp1)

DESCRIPTION

Sinh returns the real hyperbolic sine of its real argument. *Dsinh* returns the double-precision hyperbolic sine of its double-precision argument. The generic form *sinh* may be used to return a double-precision value when given a double-precision argument.

SEE ALSO

sinh(3M).

NAME

sqrt, dsqrt, csqrt — Fortran square root intrinsic function

SYNOPSIS

real r1, r2
double precision dp1, dp2
complex cx1, cx2

r2 = sqrt(r1)

dp2 = dsqrt(dp1)
dp2 = sqrt(dp1)

cx2 = csqrt(cx1)
cx2 = sqrt(cx1)

DESCRIPTION

Sqrt returns the real square root of its real argument. *Dsqrt* returns the double-precision square root of its double-precision argument. *Csqrt* returns the complex square root of its complex argument. *Sqrt*, the generic form, will become *dsqrt* or *csqrt* as required by its argument type.

SEE ALSO

exp(3M).

NAME

lge, lgt, lle, llt − string comparison intrinsic functions

SYNOPSIS

character*N a1, a2
logical l

l = lge(a1, a2)
l = lgt(a1, a2)
l = lle(a1, a2)
l = llt(a1, a2)

DESCRIPTION

These functions return .TRUE. if the inequality holds and .FALSE. otherwise.

NAME

system — issue a shell command from Fortran

SYNOPSIS

character*N c

call system(c)

DESCRIPTION

System causes its character argument to be given to *sh*(1) as input, as if the string had been typed at a terminal. The current process waits until the shell has completed.

SEE ALSO

exec(2), system(3S).
sh(1) in the *UNIX Programmer's Manual—Volume 1: Commands and Utilities*.

NAME

tan, dtan — Fortran tangent intrinsic function

SYNOPSIS

real r1, r2
double precision dp1, dp2

r2 = tan(r1)

dp2 = dtan(dp1)
dp2 = tan(dp1)

DESCRIPTION

Tan returns the real tangent of its real argument. *Dtan* returns the double-precision tangent of its double-precision argument. The generic *tan* function becomes *dtan* as required with a double-precision argument.

SEE ALSO

trig(3M).

NAME

tanh, dtanh − Fortran hyperbolic tangent intrinsic function

SYNOPSIS

real r1, r2
double precision dp1, dp2

r2 = tanh(r1)

dp2 = dtanh(dp1)
dp2 = tanh(dp1)

DESCRIPTION

Tanh returns the real hyperbolic tangent of its real argument. *Dtanh* returns the double-precision hyperbolic tangent of its double-precision argument. The generic form *tanh* may be used to return a double-precision value given a double-precision argument.

SEE ALSO

sinh(3M).

NAME

intro – introduction to file formats

DESCRIPTION

This section outlines the formats of various files. The C **struct** declarations for the file formats are given where applicable. Usually, these structures can be found in the directories **/usr/include** or **/usr/include/sys**.

References of the type *name*(1M) refer to entries found in Section 1 of the *UNIX Programmer's Manual—Volume 3: System Administration Facilities.* References of the type *Name*(1) refer to entries found in Section 1 of the *UNIX Programmer's Manual—Volume 1: Commands and Utilities.*

NAME

a.out — common assembler and link editor output

DESCRIPTION

The file name **a.out** is the output file from the assembler *as*(1) and the link editor *ld*(1). Both programs will make *a.out* executable if there were no errors in assembling or linking and no unresolved external references.

A common object file consists of a file header, a UNIX system header, a table of section headers, relocation information, (optional) line numbers, a symbol table, and a string table. The order is given below.

File header.
UNIX system header.
Section 1 header.
...
Section n header.
Section 1 data.
...
Section n data.
Section 1 relocation.
...
Section n relocation.
Section 1 line numbers.
...
Section n line numbers.
Symbol table.
String table.

The last three parts of an object file (line numbers, symbol table, and string table) may be missing if the program was linked with the −s option of *ld*(1) or if they were removed by *strip*(1). Also note that the relocation information will be absent if there were no unresolved external references after linking. The string table exists only if the symbol table contains symbols with names longer than eight characters.

The sizes of each section (contained in the header, discussed below) are in bytes and are even.

When an **a.out** file is loaded into memory for execution, three logical segments are set up: the text segment, the data segment (initialized data followed by uninitialized, the latter actually being initialized to all 0's), and a stack. On the 3B20 computers and other machines the text segment starts at location 0 in the core image or at the beginning of the next virtually addressable block past location 0. Any reference to 0 causes a memory fault (see the **−z** option of *ld*(1). On the 3B5 or 3B2 computers the text segment starts at location 0x80800000.

The **a.out** file produced by *ld*(1) by default has a number called the magic number 0413 in the first field of the UNIX system header. The headers (file header, UNIX system header, and section headers) are loaded at the beginning of the text segment and the text immediately follows the headers in the user address space. The first text address will equal the size of the headers, and will vary depending upon the number of section headers in the **a.out** file.

In an **a.out** file with three sections (.text, .data, and .bss), the first text address is at 0xA8 on most machines, 0xB0 on the 3B20 computer, and 0x808000A8 on the 3B5 computer and 3B2 computer. The text segment is not writable by the program; if other processes are executing the same **a.out** file, the processes will share a single text segment.

The data segment starts at the next segment boundary (128k on the 3B20, 512k on the 3B5 and 3B2 computers) past the last text address. The first data address is determined by the following: If an **a.out** file were split into 8k chunks, one of the chunks would contain both the end of text and the beginning of data. When the core image is created, that chunk will appear twice; once at the end of text and once at the beginning of data (with some unused space in between). The duplicated chunk of text that appears at the beginning of data is never executed; it is duplicated so that the operating system may bring in pieces of the file in multiples of the page size without having to realign the beginning of the data section to a page boundary. Therefore the first data address is the sum of the next segment boundary past the end of text plus the remainder of the last text address divided by 8k.

On the 3B20 computer a magic number of 0410 or 0407 in the UNIX system header indicates that the file was produced by a link editor from an earlier release of the UNIX system. An **a.out** file with either of these magic numbers will still be executable, although support for files with the magic number 0407 may be dropped in a future release. The magic number 0407 indicates that the text segment is not write-protected or shared, and the data segment is contiguous with the text segment. If the magic number is 0410, the text segment is write-protected and sharable. In both of these types of **a.out** files, the header is not loaded; the text segment starts at location 0 in the core image.

On the 3B20 computer, the stack begins at the end of the data section and grows toward higher addresses. On the 3B2 computer the stack begins at location 0xC0020000 and grows toward higher addresses. On the 3B5 computer the stack begins at location 0xF00000 and grows toward higher addresses. The maximum stack size on the 3B5 computer is 512k. On some computers, the stack begins at the end of memory and grows toward lower addresses. On some other machines the stack is automatically extended as required. The data segment is extended only as requested by the *brk*(2) system call.

The value of a word in the text or data portions that is not a reference to an undefined external symbol is exactly the value that will appear in memory when the file is executed. If a word in the text involves a reference to an undefined external symbol, the storage class of the symbol-table entry for that word will be marked as an "external symbol", and the section number will be set to 0. When the file is processed by the link editor and the external symbol becomes defined, the value of the symbol will be added to the word in the file.

File Header

The format of the **filehdr** header is

```
struct filehdr
{
        unsigned short  f_magic;   /* magic number */
        unsigned short  f_nscns;   /* number of sections */
        long            f_timdat;  /* time and date stamp */
        long            f_symptr;  /* file ptr to symtab */
        long            f_nsyms;   /* # symtab entries */
        unsigned short  f_opthdr;  /* sizeof(opt hdr) */
        unsigned short  f_flags;   /* flags */
};
```

UNIX System Header

The format of the **UNIX** system header on all machines other than the 3B20 computer is

```
typedef struct aouthdr
{
        short   magic;          /* magic number */
        short   vstamp;         /* version stamp */
        long    tsize;          /* text size in bytes, padded */
        long    dsize;          /* initialized data (.data) */
        long    bsize;          /* uninitialized data (.bss) */
        long    entry;          /* entry point */
        long    text_start;     /* base of text used for this file */
        long    data_start;     /* base of data used for this file */
} AOUTHDR;
```

The format of the **3B20 computer UNIX** system header is

```
typedef struct aouthdr
{
        short   magic;          /* magic number */
        short   vstamp;         /* version stamp */
        long    tsize;          /* text size in bytes, padded */
        long    dsize;          /* initialized data (.data) */
        long    bsize;          /* uninitialized data (.bss) */
        long    dum1;           /* unused fill space included */
        long    dum2;           /* for historical reasons */
        long    entry;          /* entry point */
        long    text_start;     /* base of text used for this file */
        long    data_start;     /* base of data used for this file */
} AOUTHDR;
```

Section Header

The format of the **section** header is

```
struct scnhdr
{
        char            s_name[SYMNMLEN];/* section name */
        long            s_paddr;   /* physical address */
        long            s_vaddr;   /* virtual address */
        long            s_size;    /* section size */
        long            s_scnptr;  /* file ptr to raw data */
        long            s_relptr;  /* file ptr to relocation */
        long            s_lnnoptr; /* file ptr to line numbers */
        unsigned short  s_nreloc;  /* # reloc entries */
        unsigned short  s_nlnno;   /* # line number entries */
        long            s_flags;   /* flags */
};
```

Relocation

Object files have one relocation entry for each relocatable reference in the text or data. If relocation information is present, it will be in the following format:

```
struct reloc
{
        long     r_vaddr;   /* (virtual) address of reference */
        long     r_symndx;  /* index into symbol table */
        short    r_type;    /* relocation type */
};
```

The start of the relocation information is *s_relptr* from the section header. If there is no relocation information, *s_relptr* is 0.

Symbol Table

The format of each symbol in the symbol table is

```
#define  SYMNMLEN  8
#define  FILNMLEN  14
#define  SYMESZ    18          /* the size of a SYMENT */

struct syment
{
   union                         /*  get a symbol name */
    {
       char           _n_name[SYMNMLEN]; /* name of symbol */
       struct
       {
          long        _n_zeroes;    /* == 0L if in string table */
          long        _n_offset;    /* location in string table */
       } _n_n;
       char           *_n_nptr[2];  /* allows overlaying */
    } _n;
    unsigned long     n_value;      /* value of symbol */
    short             n_scnum;      /* section number */
    unsigned short    n_type;       /* type and derived type */
    char              n_sclass;     /* storage class */
    char              n_numaux;     /* number of aux entries */
};

#define  n_name       _n._n_name
#define  n_zeroes     _n._n_n._n_zeroes
#define  n_offset     _n._n_n._n_offset
#define  n_nptr       _n._n_nptr[1]
```

Some symbols require more information than a single entry; they are followed by *auxiliary entries* that are the same size as a symbol entry. The format follows.

```
union auxent {
        struct {
                long    x_tagndx;
                union {
                        struct {
                                unsigned short  x_lnno;
                                unsigned short  x_size;
                        } x_lnsz;
                        long     x_fsize;
                } x_misc;
                union {
                        struct {
                                long    x_lnnoptr;
                                long    x_endndx;
                        }  x_fcn;
                        struct {
                                unsigned short  x_dimen[DIMNUM];
                        } x_ary;
                } x_fcnary;
                unsigned short  x_tvndx;
        } x_sym;

        struct {
                char    x_fname[FILNMLEN];
        } x_file;

        struct {
                long          x_scnlen;
                unsigned short  x_nreloc;
                unsigned short  x_nlinno;
        } x_scn;

        struct {
                long             x_tvfill;
                unsigned short  x_tvlen;
                unsigned short  x_tvran[2];
        } x_tv;
};
```

Indexes of symbol table entries begin at *zero*. The start of the symbol table is *f_symptr* (from the file header) bytes from the beginning of the file. If the symbol table is stripped, *f_symptr* is 0. The string table (if one exists) begins at *f_symptr* + (*f_nsyms* * SYMESZ) bytes from the beginning of the file.

SEE ALSO

brk(2), filehdr(4), ldfcn(4), linenum(4), reloc(4), scnhdr(4), syms(4).
as(1), cc(1), ld(1) in the *UNIX Programmer's Manual—Volume 1: Commands and Utilities.*

NAME

acct — per-process accounting file format

SYNOPSIS

#include <sys/acct.h>

DESCRIPTION

Files produced as a result of calling *acct*(2) have records in the form defined by **<sys/acct.h>**, whose contents are:

```
typedef ushort comp_t;     /* "floating point" */
                /* 13-bit fraction, 3-bit exponent */

struct  acct
{
        char    ac_flag;        /* Accounting flag */
        char    ac_stat;        /* Exit status */
        ushort  ac_uid;
        ushort  ac_gid;
        dev_t   ac_tty;
        time_t  ac_btime;       /* Beginning time */
        comp_t  ac_utime;       /* acctng user time in clock ticks */
        comp_t  ac_stime;       /* acctng system time in clock ticks */
        comp_t  ac_etime;       /* acctng elapsed time in clock ticks */
        comp_t  ac_mem;         /* memory usage in clicks */
        comp_t  ac_io;          /* chars trnsfrd by read/write */
        comp_t  ac_rw;          /* number of block reads/writes */
        char    ac_comm[8];     /* command name */
};

extern  struct  acct    acctbuf;
extern  struct  inode   *acctp;  /* inode of accounting file */

#define AFORK  01              /* has executed fork, but no exec */
#define ASU    02              /* used super-user privileges */
#define ACCTF  0300            /* record type: 00 = acct */
```

In *ac_flag*, the AFORK flag is turned on by each *fork*(2) and turned off by an *exec*(2). The *ac_comm* field is inherited from the parent process and is reset by any *exec*. Each time the system charges the process with a clock tick, it also adds to *ac_mem* the current process size, computed as follows:
(data size) + (text size) / (number of in-core processes using text)

The value of *ac_mem / (ac_stime + ac_utime)* can be viewed as an approximation to the mean process size, as modified by text-sharing.

The structure **tacct.h**, which resides with the source files of the accounting commands, represents the total accounting format used by the various accounting commands:

```
/*
 * total accounting (for acct period), also for day
 */

struct tacct {
        uid_t           ta_uid;       /* userid */
        char            ta_name[8];   /* login name */
        float           ta_cpu[2];    /* cum. cpu time, p/np (mins) */
        float           ta_kcore[2];  /* cum kcore-minutes, p/np */
        float           ta_con[2];    /* cum. connect time, p/np, mins */
        float           ta_du;        /* cum. disk usage */
        long            ta_pc;        /* count of processes */
        unsigned short  ta_sc;        /* count of login sessions */
        unsigned short  ta_dc;        /* count of disk samples */
        unsigned short  ta_fee;       /* fee for special services */
};
```

SEE ALSO

acct(2), exec(2), fork(2).

acct(1M) in the *UNIX Programmer's Manual—Volume 3: System Administration Facilities.*

acctcom(1) in the *UNIX Programmer's Manual—Volume 1: Commands and Utilities.*

BUGS

The *ac_mem* value for a short-lived command gives little information about the actual size of the command, because *ac_mem* may be incremented while a different command (e.g., the shell) is being executed by the process.

NAME

ar — common archive file format

DESCRIPTION

The archive command *ar*(1) is used to combine several files into one. Archives are used mainly as libraries to be searched by the link editor *ld*(1).

Each archive begins with the archive magic string.

```
#define ARMAG  "!<arch>\n"          /* magic string */
#define SARMAG 8                    /* length of magic string */
```

Each archive which contains common object files (see *a.out*(4)) includes an archive symbol table. This symbol table is used by the link editor *ld*(1) to determine which archive members must be loaded during the link edit process. The archive symbol table (if it exists) is always the first file in the archive (but is never listed) and is automatically created and/or updated by *ar*.

Following the archive magic string are the archive file members. Each file member is preceded by a file member header which is of the following format:

```
#define ARFMAG  "`\n"           /* header trailer string */

struct ar_hdr                   /* file member header */
{
    char  ar_name[16];          /* '/' terminated file member */
    char  ar_date[12];          /* file member date */
    char  ar_uid[6];            /* file user identification */
    char  ar_gid[6];            /* file group identification */
    char  ar_mode[8];           /* file member mode (octal) */
    char  ar_size[10];          /* file member size */
    char  ar_fmag[2];           /* header trailer string */
};
```

All information in the file member headers is in printable ASCII. The numeric information contained in the headers is stored as decimal numbers (except for *ar_mode* which is in octal). Thus, if the archive contains printable files, the archive itself is printable.

The *ar_name* field is blank-padded and slash (/) terminated. The *ar_date* field is the modification date of the file at the time of its insertion into the archive. Common format archives can be moved from system to system as long as the portable archive command *ar*(1) is used. Conversion tools such as *convert*(1) exist to aid in the transportation of non-common format archives to this format.

Each archive file member begins on an even byte boundary; a newline is inserted between files if necessary. Nevertheless the size given reflects the actual size of the file exclusive of padding.

Notice there is no provision for empty areas in an archive file.

If the archive symbol table exists, the first file in the archive has a zero length name (i.e., **ar_name[0] == '/'**). The contents of this file are as follows:

- The number of symbols. Length: 4 bytes.
- The array of offsets into the archive file. Length: 4 bytes * "the number of symbols".
- The name string table. Length: *ar_size* − (4 bytes * ("the number of symbols" + 1)).

The number of symbols and the array of offsets are managed with *sgetl* and *sputl*. The string table contains exactly as many null terminated strings as there are elements in the offsets array. Each offset from the array is associated with the corresponding name from the string table (in order). The names in the string table are all the defined global symbols found in the common object files in the archive. Each offset is the location of the archive header for the associated symbol.

SEE ALSO

sputl(3X), a.out(4).
ar(1), convert(1), ld(1), strip(1) in the *UNIX Programmer's Manual—Volume 1: Commands and Utilities.*

CAVEATS

The common archive structure is not compatible between the PDP-11 and the IBM-370, due to the different file formats. See *convert*(1) to convert between machines.

Strip(1) will remove all archive symbol entries from the header. The archive symbol entries must be restored via the **ts** option of the *ar*(1) command before the archive can be used with the link editor *ld*(1).

NAME

checklist — list of file systems processed by fsck

DESCRIPTION

Checklist resides in directory **/etc** and contains a list of, at most, 15 *special file* names. Each *special file* name is contained on a separate line and corresponds to a file system. Each file system will then be automatically processed by the *fsck* (1M) command.

SEE ALSO

fsck(1M) in the *UNIX Programmer's Manual—Volume 3: System Administration Facilities.*

NAME

core − format of core image file

DESCRIPTION

The UNIX system writes out a core image of a terminated process when any of various errors occur. See *signal*(2) for the list of reasons; the most common are memory violations, illegal instructions, bus errors, and user-generated quit signals. The core image is called **core** and is written in the process's working directory (provided it can be; normal access controls apply). A process with an effective user ID different from the real user ID will not produce a core image.

The first section of the core image is a copy of the system's per-user data for the process, including the registers as they were at the time of the fault. The size of this section depends on the parameter *usize*, which is defined in **/usr/include/sys/param.h**. The remainder represents the actual contents of the user's core area when the core image was written. If the text segment is read-only and shared, or separated from data space, it is not dumped.

The format of the information in the first section is described by the *user* structure of the system, defined in **/usr/include/sys/user.h**. The important stuff not detailed therein is the locations of the registers, which are outlined in **/usr/include/sys/reg.h**.

SEE ALSO

setuid(2), signal(2).
crash(1M) in the *UNIX Programmer's Manual—Volume 3: System Administration Facilities.*
sdb(1) in the *UNIX Programmer's Manual—Volume 1: Commands and Utilities.*

NAME

cpio — format of cpio archive

DESCRIPTION

The *header* structure, when the **−c** option of *cpio*(1) is not used, is:

```
struct {
        short   h_magic,
                h_dev;
        ushort  h_ino,
                h_mode,
                h_uid,
                h_gid;
        short   h_nlink,
                h_rdev,
                h_mtime[2],
                h_namesize,
                h_filesize[2];.
        char    h_name[h_namesize rounded to word];
} Hdr;
```

When the **−c** option is used, the *header* information is described by:

```
sscanf(Chdr,"%6o%6o%6o%6o%6o%6o%6o%6o%11lo%6o%11lo%s",
        &Hdr.h_magic, &Hdr.h_dev, &Hdr.h_ino, &Hdr.h_mode,
        &Hdr.h_uid, &Hdr.h_gid, &Hdr.h_nlink, &Hdr.h_rdev,
        &Longtime, &Hdr.h_namesize,&Longfile,Hdr.h_name);
```

Longtime and *Longfile* are equivalent to *Hdr.h_mtime* and *Hdr.h_filesize*, respectively. The contents of each file are recorded in an element of the array of varying length structures, *archive*, together with other items describing the file. Every instance of *h_magic* contains the constant 070707 (octal). The items *h_dev* through *h_mtime* have meanings explained in *stat*(2). The length of the null-terminated path name *h_name*, including the null byte, is given by *h_namesize*.

The last record of the *archive* always contains the name TRAILER!!!. Special files, directories, and the trailer are recorded with *h_filesize* equal to zero.

SEE ALSO

stat(2).

cpio(1), find(1) in the *UNIX Programmer's Manual—Volume 1: Commands and Utilities.*

NAME

dir − format of directories

SYNOPSIS

#include <sys/dir.h>

DESCRIPTION

A directory behaves exactly like an ordinary file, save that no user may write into a directory. The fact that a file is a directory is indicated by a bit in the flag word of its i-node entry (see *fs*(4)). The structure of a directory entry as given in the include file is:

```
#ifndef DIRSIZ
#define DIRSIZ      14
#endif
struct  direct
{
        ino_t  d_ino;
        char   d_name[DIRSIZ];
};
```

By convention, the first two entries in each directory are for **.** and **..**. The first is an entry for the directory itself. The second is for the parent directory. The meaning of **..** is modified for the root directory of the master file system; there is no parent, so **..** has the same meaning as **.**.

SEE ALSO

fs(4).

NAME

errfile − error-log file format

DESCRIPTION

When hardware errors are detected by the system, an error record is generated and passed to the error-logging daemon for recording in the error log for later analysis. The default error log is **/usr/adm/errfile**.

The format of an error record depends on the type of error that was encountered. Every record, however, has a header with the following format:

```
struct errhdr {
        short           e_type;         /* record type */
        short           e_len;          /* bytes in record (inc hdr) */
        time_t          e_time;         /* time of day */
        int             e_cpu;          /* proc recording error*/
};
```

The permissible record types are as follows:

```
#define E_GOTS      010     /* start for UNIX System
                             * Release 3.0*/
#define E_GORT      011     /* start for UNIX system/RT */
#define E_STOP      012     /* stop */
#define E_TCHG      013     /* time change */
#define E_CCHG      014     /* configuration change */
#define E_BLK       020     /* block device error */
#define E_STRAY     030     /* stray interrupt */
#define E_PRTY      031     /* memory parity */
#define E_PIO       041     /* 3B20 computer programmed
                             * I/O */
#define E_IOP       042     /* 3B20 computer I/O
                             * processor */
#define E_NI        0100    /* NI20 error */
```

Some records in the error file are of an administrative nature. These include the startup record that is entered into the file when logging is activated, the stop record that is written if the daemon is terminated “gracefully”, and the time-change record that is used to account for changes in the system's time-of-day. These records have the following formats:

```
struct estart {
        short           e_cpu;          /* CPU type */
        struct utsname  e_name;         /* system names */
#ifndef u3b
        short           e_mmr3;         /* contents mem mgmt reg 3 */
        long            e_syssize;      /* 11/70 system memory size */
        short           e_bconf;        /* block dev configuration */
#endif
#ifdef u3b
        int             e_mmcnt;        /* kbytes per array */
#endif
};

#define eend errhdr  /* record header */

struct etimchg {
        time_t          e_ntime;        /* new time */
};
```

Stray interrupts cause a record with the following format to be logged:

```
struct estray {
#ifdef u3b
        uint            e_saddr;        /* stray loc or device addr */
#else
        physadr         e_saddr;        /* stray loc or device addr */
        short           e_sbacty;       /* active block devices */
#endif
};
```

Memory subsystem error on 3B20 computer cause the following record to be generated:

```
struct eparity {
#ifdef u3b
        int             e_parreg[3];    /* 3B computer memory
                                         * registers */
#else
        short           e_parreg[4];    /* memory subsys registers */
#endif
};
```

Memory subsystem errors on VAX-11/780 processors cause the following record to be generated:

```
struct ememory {
        int             e_sbier;
        int             e_memcad;
};
```

Error records for block devices have the following format:

```
struct eblock {
#ifdef u3b
        ushort          e_num;          /* device number */
        struct iostat {
          long          io_ops;         /* number read/writes */
          long          io_misc;        /* number "other" operations */
          ushort        io_unlog;       /* number unlogged errors */
        }               e_stats;
        short           e_bflags;       /* read/write, error, etc */
        daddr_t         e_bnum;         /* logical block number */
        uint            e_bytes;        /* number bytes to transfer */
        union ptbl {
            int page[64];               /* page table entries */
            union ptbl *pnext;
        }               e_ptbl;
        struct ptbl     e_ptbl;         /* page table for transfer */
        uint            e_voff;         /* offset into page table */
        uint            e_stat1;        /* status word 1 */
        uint            e_stat2;        /* status word 2 */
#endif
```

```
#ifndef u3b
        dev_t           e_dev;          /* true major + minor dev # */
        physadr         e_regloc;       /* controller address */
        short           e_bacty;        /* other block I/O activity */
        struct iostat {
          long          io_ops;         /* number read/writes */
          long          io_misc;        /* number "other" operations */
          ushort        io_unlog;       /* number unlogged errors */
        }               e_stats;
        short           e_bflags;       /* read/write, error, etc */
        short           e_cyloff;       /* logical dev start cyl */
        daddr_t         e_bnum;         /* logical block number */
        ushort          e_bytes;        /* number bytes to transfer */
        paddr_t         e_memadd;       /* buffer memory address */
        ushort          e_rtry;         /* number retries */
        short           e_nreg;         /* number device registers */
#endif
#ifdef vax
        struct mba_regs {
          long mba_csr;
          long mba_cr;
          long mba_sr;
          long mba_var;
          long mba_vcr;
        } e_mba;
#endif
};
```

The following values are used in the *e_bflags* word:

```
#define E_WRITE   0             /* write operation */
#define E_READ    1             /* read operation */
#define E_NOIO    02            /* no I/O pending */
#define E_PHYS    04            /* physical I/O */
#define E_MAP     010           /* Unibus map in use */
#define E_ERROR   020           /* I/O failed */
```

The following error records are for the 3B20 computer only:

```
struct epio {                           /* programmed I/O error */
        char            e_chan;         /* which channel */
        char            e_dev;          /* which dev on channel */
        uint            e_chstat;       /* channel status */
        uint            e_cmd;          /* pio command */
}

struct eiop {                           /* I/O processor (iop) error */
        char            e_unit;         /* unit number */
        uint            e_word0;        /* iop report word */
        uint            e_word1;        /* iop report word */
}
```

The "true" major device numbers that identify the failing device are as follows:

Digital Equipment		*AT&T*	
#define RK0	0	#define DFC0	0
#define RP0	1	#define IOP0	1
#define RF0	2	#define MT0	2
#define TM0	3		
#define TC0	4		
#define HP0	5		
#define HT0	6		
#define HS0	7		
#define RL0	8		
#define HP1	9		
#define HP2	10		
#define HP3	11		

SEE ALSO

errdemon(1M) in the *UNIX Programmer's Manual—Volume 3: System Administration Facilities*.

NAME

filehdr — file header for common object files

SYNOPSIS

#include <filehdr.h>

DESCRIPTION

Every common object file begins with a 20-byte header. The following C **struct** declaration is used:

```
struct  filehdr
{
        unsigned short  f_magic ;   /* magic number */
        unsigned short  f_nscns ;   /* number of sections */
        long            f_timdat ;  /* time & date stamp */
        long            f_symptr ;  /* file ptr to symtab */
        long            f_nsyms ;   /* # symtab entries */
        unsigned short  f_opthdr ;  /* sizeof(opt hdr) */
        unsigned short  f_flags ;   /* flags */
} ;
```

F_symptr is the byte offset into the file at which the symbol table can be found. Its value can be used as the offset in *fseek*(3S) to position an I/O stream to the symbol table. The UNIX system optional header is 36 bytes on the 3B20 computer, 28 bytes otherwise. The valid magic numbers are given below:

```
#define N3BMAGIC     0550   /* 3B20 computer */
#define NTVMAGIC     0551   /* 3B20 computer */

#define VAXWRMAGIC 0570     /* writable text segments */
#define VAXROMAGIC  0575    /* readonly sharable segments */
```

The value in *f_timdat* is obtained from the *time*(2) system call. Flag bits currently defined are:

```
#define F_RELFLG   00001   /* relocation entries stripped */
#define F_EXEC     00002   /* file is executable */
#define F_LNNO     00004   /* line numbers stripped */
#define F_LSYMS    00010   /* local symbols stripped */
#define F_MINMAL   00020   /* minimal object file */
#define F_UPDATE   00040   /* update file, ogen produced */
#define F_SWABD    00100   /* file is "pre-swabbed" */
#define F_AR16WR   00200   /* 16 bit DEC host */
```

```
#define F_AR32WR  00400   /* 32 bit DEC host */
#define F_AR32W   01000   /* non-DEC host */
#define F_PATCH   02000   /* "patch" list in opt hdr */
```

SEE ALSO
time(2), fseek(3S), a.out(4).

NAME

file system − format of system volume

SYNOPSIS

#include <sys/filsys.h>
#include <sys/types.h>
#include <sys/param.h>

DESCRIPTION

Every file system storage volume has a common format for certain vital information. Every such volume is divided into a certain number of 512-byte long sectors. Sector 0 is unused and is available to contain a bootstrap program or other information.

Sector 1 is the *super-block*. The format of a super-block is:

```
/*
 * Structure of the super-block
 */
struct  filsys
{
        ushort   s_isize;              /* size in blocks of i-list */
        daddr_t  s_fsize;              /* size in blocks of entire volume */
        short    s_nfree;              /* number of addresses in s_free */
        daddr_t  s_free[NICFREE];      /* free block list */
        short    s_ninode;             /* number of i-nodes in s_inode */
        ino_t    s_inode[NICINOD];     /* free i-node list */
        char     s_flock;              /* lock during free list manipulation */
        char     s_ilock;              /* lock during i-list manipulation */
        char     s_fmod;               /* super block modified flag */
        char     s_ronly;              /* mounted read-only flag */
        time_t   s_time;               /* last super block update */
        short    s_dinfo[4];           /* device information */
        daddr_t  s_tfree;              /* total free blocks*/
        ino_t    s_tinode;             /* total free i-nodes */
        char     s_fname[6];           /* file system name */
        char     s_fpack[6];           /* file system pack name */
        long     s_fill[13];           /* ADJUST to make sizeof filsys be 512 */
        long     s_magic;              /* magic # to denote new file system */
        long     s_type;               /* type of new file system */
};
```

```
#define FsMAGIC  0xfd187e20     /* s_magic number */

#define Fs1b     1              /* 512 byte block */
#define Fs2b     2              /* 1024 byte block */
```

S_type indicates the file system type. Currently, two types of file systems are supported: the original 512-byte oriented and the new improved 1024-byte oriented. *S_magic* is used to distinguish the original 512-byte oriented file systems from the newer file systems. If this field is not equal to the magic number, *FsMAGIC*, the type is assumed to be *Fs1b*, otherwise the *s_type* field is used. In the following description, a block is then determined by the type. For the original 512-byte oriented file system, a block is 512 bytes. For the 1024-byte oriented file system, a block is 1024 bytes or two sectors. The operating system takes care of all conversions from logical block numbers to physical sector numbers.

S_isize is the address of the first data block after the i-list; the i-list starts just after the super-block, namely in block 2; thus the i-list is *s_isize*−2 blocks long. *S_fsize* is the first block not potentially available for allocation to a file. These numbers are used by the system to check for bad block numbers; if an "impossible" block number is allocated from the free list or is freed, a diagnostic is written on the on-line console. Moreover, the free array is cleared, so as to prevent further allocation from a presumably corrupted free list.

The free list for each volume is maintained as follows. The *s_free* array contains, in *s_free*[1], ..., *s_free*[*s_nfree*−1], up to 49 numbers of free blocks. *S_free*[0] is the block number of the head of a chain of blocks constituting the free list. The first long in each free-chain block is the number (up to 50) of free-block numbers listed in the next 50 longs of this chain member. The first of these 50 blocks is the link to the next member of the chain. To allocate a block: decrement *s_nfree*, and the new block is *s_free*[*s_nfree*]. If the new block number is 0, there are no blocks left, so give an error. If *s_nfree* became 0, read in the block named by the new block number, replace *s_nfree* by its first word, and copy the block numbers in the next 50 longs into the *s_free* array. To free a block, check if *s_nfree* is 50; if so, copy *s_nfree* and the *s_free* array into it, write it out, and set *s_nfree* to 0. In any event set *s_free*[*s_nfree*] to the freed block's number and increment *s_nfree*.

S_tfree is the total free blocks available in the file system.

S_ninode is the number of free i-numbers in the *s_inode* array. To allocate an i-node: if *s_ninode* is greater than 0, decrement it and return *s_inode*[*s_ninode*]. If it was 0, read the i-list and place the numbers of all free i-nodes (up to 100) into the *s_inode* array, then try again. To free an i-node, provided *s_ninode* is less than 100, place its number into *s_inode*[*s_ninode*] and increment *s_ninode*. If *s_ninode* is already 100, do not bother to enter the freed i-node into any table. This list of i-nodes is only to speed up the allocation process; the information as to whether the i-node is really free or not is maintained in the i-node itself.

S_tinode is the total free i-nodes available in the file system.

S_flock and *s_ilock* are flags maintained in the core copy of the file system while it is mounted and their values on disk are immaterial. The value of *s_fmod* on disk is likewise immaterial; it is used as a flag to indicate that the super-block has changed and should be copied to the disk during the next periodic update of file system information.

S_ronly is a read-only flag to indicate write-protection.

S_time is the last time the super-block of the file system was changed, and is the number of seconds that have elapsed since 00:00 Jan. 1, 1970 (GMT). During a reboot, the *s_time* of the super-block for the root file system is used to set the system's idea of the time.

S_fname is the name of the file system and *s_fpack* is the name of the pack.

I-numbers begin at 1, and the storage for i-nodes begins in block 2. Also, i-nodes are 64 bytes long. I-node 1 is reserved for future use. I-node 2 is reserved for the root directory of the file system, but no other i-number has a built-in meaning. Each i-node represents one file. For the format of an i-node and its flags, see *inode*(4).

FILES

/usr/include/sys/filsys.h
/usr/include/sys/stat.h

SEE ALSO

inode(4).
fsck(1M), fsdb(1M), mkfs(1M) in the *UNIX Programmer's Manual—Volume 3: System Administration Facilities.*

NAME

fspec − format specification in text files

DESCRIPTION

It is sometimes convenient to maintain text files on the UNIX system with non-standard tabs, (i.e., tabs which are not set at every eighth column). Such files must generally be converted to a standard format, frequently by replacing all tabs with the appropriate number of spaces, before they can be processed by UNIX system commands. A format specification occurring in the first line of a text file specifies how tabs are to be expanded in the remainder of the file.

A format specification consists of a sequence of parameters separated by blanks and surrounded by the brackets **<:** and **:>**. Each parameter consists of a keyletter, possibly followed immediately by a value. The following parameters are recognized:

t*tabs* The **t** parameter specifies the tab settings for the file. The value of *tabs* must be one of the following:

1. a list of column numbers separated by commas, indicating tabs set at the specified columns;
2. a − followed immediately by an integer *n*, indicating tabs at intervals of *n* columns;
3. a − followed by the name of a "canned" tab specification.

Standard tabs are specified by **t−8**, or equivalently, **t1,9,17,25,**etc. The canned tabs which are recognized are defined by the *tabs*(1) command.

s*size* The **s** parameter specifies a maximum line size. The value of *size* must be an integer. Size checking is performed after tabs have been expanded, but before the margin is prepended.

m*margin* The **m** parameter specifies a number of spaces to be prepended to each line. The value of *margin* must be an integer.

d The **d** parameter takes no value. Its presence indicates that the line containing the format specification is to be deleted from the converted file.

e The **e** parameter takes no value. Its presence indicates that the current format is to prevail only until another format specification is encountered in the file.

Default values, which are assumed for parameters not supplied, are **t−8** and **m0**. If the **s** parameter is not specified, no size checking is performed. If the first line of a file does not contain a format specification, the above defaults are assumed for the entire file. The following is an example of a line containing a format specification:

* <:t5,10,15 s72:> *

If a format specification can be disguised as a comment, it is not necessary to code the **d** parameter.

Several UNIX system commands correctly interpret the format specification for a file. Among them is *gath* (see *send*(1C)) which may be used to convert files to a standard format acceptable to other UNIX system commands.

SEE ALSO

ed(1), newform(1), send(1C), tabs(1) in the *UNIX Programmer's Manual—Volume 1: Commands and Utilities.*

NAME

gettydefs − speed and terminal settings used by getty

DESCRIPTION

The **/etc/gettydefs** file contains information used by *getty*(1M) to set up the speed and terminal settings for a line. It supplies information on what the *login* prompt should look like. It also supplies the speed to try next if the user indicates the current speed is not correct by typing a <*break*> character.

Each entry in **/etc/gettydefs** has the following format:

> label# initial-flags # final-flags # login-prompt #next-label

Each entry is followed by a blank line. The various fields can contain quoted characters of the form **\b**, **\n**, **\c**, etc., as well as *****nnn*, where *nnn* is the octal value of the desired character. The various fields are:

label This is the string against which *getty* tries to match its second argument. It is often the speed, such as **1200**, at which the terminal is supposed to run, but it need not be (see below).

initial-flags These flags are the initial *ioctl*(2) settings to which the terminal is to be set if a terminal type is not specified to *getty*. The flags that *getty* understands are the same as the ones listed in **/usr/include/sys/termio.h** (see *termio*(7)). Normally only the speed flag is required in the *initial-flags*. *Getty* automatically sets the terminal to raw input mode and takes care of most of the other flags. The *initial-flag* settings remain in effect until *getty* executes *login*(1).

final-flags These flags take the same values as the *initial-flags* and are set just prior to *getty* executes *login*. The speed flag is again required. The composite flag **SANE** takes care of most of the other flags that need to be set so that the processor and terminal are communicating in a rational fashion. The other two commonly specified *final-flags* are **TAB3**, so that tabs are sent to the terminal as spaces, and **HUPCL**, so that the line is hung up on the final close.

login-prompt This entire field is printed as the *login-prompt*. Unlike the above fields where white space is ignored (a space, tab or new-line), they are included in the *login-prompt* field.

next-label If this entry does not specify the desired speed, indicated by the user typing a <*break*> character, then *getty* will search for the entry with *next-label* as its *label* field and set up the terminal for those settings. Usually, a series of speeds are linked together in this fashion, into a closed set; For instance, **2400** linked to **1200**, which in turn is linked to **300**, which finally is linked to **2400**.

If *getty* is called without a second argument, then the first entry of **/etc/gettydefs** is used, thus making the first entry of **/etc/gettydefs** the default entry. It is also used if *getty* can not find the specified *label*. If **/etc/gettydefs** itself is missing, there is one entry built into the command which will bring up a terminal at **300** baud.

It is strongly recommended that after making or modifying **/etc/gettydefs**, it be run through *getty* with the check option to be sure there are no errors.

FILES

/etc/gettydefs

SEE ALSO

ioctl(2).
getty(1M), termio(7) in the *UNIX Programmer's Manual—Volume 3: System Administration Facilities.*
login(1) in the *UNIX Programmer's Manual—Volume 1: Commands and Utilities.*

NAME

gps — graphical primitive string, format of graphical files

DESCRIPTION

GPS is a format used to store graphical data. Several routines have been developed to edit and display GPS files on various devices. Also, higher level graphics programs such as *plot* (in *stat*(1G)) and *vtoc* (in *toc*(1G)) produce GPS format output files.

A GPS is composed of five types of graphical data or primitives.

GPS PRIMITIVES

lines The *lines* primitive has a variable number of points from which zero or more connected line segments are produced. The first point given produces a *move* to that location. (A *move* is a relocation of the graphic cursor without drawing.) Successive points produce line segments from the previous point. Parameters are available to set *color*, *weight*, and *style* (see below).

arc The *arc* primitive has a variable number of points to which a curve is fit. The first point produces a *move* to that point. If only two points are included, a line connecting the points will result; if three points a circular arc through the points is drawn; and if more than three, lines connect the points. (In the future, a spline will be fit to the points if they number greater than three.) Parameters are available to set *color*, *weight*, and *style*.

text The *text* primitive draws characters. It requires a single point which locates the center of the first character to be drawn. Parameters are *color*, *font*, *textsize*, and *textangle*.

hardware The *hardware* primitive draws hardware characters or gives control commands to a hardware device. A single point locates the beginning location of the *hardware* string.

comment A *comment* is an integer string that is included in a GPS file but causes nothing to be displayed. All GPS files begin with a comment of zero length.

GPS PARAMETERS

color *Color* is an integer value set for *arc*, *lines*, and *text* primitives.

weight *Weight* is an integer value set for *arc* and *lines* primitives to indicate line thickness. The value **0** is narrow weight, **1** is bold, and **2** is medium weight.

style *Style* is an integer value set for *lines* and *arc* primitives to give one of the five different line styles that can be drawn on TEKTRONIX 4010 series storage tubes. They are:

- **0** solid
- **1** dotted
- **2** dot dashed
- **3** dashed
- **4** long dashed

font An integer value set for *text* primitives to designate the text font to be used in drawing a character string. (Currently *font* is expressed as a four-bit *weight* value followed by a four-bit *style* value.)

textsize *Textsize* is an integer value used in *text* primitives to express the size of the characters to be drawn. *Textsize* represents the height of characters in absolute *universe-units* and is stored at one-fifth this value in the size-orientation (*so*) word (see below).

textangle *Textangle* is a signed integer value used in *text* primitives to express rotation of the character string around the beginning point. *Textangle* is expressed in degrees from the positive x-axis and can be a positive or negative value. It is stored in the size-orientation (*so*) word as a value 256/360 of it's absolute value.

ORGANIZATION

GPS primitives are organized internally as follows:

lines	*cw points sw*
arc	*cw points sw*
text	*cw point sw so* [*string*]
hardware	*cw point* [*string*]
comment	*cw* [*string*]

cw *Cw* is the control word and begins all primitives. It consists of four bits that contain a primitive-type code and twelve bits that contain the word-count for that primitive.

point(s) *Point(s)* is one or more pairs of integer coordinates. *Text* and *hardware* primitives only require a single *point*. *Point(s)* are values within a Cartesian plane or *universe* having 64K (−32K to +32K) points on each axis.

sw *Sw* is the style-word and is used in *lines, arc,* and *text* primitives. For all three, eight bits contain *color* information. In *arc* and *lines* eight bits are divided as four bits *weight* and four bits *style*. In the *text* primitive eight bits of *sw* contain the *font*.

so *So* is the size-orientation word used in *text* primitives. Eight bits contain text size and eight bits contain text rotation.

string *String* is a null-terminated character string. If the string does not end on a word boundary, an additional null is added to the GPS file to insure word-boundary alignment.

SEE ALSO

graphics(1G), stat(1G), toc(1G) in the *UNIX Programmer's Manual—Volume 1: Commands and Utilities.*

NAME

group — group file

DESCRIPTION

Group contains for each group the following information:

group name
encrypted password
numerical group ID
comma-separated list of all users allowed in the group

This is an ASCII file. The fields are separated by colons; each group is separated from the next by a new-line. If the password field is null, no password is demanded.

This file resides in directory **/etc**. Because of the encrypted passwords, it can and does have general read permission and can be used, for example, to map numerical group ID's to names.

FILES

/etc/group

SEE ALSO

crypt(3C), passwd(4).
newgrp(1), passwd(1) in the *UNIX Programmer's Manual—Volume 1: Commands and Utilities.*

NAME

inittab − script for the init process

DESCRIPTION

The *inittab* file supplies the script to *init*'s role as a general process dispatcher. The process that constitutes the majority of *init*'s process dispatching activities is the line process **/etc/getty** that initiates individual terminal lines. Other processes typically dispatched by *init* are daemons and the shell.

The *inittab* file is composed of entries that are position dependent and have the following format:

id:rstate:action:process

Each entry is delimited by a newline, however, a backslash (\) preceding a newline indicates a continuation of the entry. Up to 512 characters per entry are permitted. Comments may be inserted in the *process* field using the *sh*(1) convention for comments. Comments for lines that spawn *getty*s are displayed by the *who*(1) command. It is expected that they will contain some information about the line such as the location. There are no limits (other than maximum entry size) imposed on the number of entries within the *inittab* file. The entry fields are:

id This is one or two characters used to uniquely identify an entry.

rstate This defines the *run-level* in which this entry is to be processed. *Run-levels* effectively correspond to a configuration of processes in the system. That is, each process spawned by *init* is assigned a *run-level* or *run-levels* in which it is allowed to exist. The *run-levels* are represented by a number ranging from **0** through **6**. As an example, if the system is in *run-level* **1**, only those entries having a **1** in the *rstate* field will be processed. When *init* is requested to change *run-levels,* all processes which do not have an entry in the *rstate* field for the target *run-level* will be sent the warning signal (**SIGTERM**) and allowed a 20-second grace period before being forcibly terminated by a kill signal (**SIGKILL**). The *rstate* field can define multiple *run-levels* for a process by selecting more than one *run-level* in any combination from **0−6**. If no *run-level* is specified, then the process is assumed to be valid at all *run-levels* **0−6**. There are three other values, **a, b** and **c**, which can appear in the *rstate* field, even though they are not true *run-levels*. Entries which have these characters in the *rstate* field are processed only when the *telinit* (see *init*(1M)) process requests them to be run (regardless of the current *run-level* of the system). They differ from *run-levels* in that *init* can never enter *run-level* **a**, **b** or **c**. Also, a request for the execution of any of these processes does not change the current *run-level*. Furthermore, a process started by an **a**, **b** or **c** command is not killed when *init* changes levels. They are only killed if their line in **/etc/inittab** is marked **off** in the *action* field, their line is deleted entirely from **/etc/inittab**, or *init* goes into the *SINGLE USER* state.

action Key words in this field tell *init* how to treat the process specified in the *process* field. The actions recognized by *init* are as follows:

respawn If the process does not exist then start the process, do not wait for its termination (continue scanning the *inittab* file), and when it dies restart the process. If the process currently exists then do nothing and continue scanning the *inittab* file.

wait Upon *init*'s entering the *run-level* that matches the entry's *rstate*, start the process and wait for its termination. All subsequent reads of the *inittab* file while *init* is in the same *run-level* will cause *init* to ignore this entry.

once Upon *init*'s entering a *run-level* that matches the entry's *rstate*, start the process, do not wait for its termination. When it dies, do not restart the process. If upon entering a new *run-level*, where the process is still running from a previous *run-level* change, the program will not be restarted.

boot The entry is to be processed only at *init*'s boot-time read of the *inittab* file. *Init* is to start the process, not wait for its termination; and when it dies, not restart the process. In order for this instruction to be meaningful, the *rstate* should be the default or it must match *init*'s *run-level* at boot time. This action is useful for an initialization function following a hardware reboot of the system.

bootwait The entry is to be processed only at *init*'s boot-time read of the *inittab* file. *Init* is to start the process, wait for its termination and, when it dies, not restart the process.

powerfail Execute the process associated with this entry only when *init* receives a power fail signal (**SIGPWR** see *signal*(2)).

powerwait Execute the process associated with this entry only when *init* receives a power fail signal (**SIGPWR**) and wait until it terminates before continuing any processing of *inittab*.

off If the process associated with this entry is currently running, send the warning signal (**SIGTERM**) and wait 20 seconds before forcibly terminating the process via the kill signal (**SIGKILL**). If the process is nonexistent, ignore the entry.

ondemand This instruction is really a synonym for the **respawn** action. It is functionally identical to **respawn** but is given a different keyword in order to divorce its association with *run-levels*. This is used only with the **a**, **b** or **c** values described in the *rstate* field.

initdefault An entry with this *action* is only scanned when *init* initially invoked. *Init* uses this entry, if it exists, to determine which *run-level* to enter initially. It does this by taking the highest *run-level* specified in the **rstate** field and using that as its initial state. If the *rstate* field is empty, this is interpreted as **0123456** and so *init* will enter *run-level* **6**. Also, the **initdefault** entry cannot specify that *init* start in the *SINGLE USER* state. Additionally, if *init* does not find an **initdefault** entry in **/etc/inittab**, then it will request an initial *run-level* from the user at reboot time.

sysinit Entries of this type are executed before *init* tries to access the console. It is expected that this entry will be only used to initialize devices on which *init* might try to ask the *run-level* question. These entries are executed and waited for before continuing.

process This is a *sh* command to be executed. The entire **process** field is prefixed with *exec* and passed to a forked *sh* as **sh −c 'exec** *command'*. For this reason, any legal *sh* syntax can appear in the *process* field. Comments can be inserted with the ; #*comment* syntax.

FILES

/etc/inittab

SEE ALSO

exec(2), open(2), signal(2).
getty(1M), init(1M) in the *UNIX Programmer's Manual—Volume 3: System Administration Facilities*.
sh(1), who(1) in the *UNIX Programmer's Manual—Volume 1: Commands and Utilities*.

NAME

inode – format of an i-node

SYNOPSIS

#include <sys/types.h>
#include <sys/ino.h>

DESCRIPTION

An i-node for a plain file or directory in a file system has the following structure defined by **<sys/ino.h>**.

```
/* Inode structure as it appears on a disk block. */
struct dinode
{
        ushort  di_mode;      /* mode and type of file */
        short   di_nlink;     /* number of links to file */
        ushort  di_uid;       /* owner's user id */
        ushort  di_gid;       /* owner's group id */
        off_t   di_size;      /* number of bytes in file */
        char    di_addr[40];  /* disk block addresses */
        time_t  di_atime;     /* time last accessed */
        time_t  di_mtime;     /* time last modified */
        time_t  di_ctime;     /* time of last file status change */
};
/*
 * the 40 address bytes:
 *      39 used; 13 addresses
 *      of 3 bytes each.
 */
```

For the meaning of the defined types *off_t* and *time_t* see *types*(5).

FILES

/usr/include/sys/ino.h

SEE ALSO

stat(2), fs(4), types(5).

NAME

issue − issue identification file

DESCRIPTION

The file **/etc/issue** contains the *issue* or project identification to be printed as a login prompt. This is an ASCII file which is read by program *getty* and then written to any terminal spawned or respawned from the *lines* file.

FILES

/etc/issue

SEE ALSO

login(1) in the *UNIX Programmer's Manual—Volume 1: Commands and Utilities*.

NAME

ldfcn − common object file access routines

SYNOPSIS

#include <stdio.h>
#include <filehdr.h>
#include <ldfcn.h>

DESCRIPTION

The common object file access routines are a collection of functions for reading an object file that is in the 3B20 computer (common) object file format. Although the calling program must know the detailed structure of the parts of the object file that it processes, the routines effectively insulate the calling program from knowledge of the overall structure of the object file.

The interface between the calling program and the object file access routines is based on the defined type **LDFILE**, defined as **struct ldfile**, declared in the header file **ldfcn.h**. The primary purpose of this structure is to provide uniform access to both simple object files and to object files that are members of an archive file.

The function *ldopen*(3X) allocates and initializes the **LDFILE** structure and returns a pointer to the structure to the calling program. The fields of the **LDFILE** structure may be accessed individually through macros defined in **ldfcn.h** and contain the following information:

LDFILE *ldptr;

TYPE(ldptr)	The file magic number used to distinguish between archive members and simple object files.
IOPTR(ldptr)	The file pointer returned by *fopen* and used by the standard input/output functions.
OFFSET(ldptr)	The file address of the beginning of the object file; the offset is non-zero if the object file is a member of an archive file.
HEADER(ldptr)	The file header structure of the object file.

The object file access functions themselves may be divided into four categories:

(1) functions that open or close an object file

ldopen(3X) and *ldopen*(3X)
: open a common object file

ldclose(3X) and *ldclose*(3X)
: close a common object file

(2) functions that read header or symbol table information

ldahread(3X)
: read the archive header of a member of an archive file

ldfhread(3X)
: read the file header of a common object file

ldshread(3X) and *ldshread*(3X)
: read a section header of a common object file

ldtbread(3X)
: read a symbol table entry of a common object file

ldgetname(3X)
: retrieve a symbol name from a symbol table entry or from the string table

(3) functions that position an object file at (seek to) the start of the section, relocation, or line number information for a particular section.

ldohseek(3X)
: seek to the optional file header of a common object file

ldsseek(3X) and *ldsseek*(3X)
: seek to a section of a common object file

ldrseek(3X) and *ldrseek*(3X)
: seek to the relocation information for a section of a common object file

ldlseek(3X) and *ldlseek*(3X)
: seek to the line number information for a section of a common object file

ldtbseek(3X)
: seek to the symbol table of a common object file

(4) the function *ldtbindex*(3X) which returns the index of a particular common object file symbol table entry.

These functions are described in detail on their respective manual pages.

All the functions except *ldopen*(3X), *ldgetname*(3X), *ldopen*(3X), and *ldtbindex*(3X) return either **SUCCESS** or **FAILURE**, both constants defined in **ldfcn.h**. *Ldopen*(3X) and *ldopen*(3X) both return pointers to an **LDFILE** structure.

Additional access to an object file is provided through a set of macros defined in **ldfcn.h**. These macros parallel the standard input/output file reading and manipulating functions, translating a reference of the **LDFILE** structure into a reference to its file descriptor field.

The following macros are provided:

```
GETC(ldptr)
FGETC(ldptr)
GETW(ldptr)
UNGETC(c, ldptr)
FGETS(s, n, ldptr)
FREAD((char *) ptr, sizeof (*ptr), nitems, ldptr)
FSEEK(ldptr, offset, ptrname)
FTELL(ldptr)
REWIND(ldptr)
FEOF(ldptr)
FERROR(ldptr)
FILENO(ldptr)
SETBUF(ldptr, buf)
STROFFSET(ldptr)
```

The STROFFSET macro calculates the address of the string table in a UNIX system release 5.0 object file. See the manual entries for the corresponding standard input/output library functions for details on the use of the rest of the macros.

The program must be loaded with the object file access routine library **libld.a**.

WARNING

The macro **FSEEK** defined in the header file **ldfcn.h** translates into a call to the standard input/output function *fseek*(3S). **FSEEK** should not be used to seek from the end of an archive file since the end of an archive file may not be the same as the end of one of its object file members!

SEE ALSO

fseek(3S), ldahread(3X), ldclose(3X), ldgetname(3X), ldfhread(3X), ldlread(3X), ldlseek(3X), ldohseek(3X), ldopen(3X), ldrseek(3X), ldlseek(3X), ldshread(3X), ldtbindex(3X), ldtbread(3X), ldtbseek(3X), intro(5).

NAME

linenum — line number entries in a common object file

SYNOPSIS

#include <linenum.h>

DESCRIPTION

Compilers based on *pcc* generate an entry in the object file for each C source line on which a breakpoint is possible (when invoked with the **−g** option; see *cc*(1)). Users can then reference line numbers when using the appropriate software test system (see *sdb*(1)). The structure of these line number entries appears below.

```
struct lineno
{
        union
        {
                long     l_symndx ;
                long     l_paddr ;
        }                l_addr ;
        unsigned short   l_lnno ;
} ;
```

Numbering starts with one for each function. The initial line number entry for a function has *l_lnno* equal to zero, and the symbol table index of the function's entry is in *l_symndx*. Otherwise, *l_lnno* is non-zero, and *l_paddr* is the physical address of the code for the referenced line. Thus the overall structure is the following:

l_addr	*l_lnno*
function symtab index	0
physical address	line
physical address	line
...	
function symtab index	0
physical address	line
physical address	line
...	

SEE ALSO

a.out(4).

cc(1), sdb(1) in the *UNIX Programmer's Manual—Volume 1: Commands and Utilities.*

NAME

master − master device information table

DESCRIPTION

This file is used by the *config*(1M) program to obtain device information that enables it to generate the configuration files. The file consists of 3 parts, each separated by a line with a dollar sign ($) in column 1. Part 1 contains device information; part 2 contains names of devices that have aliases; part 3 contains tunable parameter information. Any line with an asterisk (*) in column 1 is treated as a comment.

Part 1 contains lines consisting of at least 10 fields and at most 13 fields, with the fields delimited by tabs and/or blanks:

Field 1: device name (8 chars. maximum).

Field 2: interrupt vector size (decimal, in bytes).

Field 3: device mask (octal)—each "on" bit indicates that the handler exists:

- 000100 initialization handler
- 000040 power-failure handler
- 000020 open handler
- 000010 close handler
- 000004 read handler
- 000002 write handler
- 000001 ioctl handler.

Field 4: device type indicator (octal):

- 000400 VAX-11/780 massbus adapter
- 000200 allow only one of these devices
- 000100 suppress count field in the **conf.c** file
- 000040 suppress interrupt vector
- 000020 required device
- 000010 block device
- 000004 character device
- 000002 floating vector
- 000001 fixed vector.

Field 5: handler prefix (4 chars. maximum).

Field 6: device address size (decimal).

Field 7: major device number for block-type device.

Field 8: major device number for character-type device.

Field 9:	maximum number of devices per controller (decimal).
Field 10:	maximum bus request level (4 through 7).
Fields 11-13:	optional configuration table structure declarations (8 chars. maximum).

Part 2 contains lines with 2 fields each:

Field 1:	alias name of device (8 chars. maximum).
Field 2:	reference name of device (8 chars. maximum; specified in part 1).

Part 3 contains lines with 2 or 3 fields each:

Field 1:	parameter name (as it appears in description file; 20 chars. maximum)
Field 2:	parameter name (as it appears in the **conf.c** file; 20 chars. maximum)
Field 3:	default parameter value (20 chars. maximum; parameter specification is required if this field is omitted)

Devices that are not interrupt-driven have an interrupt vector size of zero. The 040 bit in Field 4 causes *config*(1M) to record the interrupt vector although the **low.s** (**univec.c** on the VAX-11/780) file will show no interrupt vector assignment at those locations (interrupts here will be treated as strays).

SEE ALSO

config(1M) in the *UNIX Programmer's Manual—Volume 3: System Administration Facilities.*

NAME

mnttab – mounted file system table

SYNOPSIS

#include <mnttab.h>

DESCRIPTION

Mnttab resides in directory **/etc** and contains a table of devices, mounted by the *mount*(1M) command, in the following structure as defined by **<mnttab.h>**:

```
struct   mnttab {
         char       mt_dev[32];
         char       mt_filsys[32];
         short      mt_ro_flg;
         time_t     mt_time;
};
```

Each entry is 70 bytes in length; the first 32 bytes are the null-padded name of the place where the *special file* is mounted; the next 32 bytes represent the null-padded root name of the mounted special file; the remaining 6 bytes contain the mounted *special file*'s read/write permissions and the date on which it was mounted.

The maximum number of entries in *mnttab* is based on the system parameter **NMOUNT** located in **/usr/src/uts/cf/conf.c**, which defines the number of allowable mounted special files.

SEE ALSO

mount(1M), setmnt(1M) in the *UNIX Programmer's Manual—Volume 3: System Administration Facilities.*

NAME

passwd − password file

DESCRIPTION

Passwd contains for each user the following information:

login name
encrypted password
numerical user ID
numerical group ID
GCOS job number, box number, optional GCOS user ID
initial working directory
program to use as shell

This is an ASCII file. Each field within each user's entry is separated from the next by a colon. The GCOS field is used only when communicating with that system, and in other installations can contain any desired information. Each user is separated from the next by a new-line. If the password field is null, no password is demanded; if the shell field is null, the shell itself is used.

This file resides in directory **/etc**. Because of the encrypted passwords, it can and does have general read permission and can be used, for example, to map numerical user IDs to names.

The encrypted password consists of 13 characters chosen from a 64-character alphabet (., /, **0−9**, **A−Z**, **a−z**), except when the password is null, in which case the encrypted password is also null. Password aging is effected for a particular user if his encrypted password in the password file is followed by a comma and a non-null string of characters from the above alphabet. (Such a string must be introduced in the first instance by the super-user.)

The first character of the age, *M* say, denotes the maximum number of weeks for which a password is valid. A user who attempts to login after his password has expired will be forced to supply a new one. The next character, *m* say, denotes the minimum period in weeks which must expire before the password may be changed. The remaining characters define the week (counted from the beginning of 1970) when the password was last changed. (A null string is equivalent to zero.) *M* and *m* have numerical values in the range 0−63 that correspond to the 64-character alphabet shown above (i.e., **/** = 1 week; **z** = 63 weeks). If *m* = *M* = 0 (derived from the string **.** or **..**) the user will be forced to change his password the next time he logs in (and the "age" will disappear from his entry in the password file). If *m* >

M (signified, e.g., by the string ./) only the super-user will be able to change the password.

FILES

/etc/passwd

SEE ALSO

a64l(3C), crypt(3C), getpwent(3C), group(4).
login(1), passwd(1) in the *UNIX Programmer's Manual—Volume 1: Commands and Utilities.*

NAME

plot − graphics interface

DESCRIPTION

Files of this format are produced by routines described in *plot*(3X) and are interpreted for various devices by commands described in *tplot*(1G). A graphics file is a stream of plotting instructions. Each instruction consists of an ASCII letter usually followed by bytes of binary information. The instructions are executed in order. A point is designated by four bytes representing the **x** and **y** values; each value is a signed integer. The last designated point in an **l, m, n,** or **p** instruction becomes the "current point" for the next instruction.

Each of the following descriptions begins with the name of the corresponding routine in *plot*(3X).

m move: The next four bytes give a new current point.

n cont: Draw a line from the current point to the point given by the next four bytes. See *tplot*(1G).

p point: Plot the point given by the next four bytes.

l line: Draw a line from the point given by the next four bytes to the point given by the following four bytes.

t label: Place the following ASCII string so that its first character falls on the current point. The string is terminated by a new-line.

e erase: Start another frame of output.

f linemod: Take the following string, up to a new-line, as the style for drawing further lines. The styles are "dotted", "solid", "longdashed", "shortdashed", and "dotdashed". Effective only for the **−T4014** and **−Tver** options of *tplot*(1G) (TEKTRONIX 4014 terminal and Versatec plotter).

s space: The next four bytes give the lower left corner of the plotting area; the following four give the upper right corner. The plot will be magnified or reduced to fit the device as closely as possible.

Space settings that exactly fill the plotting area with unity scaling appear below for devices supported by the filters of *tplot*(1G). The upper limit is just outside the plotting area. In every case the plotting area is taken to be square; points outside may be displayable on devices whose face is not square.

DASI 300	space(0, 0, 4096, 4096);
DASI 300s	space(0, 0, 4096, 4096);
DASI 450	space(0, 0, 4096, 4096);
TEKTRONIX 4014	space(0, 0, 3120, 3120);
Versatec plotter	space(0, 0, 2048, 2048);

SEE ALSO

plot(3X), gps(4), term(5).
graph(1G), tplot(1G) in the *UNIX Programmer's Manual—Volume 1: Commands and Utilities.*

WARNING

The plotting library *plot*(3X) and the curses library *curses*(3X) both use the names erase() and move(). The curses versions are macros. If you need both libraries, put the *plot*(3X) code in a different source file than the *curses*(3X) code, and/or #undef move() and erase() in the *plot*(3X) code.

NAME

pnch — file format for card images

DESCRIPTION

The PNCH format is a convenient representation for files consisting of card images in an arbitrary code.

A PNCH file is a simple concatenation of card records. A card record consists of a single control byte followed by a variable number of data bytes. The control byte specifies the number (which must lie in the range 0-80) of data bytes that follow. The data bytes are 8-bit codes that constitute the card image. If there are fewer than 80 data bytes, it is understood that the remainder of the card image consists of trailing blanks.

SEE ALSO

send(1C) in the *UNIX Programmer's Manual—Volume 1: Commands and Utilities.*

NAME

profile — setting up an environment at login time

DESCRIPTION

If your login directory contains a file named **.profile**, that file will be executed (via **exec .profile**) before your session begins; **.profiles** are handy for setting exported environment variables and terminal modes. If the file **/etc/profile** exists, it will be executed for every user before the **.profile**. The following example is typical (except for the comments):

```
# Make some environment variables global
export MAIL PATH TERM
# Set file creation mask
umask 22
# Tell me when new mail comes in
MAIL=/usr/mail/myname
# Add my /bin directory to the shell search sequence
PATH=$PATH:$HOME/bin
# Set terminal type
echo "terminal: \c"
read TERM
case $TERM in
        300)        stty cr2 nl0 tabs; tabs;;
        300s)       stty cr2 nl0 tabs; tabs;;
        450)        stty cr2 nl0 tabs; tabs;;
        hp)         stty cr0 nl0 tabs; tabs;;
        745 | 735)  stty cr1 nl1 -tabs; TERM=745;;
        43)         stty cr1 nl0 -tabs;;
        4014 | tek) stty cr0 nl0 -tabs ff1; TERM=4014; echo "\33;";;
        *)          echo "$TERM unknown";;
esac
```

FILES

$HOME/.profile
/etc/profile

SEE ALSO

environ(5), term(5).
env(1), login(1), mail(1), sh(1), stty(1), su(1) in the *UNIX Programmer's Manual—Volume 1: Commands and Utilities*.

NAME

reloc − relocation information for a common object file

SYNOPSIS

#include <reloc.h>

DESCRIPTION

Object files have one relocation entry for each relocatable reference in the text or data. If relocation information is present, it will be in the following format.

```
struct   reloc
{
         long        r_vaddr ;    /* (virtual) address of reference */
         long        r_symndx ;   /* index into symbol table */
         short       r_type ;     /* relocation type */
} ;


/*
 * All generics
 *       reloc. already performed to symbol in the same section
 */
#define  R_ABS                    0

/*
 * 3B computer generic
 *       24-bit direct reference
 *       24-bit "relative" reference
 *       16-bit optimized "indirect" TV reference
 *       24-bit "indirect" TV reference
 *       32-bit "indirect" TV reference
 */
#define  R_DIR24    04
#define  R_REL24    05
#define  R_OPT16    014
#define  R_IND24    015
#define  R_IND32    016

/*
 * On most processors
 *
 */
#define R_RELBYTE                 017
```

```
#define R_RELWORD        020
#define R_RELLONG        021
#define R_PCRBYTE        022
#define R_PCRWORD        023
#define R_PCRLONG        024
```

As the link editor reads each input section and performs relocation, the relocation entries are read. They direct how references found within the input section are treated.

R_ABS The reference is absolute, and no relocation is necessary. The entry will be ignored.

R_DIR24 A direct, 24-bit reference to a symbol's virtual address.

R_REL24 A "PC-relative", 24-bit reference to a symbol's virtual address. Relative references occur in instructions such as jumps and calls. The actual address used is obtained by adding a constant to the value of the program counter at the time the instruction is executed.

R_OPT16 An optimized, indirect, 16-bit reference through a transfer vector. The instruction contains the offset into the transfer vector table to the transfer vector where the actual address of the referenced word is stored.

R_IND24 An indirect, 24-bit reference through a transfer vector. The instruction contains the virtual address of the transfer vector, where the actual address of the referenced word is stored.

R_IND32 An indirect, 32-bit reference through a transfer vector. The instruction contains the virtual address of the transfer vector, where the actual address of the referenced word is stored.

R_RELBYTE A direct 8-bit reference to a symbol's virtual address.

R_RELWORD
A direct 16-bit reference to a symbol's virtual address.

R_RELLONG
A direct 32-bit reference to a symbol's virtual address.

R_PCRBYTE A "PC-relative", 8-bit reference to a symbol's virtual address.

R_PCRWORD
A "PC-relative", 16-bit reference to a symbol's virtual address.

R_PCRLONG
A "PC-relative", 32-bit reference to a symbol's virtual address.

On most processors relocation of a symbol index of -1 indicates that the relative difference between the current segment's start address and the program's load address is added to the relocatable address.

Other relocation types will be defined as they are needed.

Relocation entries are generated automatically by the assembler and automatically utilized by the link editor. A link editor option exists for removing the relocation entries from an object file.

SEE ALSO

a.out(4), syms(4).
ld(1), strip(1) in the *UNIX Programmer's Manual—Volume 1: Commands and Utilities.*

NAME

sccsfile − format of SCCS file

DESCRIPTION

An file is an ASCII file. It consists of six logical parts: the *checksum*, the *delta table* (contains information about each delta), *user names* (contains login names and/or numerical group IDs of users who may add deltas), *flags* (contains definitions of internal keywords), *comments* (contains arbitrary descriptive information about the file), and the *body* (contains the actual text lines intermixed with control lines).

Throughout an file there are lines which begin with the **ASCII SOH** (start of heading) character (octal 001). This character is hereafter referred to as *the control character* and will be represented graphically as @. Any line described below which is not depicted as beginning with the control character is prevented from beginning with the control character.

Entries of the form

represent a five-digit string (a number between 00000 and 99999).

Each logical part of an file is described in detail below.

Checksum

The checksum is the first line of an file. The form of the line is:

@h

The value of the checksum is the sum of all characters, except those of the first line. The **@h** provides a *magic number* of (octal) 064001.

Delta table

The delta table consists of a variable number of entries of the form:

@s //
@d <type> <**SCCS ID**> yr/mo/da hr:mi:se <pgmr>
@i ...
@x ...
@g ...
@m < number>
.
.

.
@c <comments> ...
.
.
.
@e

The first line (@s) contains the number of lines inserted/deleted/unchanged, respectively. The second line (@d) contains the type of the delta (currently, normal: **D**, and removed: **R**), the ID of the delta, the date and time of creation of the delta, the login name corresponding to the real user ID at the time the delta was created, and the serial numbers of the delta and its predecessor, respectively.

The **@i**, **@x**, and **@g** lines contain the serial numbers of deltas included, excluded, and ignored, respectively. These lines are optional.

The **@m** lines (optional) each contain one number associated with the delta; the **@c** lines contain comments associated with the delta.

The **@e** line ends the delta table entry.

User names

The list of login names and/or numerical group IDs of users who may add deltas to the file, separated by newlines. The lines containing these login names and/or numerical group IDs are surrounded by the bracketing lines **@u** and **@U**. An empty list allows anyone to make a delta. Any line starting with a **!** prohibits the succeeding group or user from making deltas.

Flags

Keywords used internally (see *admin*(1) for more information on their use). Each flag line takes the form:

@f <flag> <optional text>

The following flags are defined:

@f t <type of program>

@f v	<program name>
@f i	<keyword string>
@f b	
@f m	<module name>
@f f	<floor>
@f c	<ceiling>
@f d	<default-sid>
@f n	
@f j	
@f l	<lock-releases>
@f q	<user defined>
@f z	<reserved for use in interfaces>

The **t** flag defines the replacement for the %**Y**% identification keyword. The **v** flag controls prompting for numbers in addition to comments; if the optional text is present it defines an number validity checking program. The **i** flag controls the warning/error aspect of the "No id keywords" message. When the **i** flag is not present, this message is only a warning; when the **i** flag is present, this message will cause a "fatal" error (the file will not be gotten, or the delta will not be made). When the **b** flag is present the **−b** keyletter may be used on the *get* command to cause a branch in the delta tree. The **m** flag defines the first choice for the replacement text of the %**M**% identification keyword. The **f** flag defines the "floor" release; the release below which no deltas may be added. The **c** flag defines the "ceiling" release; the release above which no deltas may be added. The **d** flag defines the default to be used when none is specified on a *get* command. The **n** flag causes *delta* to insert a "null" delta (a delta that applies *no* changes) in those releases that are skipped when a delta is made in a *new* release (e.g., when delta 5.1 is made after delta 2.7, releases 3 and 4 are skipped). The absence of the **n** flag causes skipped releases to be completely empty. The **j** flag causes *get* to allow concurrent edits of the same base . The **l** flag defines a *list* of releases that are *locked* against editing (*get*(1) with the **−e** keyletter). The **q** flag defines the replacement for the %**Q**% identification keyword. The **z** flag is used in certain specialized interface programs.

Comments

Arbitrary text is surrounded by the bracketing lines **@t** and **@T**. The comments section typically will contain a description of the file's purpose.

Body

The body consists of text lines and control lines. Text lines do not begin with the control character, control lines do. There are three kinds of control lines: *insert*, *delete*, and *end*, represented by:

@I
@D
@E

respectively. The digit string is the serial number corresponding to the delta for the control line.

SEE ALSO

admin(1), delta(1), get(1), prs(1) in the *UNIX Programmer's Manual—Volume 1: Commands and Utilities.*

NAME

scnhdr − section header for a common object file

SYNOPSIS

#include <scnhdr.h>

DESCRIPTION

Every common object file has a table of section headers to specify the layout of the data within the file. Each section within an object file has its own header. The C structure appears below.

```
struct scnhdr
{
        char            s_name[SYMNMLEN]; /* section name */
        long            s_paddr;    /* physical address */
        long            s_vaddr;    /* virtual address */
        long            s_size;     /* section size */
        long            s_scnptr;   /* file ptr to raw data */
        long            s_relptr;   /* file ptr to relocation */
        long            s_lnnoptr;  /* file ptr to line numbers */
        unsigned short  s_nreloc;   /* # reloc entries */
        unsigned short  s_nlnno;    /* # line number entries */
        long            s_flags;    /* flags */
};
```

File pointers are byte offsets into the file; they can be used as the offset in a call to *fseek*(3S). If a section is initialized, the file contains the actual bytes. An uninitialized section is somewhat different. It has a size, symbols defined in it, and symbols that refer to it. But it can have no relocation entries, line numbers, or data. Consequently, an uninitialized section has no raw data in the object file, and the values for *s_scnptr*, *s_relptr*, *s_lnnoptr*, *s_nreloc*, and *s_nlnno* are zero.

SEE ALSO

fseek(3S), a.out(4).
ld(1) in the *UNIX Programmer's Manual—Volume 1: Commands and Utilities*.

NAME

syms − common object file symbol table format

SYNOPSIS

#include <syms.h>

DESCRIPTION

Common object files contain information to support *symbolic* software testing (see *sdb* (1)). Line number entries, *linenum* (4), and extensive symbolic information permit testing at the C *source* level. Every object file's symbol table is organized as shown below.

```
File name 1.
        Function 1.
                Local symbols for function 1.
        Function 2.
                Local symbols for function 2.
        ...
        Static externs for file 1.

File name 2.
        Function 1.
                Local symbols for function 1.
        Function 2.
                Local symbols for function 2.
        ...
        Static externs for file 2.
...

Defined global symbols.
Undefined global symbols.
```

The entry for a symbol is a fixed-length structure. The members of the structure hold the name (null padded), its value, and other information. The C structure is given below.

```
#define  SYMNMLEN   8
#define  FILNMLEN   14

struct  syment
{
   union                                  /* all ways to get symbol name */
   {
      char           _n_name[SYMNMLEN]; /* symbol name */
      struct
      {
         long        _n_zeroes;        /* == 0L when in string table */
         long        _n_offset;        /* location of name in table */
      } _n_n;
      char           *_n_nptr[2];      /* allows overlaying */
   } _n;
   long              n_value;          /* value of symbol */
   short             n_scnum;          /* section number */
   unsigned short    n_type;           /* type and derived type */
   char              n_sclass;         /* storage class */
   char              n_numaux;         /* number of aux entries */
};

#define  n_name      _n._n_name
#define  n_zeroes    _n._n_n._n_zeroes
#define  n_offset    _n._n_n._n_offset
#define  n_nptr      _n._n_nptr[1]
```

Meaningful values and explanations for them are given in both **syms.h** and *Common Object File Format*. Anyone who needs to interpret the entries should seek more information in these sources. Some symbols require more information than a single entry; they are followed by *auxiliary entries* that are the same size as a symbol entry. The format follows.

```
union auxent
{
        struct
        {
                long            x_tagndx;
                union
                {
                        struct
                        {
                                unsigned short  x_lnno;
                                unsigned short  x_size;
                        } x_lnsz;
                        long    x_fsize;
                } x_misc;
                union
                {
                        struct
                        {
                                long    x_lnnoptr;
                                long    x_endndx;
                        }       x_fcn;
                        struct
                        {
                                unsigned short  x_dimen[DIMNUM];
                        }       x_ary;
                }               x_fcnary;
                unsigned short  x_tvndx;
        }       x_sym;
        struct
        {
                char    x_fname[FILNMLEN];
        }       x_file;
        struct
        {
                long    x_scnlen;
                unsigned short  x_nreloc;
                unsigned short  x_nlinno;
        }       x_scn;

        struct
        {
                long            x_tvfill;
```

```
                unsigned short  x_tvlen;
                unsigned short  x_tvran[2];
        }       x_tv;
};
```

Indexes of symbol table entries begin at *zero*.

SEE ALSO

a.out(4), linenum(4).
sdb(1) in the *UNIX Programmer's Manual—Volume 1: Commands and Utilities*.

CAVEATS

On machines in which longs are equivalent to ints (3B20 computer), they are converted to ints in the compiler to minimize the complexity of the compiler code generator. Thus the information about which symbols are declared as longs and which, as ints, does not show up in the symbol table.

NAME

term — format of compiled term file.

SYNOPSIS

term

DESCRIPTION

Compiled terminfo descriptions are placed under the directory **/usr/lib/terminfo**. In order to avoid a linear search of a huge UNIX system directory, a two-level scheme is used: **/usr/lib/terminfo/c/name** where *name* is the name of the terminal, and *c* is the first character of *name*. Thus, *act4* can be found in the file **/usr/lib/terminfo/a/act4**. Synonyms for the same terminal are implemented by multiple links to the same compiled file.

The format has been chosen so that it will be the same on all hardware. An 8 or more bit byte is assumed, but no assumptions about byte ordering or sign extension are made.

The compiled file is created with the *compile* program, and read by the routine *setupterm*. Both of these pieces of software are part of *curses*(3X). The file is divided into six parts: the header, terminal names, boolean flags, numbers, strings, and string table.

The header section begins the file. This section contains six short integers in the format described below. These integers are (1) the magic number (octal 0432); (2) the size, in bytes, of the names section; (3) the number of bytes in the boolean section; (4) the number of short integers in the numbers section; (5) the number of offsets (short integers) in the strings section; (6) the size, in bytes, of the string table.

Short integers are stored in two 8-bit bytes. The first byte contains the least significant 8 bits of the value, and the second byte contains the most significant 8 bits. (Thus, the value represented is 256*second+first.) The value −1 is represented by 0377, 0377, other negative value are illegal. The −1 generally means that a capability is missing from this terminal. Machines where this does not correspond to the hardware read the integers as two bytes and compute the result.

The terminal names section comes next. It contains the first line of the terminfo description, listing the various names for the terminal, separated by the '|' character. The section is terminated with an ASCII NUL character.

The boolean flags have one byte for each flag. This byte is either 0 or 1 as the flag is present or absent. The capabilities are in the same order as the file <term.h>.

Between the boolean section and the number section, a null byte will be inserted, if necessary, to ensure that the number section begins on an even byte. All short integers are aligned on a short word boundary.

The numbers section is similar to the flags section. Each capability takes up two bytes, and is stored as a short integer. If the value represented is −1, the capability is taken to be missing.

The strings section is also similar. Each capability is stored as a short integer, in the format above. A value of −1 means the capability is missing. Otherwise, the value is taken as an offset from the beginning of the string table. Special characters in ^X or \c notation are stored in their interpreted form, not the printing representation. Padding information $<nn> and parameter information %x are stored intact in uninterpreted form.

The final section is the string table. It contains all the values of string capabilities referenced in the string section. Each string is null terminated.

Note that it is possible for *setupterm* to expect a different set of capabilities than are actually present in the file. Either the database may have been updated since *setupterm* has been recompiled (resulting in extra unrecognized entries in the file) or the program may have been recompiled more recently than the database was updated (resulting in missing entries). The routine *setupterm* must be prepared for both possibilities — this is why the numbers and sizes are included. Also, new capabilities must always be added at the end of the lists of boolean, number, and string capabilities.

As an example, an octal dump of the description for the Microterm ACT 4 is included:

```
microterm|act4|microterm act iv,
    cr=^M, cud1=^J, ind=^J, bel=^G, am, cub1=^H,
    ed=^_, el=^^, clear=^L, cup=^T%p1%c%p2%c,
    cols#80, lines#24, cuf1=^X, cuu1=^Z, home=^],
```

```
000 032 001      \0 025 \0 \b \0 212 \0  " \0  m  i  c  r
020  o  t  e  r  m  |  a  c  t  4  |  m  i  c  r  o
040  t  e  r  m        a  c  t        i  v \0 \0 001 \0 \0
060 \0 \0 \0 \0 \0 \0 \0 \0 \0 \0 \0 \0 \0 \0 \0 \0
100 \0 \0  P \0 377 377 030 \0 377 377 377 377 377 377 377 377
120 377 377 377 377 \0 \0 002 \0 377 377 377 377 004 \0 006 \0
140 \b \0 377 377 377 377 \n \0 026 \0 030 \0 377 377 032 \0
160 377 377 377 377 034 \0 377 377 036 \0 377 377 377 377 377 377
200 377 377 377 377 377 377 377 377 377 377 377 377 377 377 377 377
*
520 377 377 377 377      \0 377 377 377 377 377 377 377 377 377 377
540 377 377 377 377 377 377 007 \0 \r \0 \f \0 036 \0 037 \0
560 024  %  p  1  %  c  %  p  2  %  c \0 \n \0 035 \0
600 \b \0 030 \0 032 \0 \n \0
```

Some limitations: total compiled entries cannot exceed 4096 bytes. The name field cannot exceed 128 bytes.

FILES

/usr/lib/terminfo/*/*   compiled terminal capability data base

SEE ALSO

curses(3X), terminfo(4).

NAME

terminfo — terminal capability data base

SYNOPSIS

/usr/lib/terminfo/*/*

DESCRIPTION

Terminfo is a data base describing terminals, used, *e.g.*,, by *vi*(1) and *curses*(3X). Terminals are described in *terminfo* by giving a set of capabilities which they have, and by describing how operations are performed. Padding requirements and initialization sequences are included in *terminfo.*

Entries in *terminfo* consist of a number of ',' separated fields. White space after each ',' is ignored. The first entry for each terminal gives the names which are known for the terminal, separated by '|' characters. The first name given is the most common abbreviation for the terminal, the last name given should be a long name fully identifying the terminal, and all others are understood as synonyms for the terminal name. All names but the last should be in lower case and contain no blanks; the last name may well contain upper case and blanks for readability.

Terminal names (except for the last, verbose entry) should be chosen using the following conventions. The particular piece of hardware making up the terminal should have a root name chosen, thus "hp2621". This name should not contain hyphens, except that synonyms may be chosen that do not conflict with other names. Modes that the hardware can be in, or user preferences, should be indicated by appending a hyphen and an indicator of the mode. Thus, a vt100 in 132 column mode would be vt100-w. The following suffixes should be used where possible:

Suffix	Meaning	Example
-w	Wide mode (more than 80 columns)	vt100-w
-am	With auto. margins (usually default)	vt100-am
-nam	Without automatic margins	vt100-nam
-*n*	Number of lines on the screen	aaa-60
-na	No arrow keys (leave them in local)	c100-na
-*n*p	Number of pages of memory	c100-4p
-rv	Reverse video	c100-rv

CAPABILITIES

The variable is the name by which the programmer (at the terminfo level) accesses the capability. The capname is the short name used in the text of the database, and is used by a person updating the database. The i.code is the two letter internal code used in the compiled database, and always corresponds to the old **termcap** capability name.

Capability names have no hard length limit, but an informal limit of 5 characters has been adopted to keep them short and to allow the tabs in the source file **caps** to line up nicely. Whenever possible, names are chosen to be the same as or similar to the ANSI X3.64-1979 standard. Semantics are also intended to match those of the specification.

(P) indicates that padding may be specified

(G) indicates that the string is passed through tparm with parms as given (#*i*).

(*) indicates that padding may be based on the number of lines affected

($\#_i$) indicates the ith parameter.

Variable Booleans	**Cap-name**	**I. Code**	**Description**
auto_left_margin,	bw	bw	cub1 wraps from column 0 to last column
auto_right_margin,	am	am	Terminal has automatic margins
beehive_glitch,	xsb	xb	Beehive (f1=escape, f2=ctrl C)
ceol_standout_glitch,	xhp	xs	Standout not erased by overwriting (hp)
eat_newline_glitch,	xenl	xn	newline ignored after 80 cols (Concept)
erase_overstrike,	eo	eo	Can erase overstrikes with a blank
generic_type,	gn	gn	Generic line type (e.g.,, dialup, switch).
hard_copy,	hc	hc	Hardcopy terminal
has_meta_key,	km	km	Has a meta key (shift, sets parity bit)
has_status_line,	hs	hs	Has extra "status line"
insert_null_glitch,	in	in	Insert mode distinguishes nulls
memory_above,	da	da	Display may be retained above the screen
memory_below,	db	db	Display may be retained below the screen
move_insert_mode,	mir	mi	Safe to move while in insert mode
move_standout_mode,	msgr	ms	Safe to move in standout modes
over_strike,	os	os	Terminal overstrikes
status_line_esc_ok,	eslok	es	Escape can be used on the status line
teleray_glitch,	xt	xt	Tabs ruin, magic so char (Teleray 1061)
tilde_glitch,	hz	hz	Hazeltine; can not print ~'s
transparent_underline,	ul	ul	underline character overstrikes

xon_xoff,	xon	xo	Terminal uses xon/xoff handshaking
Numbers:			
columns,	cols	co	Number of columns in a line
init_tabs,	it	it	Tabs initially every # spaces
lines,	lines	li	Number of lines on screen or page
lines_of_memory,	lm	lm	Lines of memory if > lines. 0 means varies
magic_cookie_glitch,	xmc	sg	Number of blank chars left by smso or rmso
padding_baud_rate,	pb	pb	Lowest baud where cr/nl padding is needed
virtual_terminal,	vt	vt	Virtual terminal number (UNIX system)
width_status_line,	wsl	ws	No. columns in status line
Strings:			
back_tab,	cbt	bt	Back tab (P)
bell,	bel	bl	Audible signal (bell) (P)
carriage_return,	cr	cr	Carriage return (P*)
change_scroll_region,	csr	cs	change to lines #1 through #2 (vt100) (PG)
clear_all_tabs,	tbc	ct	Clear all tab stops (P)
clear_screen,	clear	cl	Clear screen and home cursor (P*)
clr_col,	el	ce	Clear to end of line (P)
clr_eos,	ed	cd	Clear to end of display (P*)
column_address,	hpa	ch	Set cursor column (PG)
command_character,	cmdch	CC	Term. settable cmd char in prototype
cursor_address,	cup	cm	Screen rel. cursor motion row #1 col #2 (PG)
cursor_down,	cud1	do	Down one line
cursor_home,	home	ho	Home cursor (if no cup)
cursor_invisible,	civis	vi	Make cursor invisible
cursor_left,	cub1	lc	Move cursor left one space
cursor_mem_address,	mrcup	CM	Memory relative cursor addressing
cursor_normal,	cnorm	ve	Make cursor appear normal (undo vs/vi)
cursor_right,	cuf1	nd	Non-destructive space (cursor right)
cursor_to_ll,	ll	ll	Last line, first column (if no cup)
cursor_up,	cuu1	up	Upline (cursor up)
cursor_visible,	cvvis	vs	Make cursor very visible
delete_character,	dch1	dc	Delete character (P*)
delete_line,	dl1	dl	Delete line (P*)
dis_status_line,	dsl	ds	Disable status line
down_half_line,	hd	hd	Half-line down (forward 1/2 linefeed)
enter_alt_charset_mode,	smacs	as	Start alternate character set (P)
enter_blink_mode,	blink	mb	Turn on blinking

enter_bold_mode,	bold	md	Turn on bold (extra bright) mode
enter_ca_mode,	smcup	ti	String to begin programs that use cup
enter_delete_mode,	smdc	dm	Delete mode (enter)
enter_dim_mode,	dim	mh	Turn on half-bright mode
enter_insert_mode,	smir	im	Insert mode (enter);
enter_protected_mode,	prot	mp	Turn on protected mode
enter_reverse_mode,	rev	mr	Turn on reverse video mode
enter_secure_mode,	invis	mk	Turn on blank mode (chars invisible)
enter_standout_mode,	smso	so	Begin stand out mode
enter_underline_mode,	smul	us	Start underscore mode
erase_chars	ech	ec	Erase #1 characters (PG)
exit_alt_charset_mode,	rmacs	ae	End alternate character set (P)
exit_attribute_mode,	sgr0	me	Turn off all attributes
exit_ca_mode,	rmcup	te	String to end programs that use cup
exit_delete_mode,	rmdc	ed	End delete mode
exit_insert_mode,	rmir	ei	End insert mode
exit_standout_mode,	rmso	se	End stand out mode
exit_underline_mode,	rmul	ue	End underscore mode
flash_screen,	flash	vb	Visible bell (may not move cursor)
form_feed,	ff	ff	Hardcopy terminal page eject (P*)
from_status_line,	fsl	fs	Return from status line
init_1string,	is1	i1	Terminal initialization string
init_2string,	is2	i2	Terminal initialization string
init_3string,	is3	i3	Terminal initialization string
init_file,	if	if	Name of file containing is
insert_character,	ich1	ic	Insert character (P)
insert_line,	il1	al	Add new blank line (P*)
insert_padding,	ip	ip	Insert pad after character inserted (P*)
key_backspace,	kbs	kb	Sent by backspace key
key_catab,	ktbc	ka	Sent by clear-all-tabs key
key_clear,	kclr	kC	Sent by clear screen or erase key
key_ctab,	kctab	kt	Sent by clear-tab key
key_dc,	kdch1	kD	Sent by delete character key
key_dl,	kdl1	kL	Sent by delete line key
key_down,	kcud1	kd	Sent by terminal down arrow key
key_eic,	krmir	kM	Sent by rmir or smir in insert mode
key_eol,	kel	kE	Sent by clear-to-end-of-line key
key_eos,	ked	kS	Sent by clear-to-end-of-screen key
key_f0,	kf0	k0	Sent by function key f0
key_f1,	kf1	k1	Sent by function key f1

key_f10,	kf10	ka	Sent by function key f10
key_f2,	kf2	k2	Sent by function key f2
key_f3,	kf3	k3	Sent by function key f3
key_f4,	kf4	k4	Sent by function key f4
key_f5,	kf5	k5	Sent by function key f5
key_f6,	kf6	k6	Sent by function key f6
key_f7,	kf7	k7	Sent by function key f7
key_f8,	kf8	k8	Sent by function key f8
key_f9,	kf9	k9	Sent by function key f9
key_home,	khome	kh	Sent by home key
key_ic,	kich1	kI	Sent by ins char/enter ins mode key
key_il,	kil1	kA	Sent by insert line
key_left,	kcub1	kl	Sent by terminal left arrow key
key_ll,	kll	kH	Sent by home-down key
key_npage,	knp	kN	Sent by next-page key
key_ppage,	kpp	kP	Sent by previous-page key
key_right,	kcuf1	kr	Sent by terminal right arrow key
key_sf,	kind	kF	Sent by scroll-forward/down key
key_sr,	kri	kR	Sent by scroll-backward/up key
key_stab,	khts	kT	Sent by set-tab key
key_up,	kcuu1	ku	Sent by terminal up arrow key
keypad_local,	rmkx	ke	Out of "keypad transmit" mode
keypad_xmit,	smkx	ks	Put terminal in "keypad transmit" mode
lab_f0,	lf0	l0	Labels on function key f0 if not f0
lab_f1,	lf1	l1	Labels on function key f1 if not f1
lab_f10,	lf10	la	Labels on function key f10 if not f10
lab_f2,	lf2	l2	Labels on function key f2 if not f2
lab_f3,	lf3	l3	Labels on function key f3 if not f3
lab_f4,	lf4	l4	Labels on function key f4 if not f4
lab_f5,	lf5	l5	Labels on function key f5 if not f5
lab_f6,	lf6	l6	Labels on function key f6 if not f6
lab_f7,	lf7	l7	Labels on function key f7 if not f7
lab_f8,	lf8	l8	Labels on function key f8 if not f8
lab_f9,	lf9	l9	Labels on function key f9 if not f9
meta_on,	smm	mm	Turn on "meta mode" (8th bit)
meta_off,	rmm	mo	Turn off "meta mode"
newline,	nel	nw	Newline (behaves like cr followed by lf)
pad_char,	pad	pc	Pad character (rather than null)
parm_dch,	dch	DC	Delete #1 chars (PG*)
parm_delete_line,	dl	DL	Delete #1 lines (PG*)

parm_down_cursor,	cud	DO	Move cursor down #1 lines (PG*)
parm_ich,	ich	IC	Insert #1 blank chars (PG*)
parm_index,	indn	SF	Scroll forward #1 lines (PG)
parm_insert_line,	il	AL	Add #1 new blank lines (PG*)
parm_left_cursor,	cub	LE	Move cursor left #1 spaces (PG)
parm_right_cursor,	cuf	RI	Move cursor right #1 spaces (PG*)
parm_rindex,	rin	SR	Scroll backward #1 lines (PG)
parm_up_cursor,	cuu	UP	Move cursor up #1 lines (PG*)
pkey_key,	pfkey	pk	Prog funct key #1 to type string #2
pkey_local,	pfloc	pl	Prog funct key #1 to execute string #2
pkey_xmit,	pfx	px	Prog funct key #1 to xmit string #2
print_screen,	mc0	ps	Print contents of the screen
prtr_off,	mc4	pf	Turn off the printer
prtr_on,	mc5	po	Turn on the printer
repeat_char,	rep	rp	Repeat char #1 #2 times. (PG*)
reset_1string,	rs1	r1	Reset terminal completely to sane modes.
reset_2string,	rs2	r2	Reset terminal completely to sane modes.
reset_3string,	rs3	r3	Reset terminal completely to sane modes.
reset_file,	rf	rf	Name of file containing reset string
restore_cursor,	rc	rc	Restore cursor to position of last sc
row_address,	vpa	cv	Vertical position absolute (set row) (PG)
save_cursor,	sc	sc	Save cursor position (P)
scroll_forward,	ind	sf	Scroll text up (P)
scroll_reverse,	ri	sr	Scroll text down (P)
set_attributes,	sgr	sa	Define the video attributes (PG9)
set_tab,	hts	st	Set a tab in all rows, current column
set_window,	wind	wi	Current window is lines #1-#2 cols #3-#4
tab,	ht	ta	Tab to next 8 space hardware tab stop
to_status_line,	tsl	ts	Go to status line, column #1
underline_char,	uc	uc	Underscore one char and move past it
up_half_line,	hu	hu	Half-line up (reverse 1/2 linefeed)
init_prog,	iprog	iP	Path name of program for init
key_a1,	ka1	K1	Upper left of keypad
key_a3,	ka3	K3	Upper right of keypad
key_b2,	kb2	K2	Center of keypad
key_c1,	kc1	K4	Lower left of keypad
key_c3,	kc3	K5	Lower right of keypad
prtr_non,	mc5p	pO	Turn on the printer for #1 bytes

A Sample Entry

The following entry, which describes the Concept−100, is among the more complex entries in the *terminfo* file as of this writing.

```
concept100|c100|concept|c104|c100-4p|concept 100,
        am, bel=^G, blank=\EH, blink=\EC, clear=^L$<2*>, cnorm=\Ew,
        cols#80, cr=^M$<9>, cub1=^H, cud1=^J, cuf1=\E=,
        cup=\Ea%p1%' '%+%c%p2%' '%+%c,
        cuu1=\E;, cvvis=\EW, db, dch1=\E^A$<16*>, dim=\EE, dl1=\E^B$<3*>,
        ed=\E^C$<16*>, el=\E^U$<16>, eo, flash=\Ek$<20>\EK, ht=\t$<8>,
        il1=\E^R$<3*>, in, ind=^J, .ind=^J$<9>, ip=$<16*>,
        is2=\EU\Ef\E7\E5\E8\El\ENH\EK\E\200\Eo&\200\Eo\47\E,
        kbs=^h, kcub1=\E>, kcud1=\E<, kcuf1=\E=, kcuu1=\E;,
        kf1=\E5, kf2=\E6, kf3=\E7, khome=\E?,
        lines#24, mir, pb#9600, prot=\EI, rep=\Er%p1%c%p2%' '%+%c$<.2*>,
        rev=\ED, rmcup=\Ev    $<6>\Ep\r\n, rmir=\E\200, rmkx=\Ex,
        rmso=\Ed\Ee, rmul=\Eg, rmul=\Eg, sgr0=\EN\200,
        smcup=\EU\Ev  8p\Ep\r, smir=\E^P, smkx=\EX, smso=\EE\ED,
        smul=\EG, tabs, ul, vt#8, xenl,
```

Entries may continue onto multiple lines by placing white space at the beginning of each line except the first. Comments may be included on lines beginning with "#". Capabilities in *terminfo* are of three types: Boolean capabilities which indicate that the terminal has some particular feature, numeric capabilities giving the size of the terminal or the size of particular delays, and string capabilities, which give a sequence which can be used to perform particular terminal operations.

Types of Capabilities

All capabilities have names. For instance, the fact that the Concept has *automatic margins* (i.e., an automatic return and linefeed when the end of a line is reached) is indicated by the capability **am**. Hence the description of the Concept includes **am**. Numeric capabilities are followed by the character '#' and then the value. Thus **cols**, which indicates the number of columns the terminal has, gives the value '80' for the Concept.

Finally, string valued capabilities, such as **el** (clear to end of line sequence) are given by the two-character code, an '=', and then a string ending at the next following ','. A delay in milliseconds may appear anywhere in such a capability, enclosed in $<..> brackets, as in **el**=\EK$<3>, and padding characters are supplied by *tputs* to provide this delay. The delay can be either a number, e.g., '20', or a number followed by an '*', i.e., '3*'. A '*' indicates that the padding required is proportional to the number of lines affected by the operation, and the amount given is the per-affected-unit padding required. (In the case of insert character, the factor is still the number of *lines* affected. This is always one unless the terminal has **xenl** and the software uses it.) When a '*' is specified, it is sometimes useful to give a delay of the form '3.5' to specify a delay per unit to tenths of milliseconds. (Only one decimal place is allowed.)

A number of escape sequences are provided in the string valued capabilities for easy encoding of characters there. Both **\E** and **\e** map to an ESCAPE character, **^x** maps to a control-x for any appropriate x, and the sequences **\n \l \r \t \b \f \s** give a newline, linefeed, return, tab, backspace, formfeed, and space. Other escapes include \^ for ^, \\ for \, \, for comma, \: for :, and \0 for null. (\0 will produce \200, which does not terminate a string but behaves as a null character on most terminals.) Finally, characters may be given as three octal digits after a \.

Sometimes individual capabilities must be commented out. To do this, put a period before the capability name. For example, see the second **ind** in the example above.

Preparing Descriptions

We now outline how to prepare descriptions of terminals. The most effective way to prepare a terminal description is by imitating the description of a similar terminal in *terminfo* and to build up a description gradually, using partial descriptions with *vi* to check that they are correct. Be aware that a very unusual terminal may expose deficiencies in the ability of the *terminfo* file to describe it or bugs in *vi*. To easily test a new terminal description you can set the environment variable TERMINFO to a pathname of a directory containing the compiled description you are working on and programs will look there rather than in */usr/lib/terminfo*. To get the padding for insert line right (if the terminal manufacturer did not document it) a severe test is to edit /etc/passwd at 9600 baud, delete 16 or so lines from the middle of the screen, then hit the 'u' key several times quickly. If the terminal messes up, more padding is usually needed. A similar test can be used for insert character.

Basic Capabilities

The number of columns on each line for the terminal is given by the **cols** numeric capability. If the terminal is a CRT, then the number of lines on the screen is given by the **lines** capability. If the terminal wraps around to the beginning of the next line when it reaches the right margin, then it should have the **am** capability.

If the terminal can clear its screen, leaving the cursor in the home position, then this is given by the **clear** string capability. If the terminal overstrikes (rather than clearing a position when a character is struck over) then it should have the **os** capability. If the terminal is a printing terminal, with no soft copy unit, give it both **hc** and **os**. (**os** applies to storage scope terminals, such as TEKTRONIX 4010 series, as well as hard copy and APL terminals.) If there is a code to move the cursor to the left edge of the current row, give this as **cr**. (Normally this will be carriage return, control M.) If there is a code to produce an audible signal (bell, beep, etc) give this as **bel**.

If there is a code to move the cursor one position to the left (such as backspace) that capability should be given as **cub1**. Similarly, codes to move to the right, up, and down should be given as **cuf1**, **cuu1**, and **cud1**. These local cursor motions should not alter the text they pass over, for example, you would not normally use '**cuf1=** ' because the space would erase the character moved over.

A very important point here is that the local cursor motions encoded in *terminfo* are undefined at the left and top edges of a CRT terminal. Programs should never attempt to backspace around the left edge, unless **bw** is given, and never attempt to go up locally off the top. In order to scroll text up, a program will go to the bottom left corner of the screen and send the **ind** (index) string.

To scroll text down, a program goes to the top left corner of the screen and sends the **ri** (reverse index) string. The strings **ind** and **ri** are undefined when not on their respective corners of the screen.

Parameterized versions of the scrolling sequences are **indn** and **rin** which have the same semantics as **ind** and **ri** except that they take one parameter, and scroll that many lines. They are also undefined except at the appropriate edge of the screen.

The **am** capability tells whether the cursor sticks at the right edge of the screen when text is output, but this does not necessarily apply to a **cuf1** from the last column. The only local motion which is defined from the left edge is if **bw** is given, then a **cub1** from the left edge will move to the right edge of the previous row. If **bw** is not given, the effect is undefined. This is useful for drawing a box around the edge of the screen, for example. If the terminal has switch selectable automatic margins, the *terminfo* file usually assumes that this is on; i.e., **am**. If the terminal has a command which moves to the first column of the next line, that command can be given as **nel** (newline). It does not matter if the command clears the remainder of the current line, so if the terminal has no **cr** and **lf** it may still be possible to craft a working **nel** out of one or both of them.

These capabilities suffice to describe hardcopy and glass-tty terminals. Thus the model 33 teletype is described as

```
33¦tty33¦tty¦model 33 teletype,
bel=^G, cols#72, cr=^M, cud1=^J, hc, ind=^J, os,
```

while the Lear Siegler ADM−3 is described as

```
adm3¦3¦lsi adm3,
am, bel=^G, clear=^Z, cols#80, cr=^M, cub1=^H, cud1=^J,
ind=^J, lines#24,
```

Parameterized Strings

Cursor addressing and other strings requiring parameters in the terminal are described by a parameterized string capability, with *printf*(3S) like escapes **%x** in it. For example, to address the cursor, the **cup** capability is given, using two parameters: the row and column to address to. (Rows and columns are numbered from zero and refer to the physical screen visible to the user, not to any unseen memory.) If the terminal has memory relative cursor addressing, that can be indicated by **mrcup**.

The parameter mechanism uses a stack and special % codes to manipulate it. Typically a sequence will push onc of the parameters onto the stack and then print it in some format. Often more complex operations are necessary.

The % encodings have the following meanings:

%%	outputs '%'
%d	print pop() as in printf
%2d	print pop() like %2d
%3d	print pop() like %3d
%02d	
%03d	as in printf
%c	print pop() gives %c
%s	print pop() gives %s
%p[1-9]	push ith parm
%P[a-z]	set variable [a-z] to pop()
%g[a-z]	get variable [a-z] and push it

%'c'	char constant c
%{nn}	integer constant nn
%+ %- %* %/ %m	arithmetic (%m is mod): push(pop() op pop())
%& %| %^	bit operations: push(pop() op pop())
%= %> %<	logical operations: push(pop() op pop())
%! %~	unary operations push(op pop())
%i	add 1 to first two parms (for ANSI terminals)
%? expr %t thenpart %e elsepart %;	if-then-else, %e elsepart is optional. else-if's are possible ala Algol 68: %? c_1 %t b_1 %e c_2 %t b_2 %e c_3 %t b_3 %e c_4 %t b_4 %e %; c_i are conditions, b_i are bodies.

Binary operations are in postfix form with the operands in the usual order. That is, to get x-5 one would use "%gx%{5}%-".

Consider the Hewlett-Packard 2645, which, to get to row 3 and column 12, needs to be sent \E&a12c03Y padded for 6 milliseconds. Note that the order of the rows and columns is inverted here, and that the row and column are printed as two digits. Thus its **cup** capability is cup=6\E&%p2%2dc%p1%2dY.

The Microterm ACT-IV needs the current row and column sent preceded by a **^T**, with the row and column simply encoded in binary, cup=^T%p1%c%p2%c. Terminals which use %c need to be able to backspace the cursor (**cub1**), and to move the cursor up one line on the screen (**cuu1**). This is necessary because it is not always safe to transmit **\n** **^D** and **\r**, as the system may change or discard them. (The library routines dealing with terminfo set tty modes so that tabs are never expanded, so \t is safe to send. This turns out to be essential for the Ann Arbor 4080.)

A final example is the LSI ADM-3a, which uses row and column offset by a blank character, thus cup=\E=%p1%' '%+%c%p2%' '%+%c. After sending '\E=', this pushes the first parameter, pushes the ASCII value for a space (32), adds them (pushing the sum on the stack in place of the two previous values) and outputs that value as a character. Then the same is done for the second parameter. More complex arithmetic is possible using the stack.

If the terminal has row or column absolute cursor addressing, these can be given as single parameter capabilities **hpa** (horizontal position absolute) and **vpa** (vertical position absolute). Sometimes these are shorter than the more general two parameter sequence (as with the hp2645) and can be used in preference to **cup** . If there are parameterized local motions (e.g., move *n* spaces to the right) these can be given as **cud**, **cub**, **cuf**, and **cuu** with a single parameter indicating how many spaces to move. These are primarily useful if the terminal does not have **cup**, such as the TEKTRONIX 4025.

Cursor Motions

If the terminal has a fast way to home the cursor (to very upper left corner of screen) then this can be given as **home**; similarly a fast way of getting to the lower left-hand corner can be given as **ll**; this may involve going up with **cuu1** from the home position, but a program should never do this itself (unless **ll** does) because it can make no assumption about the effect of moving up from the home position. Note that the home position is the same as addressing to (0,0): to the top left corner of the screen, not of memory. (Thus, the \EH sequence on Hewlett-Packard terminals cannot be used for **home**.)

Area Clears

If the terminal can clear from the current position to the end of the line, leaving the cursor where it is, this should be given as **el**. If the terminal can clear from the current position to the end of the display, then this should be given as **ed**. **Ed** is only defined from the first column of a line. (Thus, it can be simulated by a request to delete a large number of lines, if a true **ed** is not available.)

Insert/delete line

If the terminal can open a new blank line before the line where the cursor is, this should be given as **il1**; this is done only from the first position of a line. The cursor must then appear on the newly blank line. If the terminal can delete the line which the cursor is on, then this should be given as **dl1**; this is done only from the first position on the line to be deleted. Versions of **il1** and **dl1** which take a single parameter and insert or delete that many lines can be given as **il** and **dl**. If the terminal has a settable scrolling region (like the vt100) the command to set this can be described with the **csr** capability, which takes two parameters: the top and bottom lines of the scrolling region. The cursor position is, alas, undefined after using this command. It is possible to get the effect of insert or delete line using this command — the **sc** and **rc** (save and restore cursor) commands are also useful. Inserting lines at the top or bottom of the screen can also be done using **ri** or **ind** on many terminals without a true insert/delete line, and is often faster even on terminals with those features.

If the terminal has the ability to define a window as part of memory, which all commands affect, it should be given as the parameterized string **wind**. The four parameters are the starting and ending lines in memory and the starting and ending columns in memory, in that order.

If the terminal can retain display memory above, then the **da** capability should be given; if display memory can be retained below, then **db** should be given. These indicate that deleting a line or scrolling may bring non-blank lines up from below or that scrolling back with **ri** may bring down non-blank lines.

Insert/Delete Character

There are two basic kinds of intelligent terminals with respect to insert/delete character which can be described using *terminfo*. The most common insert/delete character operations affect only the characters on the current line and shift characters off the end of the line rigidly. Other terminals, such as the Concept 100 and the Perkin Elmer Owl, make a distinction between typed and untyped blanks on the screen, shifting upon an insert or delete only to an untyped blank on the screen which is either eliminated, or expanded to two untyped blanks. You can determine the kind of terminal you have by clearing the screen and then typing text separated by cursor motions. Type abc def using local cursor motions (not spaces) between the abc and the def. Then position the cursor before the abc and put the terminal in insert mode. If typing characters causes the rest of the line to shift rigidly and characters to fall off the end, then your terminal does not distinguish between blanks and untyped positions. If the abc shifts over to the def which then move together around the end of the current line and onto the next as you insert, you have the second type of terminal, and should give the capability **in**, which stands for insert null. While these are two logically separate attributes (one line vs. multiline insert mode, and special treatment of untyped spaces) we have seen no terminals whose insert mode cannot be described with the single attribute.

Terminfo can describe both terminals which have an insert mode, and terminals which send a simple sequence to open a blank position on the current line. Give as **smir** the sequence to get into insert mode. Give as **rmir** the sequence to leave insert mode. Now give as **ich1** any sequence needed to be sent just before sending the character to be inserted. Most terminals with a true insert mode will not give **ich1**; terminals which send a sequence to open a screen position should give it here. (If your terminal has both, insert mode is usually preferable to **ich1**. Do not give both unless the terminal actually requires both to be used in combination.) If post insert padding is needed, give this as a number of milliseconds in **ip** (a string option). Any other sequence which may need to be sent after an insert of a single character may also be given in **ip**. If your terminal needs both to be placed into an 'insert mode' and a special code to precede each inserted character, then both **smir/rmir** and **ich1** can be given, and both will be used. The **ich** capability, with one parameter, *n*, will repeat the effects of **ich1** *n* times.

It is occasionally necessary to move around while in insert mode to delete characters on the same line (e.g., if there is a tab after the insertion position). If your terminal allows motion while in insert mode you can give the capability **mir** to speed up inserting in this case. Omitting **mir** will affect only speed. Some terminals (notably Datamedia's) must not have **mir** because of the way their insert mode works.

Finally, you can specify **dch1** to delete a single character, **dch** with one parameter, *n*, to delete *n characters,* and delete mode by giving **smdc** and **rmdc** to enter and exit delete mode (any mode the terminal needs to be placed in for **dch1** to work).

A command to erase *n* characters (equivalent to outputting *n* blanks without moving the cursor) can be given as **ech** with one parameter.

Highlighting, Underlining, and Visible Bells

If your terminal has one or more kinds of display attributes, these can be represented in a number of different ways. You should choose one display form as *standout mode*, representing a good, high contrast, easy-on-the-eyes, format for highlighting error messages and other attention getters. (If you have a choice, reverse video plus half-bright is good, or reverse video alone.) The sequences to enter and exit standout mode are given as **smso** and

rmso, respectively. If the code to change into or out of standout mode leaves one or even two blank spaces on the screen, as the TVI 912 and Teleray 1061 do, then **xmc** should be given to tell how many spaces are left.

Codes to begin underlining and end underlining can be given as **smul** and **rmul** respectively. If the terminal has a code to underline the current character and move the cursor one space to the right, such as the Microterm Mime, this can be given as **uc**.

Other capabilities to enter various highlighting modes include **blink** (blinking) **bold** (bold or extra bright) **dim** (dim or half-bright) **invis** (blanking or invisible text) **prot** (protected) **rev** (reverse video) **sgr0** (turn off *all* attribute modes) **smacs** (enter alternate character set mode) and **rmacs** (exit alternate character set mode). Turning on any of these modes singly may or may not turn off other modes.

If there is a sequence to set arbitrary combinations of modes, this should be given as **sgr** (set attributes), taking 9 parameters. Each parameter is either 0 or 1, as the corresponding attribute is on or off. The 9 parameters are, in order: standout, underline, reverse, blink, dim, bold, blank, protect, alternate character set. Not all modes need be supported by **sgr**, only those for which corresponding separate attribute commands exist.

Terminals with the "magic cookie" glitch (**xmc**) deposit special "cookies" when they receive mode-setting sequences, which affect the display algorithm rather than having extra bits for each character. Some terminals, such as the Hewlett-Packard 2621, automatically leave standout mode when they move to a new line or the cursor is addressed. Programs using standout mode should exit standout mode before moving the cursor or sending a newline, unless the **msgr** capability, asserting that it is safe to move in standout mode, is present.

If the terminal has a way of flashing the screen to indicate an error quietly (a bell replacement) then this can be given as **flash**; it must not move the cursor.

If the cursor needs to be made more visible than normal when it is not on the bottom line (to make, for example, a non-blinking underline into an easier to find block or blinking underline) give this sequence as **cvvis**. If there is a way to make the cursor completely invisible, give that as **civis**. The capability **cnorm** should be given which undoes the effects of both of these modes.

If the terminal needs to be in a special mode when running a program that uses these capabilities, the codes to enter and exit this mode can be given as **smcup** and **rmcup**. This arises, for example, from terminals like the Concept with more than one page of memory. If the terminal has only memory relative cursor addressing and not screen relative cursor addressing, a one screen-sized window must be fixed into the terminal for cursor addressing to work properly. This is also used for the TEKTRONIX 4025, where **smcup** sets the command character to be the one used by terminfo.

If your terminal correctly generates underlined characters (with no special codes needed) even though it does not overstrike, then you should give the capability **ul**. If overstrikes are erasable with a blank, then this should be indicated by giving **eo**.

Keypad

If the terminal has a keypad that transmits codes when the keys are pressed, this information can be given. Note that it is not possible to handle terminals where the keypad only works in local (this applies, for example, to the unshifted Hewlett-Packard 2621 keys). If the keypad can be set to transmit or not transmit, give these codes as **smkx** and **rmkx**. Otherwise the keypad is assumed to always transmit. The codes sent by the left arrow, right arrow, up arrow, down arrow, and home keys can be given as **kcub1, kcuf1, kcuu1, kcud1,** and **khome** respectively. If there are function keys such as f0, f1, ..., f10, the codes they send can be given as **kf0, kf1, ..., kf10**. If these keys have labels other than the default f0 through f10, the labels can be given as **lf0, lf1, ..., lf10**. The codes transmitted by certain other special keys can be given: **kll** (home down), **kbs** (backspace), **ktbc** (clear all tabs), **kctab** (clear the tab stop in this column), **kclr** (clear screen or erase key), **kdch1** (delete character), **kdl1** (delete line), **krmir** (exit insert mode), **kel** (clear to end of line), **ked** (clear to end of screen), **kich1** (insert character or enter insert mode), **kil1** (insert line), **knp** (next page), **kpp** (previous page), **kind** (scroll forward/down), **kri** (scroll backward/up), **khts** (set a tab stop in this column). In addition, if the keypad has a 3 by 3 array of keys including the four arrow keys, the other five keys can be given as **ka1**, **ka3**, **kb2**, **kc1**, and **kc3**. These keys are useful when the effects of a 3 by 3 directional pad are needed.

Tabs and Initialization

If the terminal has hardware tabs, the command to advance to the next tab stop can be given as **ht** (usually control I). A "backtab" command which moves leftward to the next tab stop can be given as **cbt**. By convention, if the teletype modes indicate that tabs are being expanded by the computer rather than being sent to the terminal, programs should not use **ht** or **cbt** even if they are present, since the user may not have the tab stops properly set. If the terminal has hardware tabs which are initially set every *n* spaces when the terminal is powered up, the numeric parameter **it** is given, showing the number of spaces the tabs are set to. This is normally used by the *tset* command to determine whether to set the mode for hardware tab expansion, and whether to set the tab stops. If the terminal has tab stops that can be saved in nonvolatile memory, the terminfo description can assume that they are properly set.

Other capabilities include **is1**, **is2**, and **is3**, initialization strings for the terminal, **iprog**, the path name of a program to be run to initialize the terminal, and **if**, the name of a file containing long initialization strings. These strings are expected to set the terminal into modes consistent with the rest of the terminfo description. They are normally sent to the terminal, by the *tset* program, each time the user logs in. They will be printed in the following order: **is1**; **is2**; setting tabs using **tbc** and **hts**; **if**; running the program **iprog**; and finally **is3**. Most initialization is done with **is2**. Special terminal modes can be set up without duplicating strings by putting the common sequences in **is2** and special cases in **is1** and **is3**. A pair of sequences that does a harder reset from a totally unknown state can be analogously given as **rs1**, **rs2**, **rf**, and **rs3**, analogous to **is2** and **if**. These strings are output by the *reset* program, which is used when the terminal gets into a wedged state. Commands are normally placed in **rs2** and **rf** only if they produce annoying effects on the screen and are not necessary when logging in. For example, the command to set the vt100 into 80-column mode would normally be part of **is2**, but it causes an annoying glitch of the screen and is not normally needed since the terminal is usually already in 80 column mode.

If there are commands to set and clear tab stops, they can be given as **tbc** (clear all tab stops) and **hts** (set a tab stop in the current column of every row). If a more complex sequence is needed to set the tabs than can be described by this, the sequence can be placed in **is2** or **if**.

Delays

Certain capabilities control padding in the teletype driver. These are primarily needed by hard copy terminals, and are used by the *tset* program to set teletype modes appropriately. Delays embedded in the capabilities **cr**, **ind**, **cub1**, **ff**, and **tab** will cause the appropriate delay bits to be set in the teletype driver. If **pb** (padding baud rate) is given, these values can be ignored at baud rates below the value of **pb**.

Miscellaneous

If the terminal requires other than a null (zero) character as a pad, then this can be given as **pad**. Only the first character of the **pad** string is used.

If the terminal has an extra "status line" that is not normally used by software, this fact can be indicated. If the status line is viewed as an extra line below the bottom line, into which one can cursor address normally (such as the Heathkit h19's 25th line, or the 24th line of a vt100 which is set to a 23-line scrolling region), the capability **hs** should be given. Special strings to go to the beginning of the status line and to return from the status line can be given as **tsl** and **fsl**. (**fsl** must leave the cursor position in the same place it was before **tsl**. If necessary, the **sc** and **rc** strings can be included in **tsl** and **fsl** to get this effect.) The parameter **tsl** takes one parameter, which is the column number of the status line the cursor is to be moved to. If escape sequences and other special commands, such as tab, work while in the status line, the flag **eslok** can be given. A string which turns off the status line (or otherwise erases its contents) should be given as **dsl**. If the terminal has commands to save and restore the position of the cursor, give them as **sc** and **rc**. The status line is normally assumed to be the same width as the rest of the screen, e.g., **cols**. If the status line is a different width (possibly because the terminal does not allow an entire line to be loaded) the width, in columns, can be indicated with the numeric parameter **wsl**.

If the terminal can move up or down half a line, this can be indicated with **hu** (half-line up) and **hd** (half-line down). This is primarily useful for superscripts and subscripts on hardcopy terminals. If a hardcopy terminal can eject to the next page (form feed), give this as **ff** (usually control L).

If there is a command to repeat a given character a given number of times (to save time transmitting a large number of identical characters) this can be indicated with the parameterized string **rep**. The first parameter is the character to be repeated and the second is the number of times to repeat it. Thus, tparm(repeat_char, 'x', 10) is the same as 'xxxxxxxxxx'.

If the terminal has a settable command character, such as the TEKTRONIX 4025, this can be indicated with **cmdch**. A prototype command character is chosen which is used in all capabilities. This character is given in the **cmdch** capability to identify it. The following convention is supported on some UNIX systems: The environment is to be searched for a **CC** variable, and if found, all occurrences of the prototype character are replaced with the character in the environment variable.

Terminal descriptions that do not represent a specific kind of known terminal, such as *switch*, *dialup*, *patch*, and *network*, should include the **gn** (generic) capability so that programs can complain that they do not know how to talk to the terminal. (This capability does not apply to *virtual* terminal descriptions for which the escape sequences are known.)

If the terminal uses xon/xoff handshaking for flow control, give **xon**. Padding information should still be included so that routines can make better decisions about costs, but actual pad characters will not be transmitted.

If the terminal has a "meta key" which acts as a shift key, setting the 8th bit of any character transmitted, this fact can be indicated with **km**. Otherwise, software will assume that the 8th bit is parity and it will usually be cleared. If strings exist to turn this "meta mode" on and off, they can be given as **smm** and **rmm**.

If the terminal has more lines of memory than will fit on the screen at once, the number of lines of memory can be indicated with **lm**. A value of **lm#**0 indicates that the number of lines is not fixed, but that there is still more memory than fits on the screen.

If the terminal is one of those supported by the UNIX system virtual terminal protocol, the terminal number can be given as **vt**.

Media copy strings which control an auxiliary printer connected to the terminal can be given as **mc0**: print the contents of the screen, **mc4**: turn off the printer, and **mc5**: turn on the printer. When the printer is on, all text sent to the terminal will be sent to the printer. It is undefined whether the text is also displayed on the terminal screen when the printer is on. A variation **mc5p** takes one parameter, and leaves the printer on for as many characters as the value of the parameter, then turns the printer off. The parameter should not exceed 255. All text, including **mc4**, is transparently passed to the printer while an **mc5p** is in effect.

Strings to program function keys can be given as **pfkey**, **pfloc**, and **pfx**. Each of these strings takes two parameters: the function key number to program (from 0 to 10) and the string to program it with. Function key numbers out of this range may program undefined keys in a terminal dependent manner. The difference between the capabilities is that **pfkey** causes pressing the given key to be the same as the user typing the given string; **pfloc** causes the string to be executed by the terminal in local; and **pfx** causes the string to be transmitted to the computer.

Glitches and Braindamage

Hazeltine terminals, which do not allow '~' characters to be displayed should indicate **hz**.

Terminals which ignore a linefeed immediately after an **am** wrap, such as the Concept and vt100, should indicate **xenl**.

If **el** is required to get rid of standout (instead of merely writing normal text on top of it), **xhp** should be given.

Teleray terminals, where tabs turn all characters moved over to blanks, should indicate **xt** (destructive tabs). This glitch is also taken to mean that it is not possible to position the cursor on top of a "magic cookie", that to erase standout mode it is instead necessary to use delete and insert line.

The Beehive Superbee, which is unable to correctly transmit the escape or control C characters, has **xsb**, indicating that the f1 key is used for escape and f2 for control C. (Only certain Superbees have this problem, depending on the ROM.)

Other specific terminal problems may be corrected by adding more capabilities of the form **x***x*.

Similar Terminals

If there are two very similar terminals, one can be defined as being just like the other with certain exceptions. The string capability **use** can be given with the name of the similar terminal. The capabilities given before **use** override those in the terminal type invoked by **use**. A capability can be cancelled by placing **xx@** to the left of the capability definition, where xx is the capability. For example, the entry

2621-nl, smkx@, rmkx@, use=2621,

defines a 2621-nl that does not have the **smkx** or **rmkx** capabilities, and hence does not turn on the function key labels when in visual mode. This is useful for different modes for a terminal, or for different user preferences.

FILES

/usr/lib/terminfo/?/* files containing terminal descriptions

SEE ALSO

curses(3X), printf(3S), term(5).
tic(1M) in the *UNIX Programmer's Manual—Volume 3: System Administration Facilities.*

NAME

utmp, wtmp – utmp and wtmp entry formats

SYNOPSIS

#include <sys/types.h>
#include <utmp.h>

DESCRIPTION

These files, which hold user and accounting information for such commands as *who*(1), *write*(1), and *login*(1), have the following structure as defined by **<utmp.h>**:

```
#define    UTMP_FILE     "/etc/utmp"
#define    WTMP_FILE     "/etc/wtmp"
#define    ut_name       ut_user

struct utmp {
        char      ut_user[8];          /* User login name */
        char      ut_id[4];            /* /etc/inittab id (usually line #) */
        char      ut_line[12];         /* device name (console, lnxx) */
        short     ut_pid;              /* process id */
        short     ut_type;             /* type of entry */
        struct    exit_status {
            short     e_termination;   /* Process termination status */
            short     e_exit;          /* Process exit status */
        } ut_exit;                     /* The exit status of a process
                                        * marked as DEAD_PROCESS. */
        time_t    ut_time;             /* time entry was made */
};

/*  Definitions for ut_type  */
#define  EMPTY            0
#define  RUN_LVL          1
#define  BOOT_TIME        2
#define  OLD_TIME         3
#define  NEW_TIME         4
#define  INIT_PROCESS     5
#define  LOGIN_PROCESS    6
#define  USER_PROCESS     7
#define  DEAD_PROCESS     8
#define  ACCOUNTING       9
#define  UTMAXTYPE        ACCOUNTING
```

```
/* Special strings or formats used in the "ut_line" field when */
/* accounting for something other than a process */
/* No string for the ut_line field can be more than 11 chars + */
/* a NULL in length */
#define RUNLVL_MSG "run-level %c"
#define BOOT_MSG    "system boot"
#define OTIME_MSG   "old time"
#define NTIME_MSG   "new time"
```

FILES

/usr/include/utmp.h
/etc/utmp
/etc/wtmp

SEE ALSO

getut(3C).
login(1), who(1), write(1) in the *UNIX Programmer's Manual—Volume 1: Commands and Utilities.*

NAME

intro − introduction to miscellany

DESCRIPTION

This section describes miscellaneous facilities such as macro packages, character set tables, etc.

NAME

ascii – map of ASCII character set

SYNOPSIS

cat /usr/pub/ascii

DESCRIPTION

Ascii is a map of the ASCII character set, giving both octal and hexadecimal equivalents of each character, to be printed as needed. It contains:

000 nul	001 soh	002 stx	003 etx
004 eot	005 enq	006 ack	007 bel
010 bs	011 ht	012 nl	013 vt
014 np	015 cr	016 so	017 si
020 dle	021 dc1	022 dc2	023 dc3
024 dc4	025 nak	026 syn	027 etb
030 can	031 em	032 sub	033 esc
034 fs	035 gs	036 rs	037 us
040 sp	041 !	042 "	043 #
044 $	045 %	046 &	047 ′
050 (	051)	052 *	053 +
054 ,	055 −	056 .	057 /
060 0	061 1	062 2	063 3
064 4	065 5	066 6	067 7
070 8	071 9	072 :	073 ;
074 <	075 =	076 >	077 ?
100 @	101 A	102 B	103 C
104 D	105 E	106 F	107 G
110 H	111 I	112 J	113 K
114 L	115 M	116 N	117 O
120 P	121 Q	122 R	123 S
124 T	125 U	126 V	127 W
130 X	131 Y	132 Z	133 [
134 \	135]	136 ^	137 _
140 `	141 a	142 b	143 c
144 d	145 e	146 f	147 g
150 h	151 i	152 j	153 k
154 l	155 m	156 n	157 o
160 p	161 q	162 r	163 s
164 t	165 u	166 v	167 w
170 x	171 y	172 z	173 {

174	175 }	176 ~	177 del

00 nul	01 soh	02 stx	03 etx
04 eot	05 enq	06 ack	07 bel
08 bs	09 ht	0a nl	0b vt
0c np	0d cr	0e so	0f si
10 dle	11 dc1	12 dc2	13 dc3
14 dc4	15 nak	16 syn	17 etb
18 can	19 em	1a sub	1b esc
1c fs	1d gs	1e rs	1f us
20 sp	21 !	22 "	23 #
24 $	25 %	26 &	27 '
28 (	29)	2a *	2b +
2c ,	2d −	2e .	2f /
30 0	31 1	32 2	33 3
34 4	35 5	36 6	37 7
38 8	39 9	3a :	3b ;
3c <	3d =	3e >	3f ?
40 @	41 A	42 B	43 C
44 D	45 E	46 F	47 G
48 H	49 I	4a J	4b K
4c L	4d M	4e N	4f O
50 P	51 Q	52 R	53 S
54 T	55 U	56 V	57 W
58 X	59 Y	5a Z	5b [
5c \	5d]	5e ^	5f _
60 `	61 a	62 b	63 c
64 d	65 e	66 f	67 g
68 h	69 i	6a j	6b k
6c l	6d m	6e n	6f o
70 p	71 q	72 r	73 s
74 t	75 u	76 v	77 w
78 x	79 y	7a z	7b {
7c	7d }	7e ~	7f del

FILES

/usr/pub/ascii

NAME

environ − user environment

DESCRIPTION

An array of strings called the "environment" is made available by *exec*(2) when a process begins. By convention, these strings have the form "name=value". The following names are used by various commands:

PATH The sequence of directory prefixes that *sh*(1), *time*(1), *nice*(1), *nohup*(1), etc., apply in searching for a file known by an incomplete path name. The prefixes are separated by colons (:). *Login*(1) sets **PATH=:/bin:/usr/bin.**

HOME Name of the user's login directory, set by *login*(1) from the password file *passwd*(4).

TERM The kind of terminal for which output is to be prepared. This information is used by commands, such as *mm*(1) or *tplot*(1G), which may exploit special capabilities of that terminal.

TZ Time zone information. The format is **xxx***n***zzz** where **xxx** is standard local time zone abbreviation, *n* is the difference in hours from GMT, and **zzz** is the abbreviation for the daylight-saving local time zone, if any; for example, **EST5EDT**.

Further names may be placed in the environment by the *export* command and "name=value" arguments in *sh*(1), or by *exec*(2). It is unwise to conflict with certain shell variables that are frequently exported by **.profile** files: **MAIL, PS1, PS2, IFS.**

SEE ALSO

exec(2).
env(1), login(1), sh(1), mm(1), nice(1), nohup(1), time(1), tplot(1G) in the *UNIX Programmer's Manual—Volume 1: Commands and Utilities.*

NAME

eqnchar − special character definitions for eqn and neqn

SYNOPSIS

eqn /usr/pub/eqnchar [files] | **troff** [options]

neqn /usr/pub/eqnchar [files] | **nroff (1)** [options]

eqn -Taps /usr/pub/apseqnchar [files] | **troff** [options]

eqn -Tcat /usr/pub/cateqnchar [files] | **otroff** [options]

DESCRIPTION

Eqnchar contains *troff*(1) and *nroff*(1) character definitions for constructing characters that are not available on a phototypesetter. These definitions are primarily intended for use with *eqn*(1) and *neqn*; *eqnchar* contains definitions for the following characters:

<table>
<tr><td>ciplus</td><td>ciplus</td><td>||</td><td>||</td><td>square</td><td>square</td></tr>
<tr><td>citimes</td><td>citimes</td><td>langle</td><td>langle</td><td>circle</td><td>circle</td></tr>
<tr><td>wig</td><td>wig</td><td>rangle</td><td>rangle</td><td>blot</td><td>blot</td></tr>
<tr><td>−wig</td><td>−wig</td><td>hbar</td><td>hbar</td><td>bullet</td><td>bullet</td></tr>
<tr><td>>wig</td><td>>wig</td><td>ppd</td><td>ppd</td><td>prop</td><td>prop</td></tr>
<tr><td><wig</td><td><wig</td><td><−></td><td><→</td><td>empty</td><td>empty</td></tr>
<tr><td>=wig</td><td>=wig</td><td><=></td><td>⩽></td><td>member</td><td>member</td></tr>
<tr><td>star</td><td>star</td><td>|<</td><td>|<</td><td>nomem</td><td>nomem</td></tr>
<tr><td>bigstar</td><td>bigstar</td><td>|></td><td>|></td><td>cup</td><td>cup</td></tr>
<tr><td>=dot</td><td>=dot</td><td>ang</td><td>ang</td><td>cap</td><td>cap</td></tr>
<tr><td>orsign</td><td>orsign</td><td>rang</td><td>rang</td><td>incl</td><td>incl</td></tr>
<tr><td>andsign</td><td>andsign</td><td>3dot</td><td>3dot</td><td>subset</td><td>subset</td></tr>
<tr><td>=del</td><td>=del</td><td>thf</td><td>thf</td><td>supset</td><td>supset</td></tr>
<tr><td>oppA</td><td>oppA</td><td>quarter</td><td>quarter</td><td>!subset</td><td>!subset</td></tr>
<tr><td>oppE</td><td>oppE</td><td>3quarter</td><td>3quarter</td><td></td><td>!supset!supset</td></tr>
<tr><td>angstrom</td><td>angstrom</td><td></td><td>degree</td><td>degree</td><td>scrLscrL</td></tr>
<tr><td>==<</td><td>==<</td><td>==></td><td>==></td><td></td><td></td></tr>
</table>

Apseqnchar is a version of *eqnchar* tailored for the Autologic APS-5 phototypesetter. This will not look optimal on other phototypesetters. Similarly, *cateqnchar* is the old *eqnchar* tailored for the Wang CAT and the old *otroff*. Until a phototypesetter-independent version of *eqnchar* is available, *eqnchar* should be a link to the default version on each system. The standard default is *apseqnchar*.

FILES

/usr/pub/eqnchar
/usr/pub/apseqnchar
/usr/pub/cateqnchar

SEE ALSO

eqn(1), nroff(1), troff(1) in the *UNIX Programmer's Manual—Volume 1: Commands and Utilities.*

NAME

fcntl − file control options

SYNOPSIS

#include <fcntl.h>

DESCRIPTION

The *fcntl*(2) function provides for control over open files. The *include* file describes *requests* and *arguments* to *fcntl* and *open*(2).

```
/* Flag values accessible to open(2) and fcntl(2) */
/*  (The first three can only be set by open) */
#define    O_RDONLY    0
#define    O_WRONLY    1
#define    O_RDWR      2
#define    O_NDELAY    04      /* Non-blocking I/O */
#define    O_APPEND    010     /* append (writes guaranteed at the end) */

/* Flag values accessible only to open(2) */
#define    O_CREAT    00400    /* open with file create (uses third open arg) */
#define    O_TRUNC    01000    /* open with truncation */
#define    O_EXCL     02000    /* exclusive open */

/* fcntl(2) requests */
#define    F_DUPFD     0    /* Duplicate fildes */
#define    F_GETFD     1    /* Get fildes flags */
#define    F_SETFD     2    /* Set fildes flags */
#define    F_GETFL     3    /* Get file flags */
#define    F_SETFL     4    /* Set file flags */
#define    F_GETLK     5    /* Get blocking file locks */
#define    F_SETLK     6    /* Set or clear file locks and fail on busy */
#define    F_SETLKW    7    /*Set or clear file locks and wait on busy */

/* file segment locking control structure */
struct flock
    short    l_type;
    short    l_whence;
    long     l_start;
    long     l_len;        /* if 0 then until EOF */
    int      l_pid;        /* returned with F_GETLK */

/* file segment locking types */
#define    F_RDLCK    01    /* Read lock */
#define    F_WRLCK    02    /* Write lock */
#define    F_UNLCK    03    /* Remove locks */
```

SEE ALSO

fcntl(2), open(2).

NAME

font — description files for device-independent troff

SYNOPSIS

troff −Tptty ...

DESCRIPTION

For each phototypesetter supported by *troff*(1) and available on this system, there is a directory containing files describing the device and its fonts. This directory is named **/usr/lib/font/dev***ptty* where *ptty* is the name of the phototypesetter. Currently the only *ptty* supported is **aps** for the Autologic APS−5.

For a particular phototypesetter, *ptty*, the ASCII file *DESC* in the directory **/usr/lib/font/dev***ptty* describes its characteristics. Each line starts with a word identifying the characteristic and followed by appropriate specifiers. Blank lines and lines beginning with a # are ignored.

The legal lines for *DESC* are:

res *num*	resolution of device in basic increments per inch
hor *num*	smallest unit of horizontal motion
vert *num*	smallest unit of vertical motion
unitwidth *num*	pointsize in which widths are specified
sizescale *num*	scaling for fractional pointsizes
paperwidth *num*	width of paper in basic increments
paperlength *num*	length of paper in basic increments
spare1 *num*	available for use
spare2 *num*	available for use
sizes *num num ...*	list of pointsizes available on typesetter
fonts *num name ...*	number of initial fonts followed by the names of the fonts. For example: fonts 4 R I B S
charset	this always comes last in the file and is on a line by itself. Following it is the list of special character

names for this device. Names are separated by a space or a newline. The list can be as long as necessary. Names not in this list are not allowed in the font description files.

Res is the basic resolution of the device in increments per inch. **Hor** and **vert** describe the relationships between motions in the horizontal and vertical directions. If the device is capable of moving in single basic increments in both directions, both **hor** and **vert** would have values of 1. If the vertical motions only take place in multiples of two basic units while the horizontal motions take place in the basic increments, then **hor** would be 1, while **vert** would be 2. **Unitwidth** is the pointsize in which all width tables in the font description files are given. *Troff* automatically scales the widths from the **unitwidth** size to the pointsize it is working with. **Sizescale** is not currently used and is 1. **Paperwidth** is the width of the paper in basic increments. The APS-5 is 6120 increments wide. **Paperlength** is the length of a sheet of paper in the basic increments.

For each font supported by the phototypesetter, there is also an ASCII file with the same name as the font (e.g., **R**, **I**, **CW**). The format for a font description file is:

name *name*	name of the font, such as **R** or **CW**
internalname *name*	internal name of font
special	sets flag indicating that the font is special
ligatures *name* ... **0**	Sets flag indicating font has ligatures. The list of ligatures follows and is terminated by a zero. Accepted ligatures are: **ff fi fl ffi ffl**.
spare1	available for use
spacewidth *num*	width of space if something other than 1/3 of \(em is desired as a space.
charset	The charset must come at the end. Each line following the word *charset* describes one character in the

font. Each line has one of two formats:

name *width* *kerning code*
name "

where *name* is either a single ASCII character or a special character name from the list found in *DESC*. The width is in basic increments. The kerning information is 1 if the character descends below the line, 2 if it rises above the letter 'a', and 3 if it both rises and descends. The kerning information for special characters is not used and so may be 0. The code is the number sent to the typesetter to produce the character. The second format is used to indicate that the character has more than one name. The double quote indicates that this name has the same values as the preceding line. The kerning and code fields are not used if the width field is a double quote character.

Troff and its postprocessors read this information from binary files produced from the ASCII files by a program distributed with *troff* called *makedev*. For those with a need to know, a description of the format of these files follows:

The file *DESC.out* starts with the *dev* structure, defined by *dev.h*:

```
/*
dev.h: characteristics of a typesetter
* /

struct dev {
short    filesize;   /* number of bytes in file, */
                          /* excluding dev part */
short    res;             /* basic resolution in goobies/inch */
short    hor;             /* goobies horizontally */
short    vert;
short    unitwidth;       /* size at which widths are given*/
short    nfonts;     /* number fonts physically available */
short    nsizes;     /* number of pointsizes */
short    sizescale; /* scaling for fractional pointsizes */
short    paperwidth;      /* max line length in units */
short    paperlength;  /* max paper length in units */
short    nchtab;   /* number of funny names in chtab */
short    lchname; /* length of chname table */
```

```
short   spare1;  /* in case of expansion */
short   spare2;
};
```

Filesize is just the size of everything in *DESC.out* excluding the *dev* structure. *Nfonts* is the number of different font positions available. *Nsizes* is the number of different pointsizes supported by this typesetter. *Nchtab* is the number of special character names. *Lchname* is the total number of characters, including nulls, needed to list all the special character names. At the end of the structure are two spares for later expansions.

Immediately following the *dev* structure are a number of tables. First is the *sizes* table, which contains *nsizes* + 1 shorts(a null at the end), describing the pointsizes of text available on this device. The second table is the *funny_char_index_table*. It contains indices into the the table which follows it, the *funny_char_strings*. The indices point to the beginning of each special character name which is stored in the *funny_char_strings* table. The *funny_char_strings* table is *lchname* characters long, while the *funny_char_index_table* is *nchtab* shorts long.

Following the *dev* structure will occur *nfonts* {*font*}.*out* files, which are used to initialize the font positions. These {*font*}.*out* files, which also exist as separate files, begin with a *font* structure and then are followed by four character arrays:

```
struct font {         /* characteristics of a font */
char     nwfont;  /* number of width entries */
char     specfont;          /* 1 == special font */
char      ligfont;  /* 1 == ligatures exist on this font */
char     spare1;  /* unused for now */
char     namefont[10]; /* name of this font, e.g., R */
char     intname[10];  /* internal name of font, in ASCII */
};
```

The *font* structure tells how many defined characters there are in the font, whether the font is a "special" font and if it contains ligatures. It also has the ASCII name of the font, which should match the name of the file it appears in, and the internal name of the font on the typesetting device (*intname*). The internal name is independent of the font position and name that *troff* knows about. For example, you might say mount R in position 4, but when asking the typesetter to actually produce a character from the R font, the postprocessor which instructs the typesetter would use *intname*.

The first three character arrays are specific for the font and run in parallel. The first array, *widths*, contains the width of each character relative to *unitwidth*. *Unitwidth* is defined in *DESC*. The second array, *kerning*, contains kerning information. If a character rises above the letter 'a', 02 is set. If it descends below the line, 01 is set. The third array, *codes*, contains the code that is sent to the typesetter to produce the character.

The fourth array is defined by the device description in *DESC*. It is the *font_index_table*. This table contains indices into the *width*, *kerning*, and *code* tables for each character. The order that characters appear in these three tables is arbitrary and changes from one font to the next. In order for *troff* to be able to translate from ASCII and the special character names to these arbitrary tables, the *font_index_table* is created with an order which is constant for each device. The number of entries in this table is 96 plus the number of special character names for this device. The value 96 is 128 - 32, the number of printable characters in the ASCII alphabet. To determine whether a normal ASCII character exists, *troff* takes the ASCII value of the character, subtracts 32, and looks in the *font_index_table*. If it finds a 0, the character is not defined in this font. If it finds anything else, that is the index into *widths*, *kerning*, and *codes* that describe that character.

To look up a special character name, for example **\(pl**, the mathematical plus sign, and determine whether it appears in a particular font or not, the following procedure is followed. A *counter* is set to 0 and an index to a special character name is picked out of the *counter'th* position in the *funny_char_index_table*. A string comparision is performed between *funny_char_strings [funny_char_index_table [counter]]* and the special character name, in our example **pl**, and if it matches, then *troff* refers to this character as (96 + *counter*). When it wants to determine whether a specific font supports this character, it looks in *font_index_table[(96+counter)]*, (see below), to see whether there is a 0, meaning the character does not appear in this font, or number, which is the index into the *widths*, *kerning*, and *codes* tables.

Notice that since a value of 0 in the *font_index_table* indicates that a character does not exist, the 0th element of the *width*, *kerning*, and *codes* arrays are not used. For this reason the 0th element of the *width* array can be used for a special purpose, defining the width of a space for a font. Normally a space is defined by *troff* to be 1/3 of the width of the \(em character, but if the 0th element of the *width* array is non-zero, then that value is used for the width of a space.

SEE ALSO

troff(5).
troff(1) in the *UNIX Programmer's Manual—Volume 1: Commands and Utilities.*

FILES

/usr/lib/font/dev{X}/DESC.out description file for phototypesetter X
/usr/lib/font/dev{X}/{font}.out font description files for phototypesetter X

NAME

man − macros for formatting entries in this manual

SYNOPSIS

nroff −man files

troff −man [**−rs1**] files

DESCRIPTION

These *troff*(1) macros are used to lay out the format of the entries of this manual. A skeleton entry may be found in the file **/usr/man/u_man/man0/skeleton**. These macros are used by the *man*(1) command.

The default page size is 8.5″×11″, with a 6.5″×10″ text area; the **−rs1** option reduces these dimensions to 6″×9″ and 4.75″×8.375″, respectively; this option (which is *not* effective in *nroff*(1)) also reduces the default type size from 10-point to 9-point, and the vertical line spacing from 12-point to 10-point. The **−rV2** option may be used to set certain parameters to values appropriate for certain Versatec printers: it sets the line length to 82 characters, the page length to 84 lines, and it inhibits underlining; this option should not be confused with the **−Tvp** option of the *man*(1) command, which is available at some UNIX system sites.

Any *text* argument below may be one to six "words". Double quotes ("") may be used to include blanks in a "word". If *text* is empty, the special treatment is applied to the next line that contains text to be printed. For example, **.I** may be used to italicize a whole line, or **.SM** followed by **.B** to make small bold text. By default, hyphenation is turned off for *nroff*(1), but remains on for *troff*(1).

Type font and size are reset to default values before each paragraph and after processing font- and size-setting macros, e.g., **.I**, **.RB**, **.SM**. Tab stops are neither used nor set by any macro except **.DT** and **.TH**.

Default units for indents *in* are ens. When *in* is omitted, the previous indent is used. This remembered indent is set to its default value (7.2 ens in *troff*(1), 5 ens in *nroff*this corresponds to 0.5″ in the default page size) by **.TH**, **.P**, and **.RS**, and restored by **.RE**.

.TH *t s c n* Set the title and entry heading; *t* is the title, *s* is the section number, *c* is extra commentary, e.g., "local", *n* is new manual name. Invokes **.DT** (see below).

.SH *text*	Place subhead *text*, e.g., **SYNOPSIS**, here.
.SS *text*	Place sub-subhead *text*, e.g., **Options**, here.
.B *text*	Make *text* bold.
.I *text*	Make *text* italic.
.SM *text*	Make *text* 1 point smaller than default point size.
.RI *a b*	Concatenate roman *a* with italic *b*, and alternate these two fonts for up to six arguments. Similar macros alternate between any two of roman, italic, and bold: **.IR .RB .BR .IB .BI**
.P	Begin a paragraph with normal font, point size, and indent. **.PP** is a synonym for **.P**.
.HP *in*	Begin paragraph with hanging indent.
.TP *in*	Begin indented paragraph with hanging tag. The next line that contains text to be printed is taken as the tag. If the tag does not fit, it is printed on a separate line.
.IP *t in*	Same as **.TP** *in* with tag *t*; often used to get an indented paragraph without a tag.
.RS *in*	Increase relative indent (initially zero). Indent all output an extra *in* units from the current left margin.
.RE *k*	Return to the *k*th relative indent level (initially, *k*=1; *k*=0 is equivalent to *k*=1); if *k* is omitted, return to the most recent lower indent level.
.PM *m*	Produces proprietary markings; where *m* may be **P** for **PRIVATE**, **N** for **NOTICE**, **BP** for **BELL LABORATORIES PROPRIETARY**, or **BR** for **BELL LABORATORIES RESTRICTED**.
.DT	Restore default tab settings (every 7.2 ens in *troff*(1), 5 ens in *nroff*(1)).
.PD *v*	Set the interparagraph distance to *v* vertical spaces. If *v* is omitted, set the interparagraph distance to the default value (0.4v in *troff*(1), 1v in *nroff*(1)).

The following *strings* are defined:

***R**	® in *troff*(1), **(Reg.)** in *nroff*.
***S**	Change to default type size.
***(Tm**	Trademark indicator.

The following *number registers* are given default values by **.TH**:

IN	Left margin indent relative to subheads (default is 7.2 ens in *troff*(1), 5 ens in *nroff*(1)).

LL	Line length including **IN**.
PD	Current interparagraph distance.

CAVEATS

In addition to the macros, strings, and number registers mentioned above, there are defined a number of *internal* macros, strings, and number registers. Except for names predefined by *troff (1)* and number registers **d**, **m**, and **y**, all such internal names are of the form *XA*, where *X* is one of **)**, **]**, and **}**, and *A* stands for any alphanumeric character.

If a manual entry needs to be preprocessed by *eqn*(1) (or *neqn*), and/or *tbl*(1), it must begin with a special line (described in *man*(1)), causing the *man* command to invoke the appropriate preprocessor(s).

The programs that prepare the Table of Contents and the Permuted Index for this Manual assume the *NAME* section of each entry consists of a single line of input that has the following format:

name[, name, name ...] \− explanatory text

The macro package increases the inter-word spaces (to eliminate ambiguity) in the *SYNOPSIS* section of each entry.

The macro package itself uses only the roman font (so that one can replace, for example, the bold font by the constant-width font (**CW**). Of course, if the input text of an entry contains requests for other fonts (e.g., **.I**, **.RB**, **\fI**), the corresponding fonts must be mounted.

FILES

/usr/lib/tmac/tmac.an
/usr/lib/macros/cmp.n.[dt].an
/usr/lib/macros/ucmp.n.an
/usr/man/[uap]_man/man0/skeleton

SEE ALSO

eqn(1), man(1), nroff(1), tbl(1), tc(1), troff(1) in the *UNIX Programmer's Manual—Volume 1: Commands and Utilities.*

BUGS

If the argument to **.TH** contains *any* blanks and is *not* enclosed by double quotes (**""**), there will be strange irregular dots on the output.

NAME

math − math functions and constants

SYNOPSIS

#include <math.h>

DESCRIPTION

This file contains declarations of all the functions in the Math Library (described in Section 3M), as well as various functions in the C Library (Section 3C) that return floating-point values.

It defines the structure and constants used by the *matherr*(3M) error-handling mechanisms, including the following constant used as an error-return value:

HUGE	The maximum value of a single-precision floating-point number.

The following mathematical constants are defined for user convenience:

M_E	The base of natural logarithms (e).
M_LOG2E	The base-2 logarithm of e.
M_LOG10E	The base-10 logarithm of e.
M_LN2	The natural logarithm of 2.
M_LN10	The natural logarithm of 10.
M_PI	π, the ratio of the circumference of a circle to its diameter. (There are also several fractions of π, its reciprocal, and its square root.)
M_SQRT2	The positive square root of 2.
M_SQRT1_2	The positive square root of 1/2.

For the definitions of various machine-dependent "constants," see the description of the *<values.h>* header file.

FILES

/usr/include/math.h

SEE ALSO

intro(3), matherr(3M), values(5).

NAME

mm − the MM macro package for formatting documents

SYNOPSIS

mm [options] [files]

nroff −mm [options] [files]

nroff −cm [options] [files]

mmt [options] [files]

troff −mm [options] [files]

DESCRIPTION

This package provides a formatting capability for a very wide variety of documents. It is the standard package used by the BTL typing pools and documentation centers. The manner in which a document is typed in and edited is essentially independent of whether the document is to be eventually formatted at a terminal or is to be phototypeset. See the references below for further details.

The **−mm** option causes *nroff*(1) and *troff*(1) to use the non-compacted version of the macro package, while the **−cm** option results in the use of the compacted version, thus speeding up the process of loading the macro package.

FILES

/usr/lib/tmac/tmac.m	pointer to the non-compacted version of the package
/usr/lib/macros/mm[nt]	non-compacted version of the package
/usr/lib/macros/cmp.n.[dt].m	compacted version of the package
/usr/lib/macros/ucmp.n.m	initializers for the compacted version of the package

SEE ALSO

mm(1), mmt(1), nroff(1), troff(1) in the *UNIX Programmer's Manual—Volume 1: Commands and Utilities.*

NAME

mosd − the OSDD adapter macro package for formatting documents

SYNOPSIS

osdd [options] [files]

mm −mosd [options] [files]

nroff −mm −mosd [options] [files]

nroff −cm −mosd [options] [files]

mmt −mosd [options] [files]

troff −mm −mosd [options] [files]

DESCRIPTION

The OSDD adapter macro package is a tool used in conjunction with the MM macro package to prepare Operations Systems Deliverable Documentation. Many of the OSDD Standards are different from the default format provided by MM. The OSDD adapter package sets the appropriate MM options for automatic production of the OSDD Standards. The OSDD adapter package also generates the correct OSDD page headers and footers, heading styles, Table of Contents format, etc.

OSDD document (input) files are prepared with the MM macros. Additional information which must be given at the beginning of the document file is specified by the following string definitions:

```
.ds H1 document-number
.ds H2 section-number
.ds H3 issue-number
.ds H4 date
.ds H5 rating
```

The *document-number* should be of the standard 10-character format. The words "Section" and "Issue" should not be included in the string definitions; they will be supplied automatically when the document is printed. For example:

```
.ds H1 OPA−1P135−01
.ds H2 4
.ds H3 2
```

automatically produces

```
OPA-1P135-01
Section 4
Issue 2
```

as the document page header. Quotation marks are not used in string definitions.

If certain information is not to be included in a page header, then the string is defined as null; e.g.,

    .ds H2

means that there is no *section-number*.

The OSDD Standards require that the *Table of Contents* be numbered beginning with *Page 1*. By default, the first page of text will be numbered *Page 2*. If the *Table of Contents* has more than one page, for example *n*, then either **−rP***n+1* must be included as a command line option or **.nr P n** must be included in the document file. For example, if the *Table of Contents* is four pages then use **−rP5** on the command line or **.nr P 4** in the document file.

The OSDD Standards require that certain information such as the document *rating* appear on the *Document Index* or on the *Table of Contents* page if there is no index. By default, it is assumed that an index has been prepared separately. If there is no index, the following must be included in the document file:

    .nr Di 0

This will ensure that the necessary information is included on the *Table of Contents* page.

The OSDD Standards require that all numbered figures be placed at the end of the document. The **.Fg** macro is used to produce full page figures. This macro produces a blank page with the appropriate header, footer, and figure caption. Insertion of the actual figure on the page is a manual operation. The macro usage is

    .Fg page-count "figure caption"

where *page-count* is the number of pages required for a multi-page figure (default 1 page).

The **.Fg** macro cannot be used within the document unless the final **.Fg** in a series of figures is followed by a **.SK** macro to force out the last figure page.

The *Table of Contents* for OSDD documents (see Figure 4 in Section 4.1 of the OSDD Standards) is produced with:

    .Tc
    System Type
    System Name
    Document Type
    .Td

The **.Tc/.Td** macros are used instead of the **.TC** macro from MM.

The **.PM** macro may be used to generate proprietary markings – see the MM document for legal styles.

The **.P** macro is used for paragraphs. The **Np** register is set automatically to indicate the paragraph numbering style. It is very important that the **.P** macro be used correctly. All paragraphs (including those immediately following a **.H** macro) must use a **.P** macro. Unless there is a **.P** macro, there will not be a number generated for the paragraph. Similarly, the **.P** macro should not be used for text which is not a paragraph. The **.SP** macro may be appropriate for these cases, e.g., for "paragraphs" within a list item.

The page header format is produced automatically in accordance with the OSDD Standards. The OSDD Adapter macro package uses the **.TP** macro for this purpose. Therefore the **.TP** macro normally available in MM is not available for users.

FILES

/usr/lib/tmac/tmac.osd

SEE ALSO

mm(5).
mm(1), mmt(1), nroff(1), troff(1) in the *UNIX Programmer's Manual—Volume 1: Commands and Utilities.*

NAME

mptx − the macro package for formatting a permuted index

SYNOPSIS

nroff −mptx [options] [files]

troff −mptx [options] [files]

DESCRIPTION

This package provides a definition for the **.xx** macro used for formatting a permuted index as produced by *ptx*(1). This package does not provide any other formatting capabilities such as headers and footers. If these or other capabilities are required, the *mptx* macro package may be used in conjuction with the *MM* macro package. In this case, the **−mptx** option must be invoked *after* the **−mm** call. For example:

nroff −cm −mptx file

or

mm −mptx file

FILES

/usr/lib/tmac/tmac.ptx	pointer to the non-compacted version of the package
/usr/lib/macros/ptx	non-compacted version of the package

SEE ALSO

mm(5).
mm(1), nroff(1), ptx(1), troff(1) in the *UNIX Programmer's Manual—Volume 1: Commands and Utilities.*

NAME

mv − a troff macro package for typesetting viewgraphs and slides

SYNOPSIS

mvt [**−a**] [options] [files]

troff [**−a**] [**−rX1**] **−mv** [options] [files]

DESCRIPTION

This package makes it easy to typeset viewgraphs and projection slides in a variety of sizes. A few macros (briefly described below) accomplish most of the formatting tasks needed in making transparencies. All of the facilities of *troff*(1), *eqn*(1), and *tbl*(1) are available for more difficult tasks.

The output can be previewed on most terminals, and, in particular, on the TEKTRONIX 4014. For this device, specify the **−rX1** option (this option is automatically specified by the *mvt* command−q.v.−when that command is invoked with the **−T4014** option). To preview output on other terminals, specify the **−a** option.

The available macros are:

.VS [*n*] [*i*] [*d*] Foil-start macro; foil size is to be 7″×7″; *n* is the foil number, *i* is the foil identification, *d* is the date; the foil-start macro resets all parameters (indent, point size, etc.) to initial default values, except for the values of *i* and *d* arguments inherited from a previous foil-start macro; it also invokes the **.A** macro (see below).

The naming convention for this and the following eight macros is that the first character of the name (**V** or **S**) distinguishes between viewgraphs and slides, respectively, while the second character indicates whether the foil is square (**S**), small wide (**w**), small high (**h**), big wide (**W**), or big high (**H**). Slides are "skinnier" than the corresponding viewgraphs: the ratio of the longer dimension to the shorter one is larger for slides than for viewgraphs. As a result, slide foils can be used for viewgraphs, but not vice versa; on the other hand, viewgraphs can accommodate a bit more text.

.Vw [*n*] [*i*] [*d*]	Same as **.VS**, except that foil size is 7″ wide × 5″ high.
.Vh [*n*] [*i*] [*d*]	Same as **.VS**, except that foil size is 5″×7″.
.VW [*n*] [*i*] [*d*]	Same as **.VS**, except that foil size is 7″×5.4″.
.VH [*n*] [*i*] [*d*]	Same as **.VS**, except that foil size is 7″×9″.
.Sw [*n*] [*i*] [*d*]	Same as **.VS**, except that foil size is 7″×5″.
.Sh [*n*] [*i*] [*d*]	Same as **.VS**, except that foil size is 5″×7″.
.SW [*n*] [*i*] [*d*]	Same as **.VS**, except that foil size is 7″×5.4″.
.SH [*n*] [*i*] [*d*]	Same as **.VS**, except that foil size is 7″×9″.
.A [*x*]	Place text that follows at the first indentation level (left margin); the presence of *x* suppresses the ½ line spacing from the preceding text.
.B [*m* [*s*]]	Place text that follows at the second indentation level; text is preceded by a mark; *m* is the mark (default is a large bullet); *s* is the increment or decrement to the point size of the mark with respect to the *prevailing* point size (default is 0); if *s* is 100, it causes the point size of the mark to be the same as that of the *default* mark.
.C [*m* [*s*]]	Same as **.B**, but for the third indentation level; default mark is a dash.
.D [*m* [*s*]]	Same as **.B**, but for the fourth indentation level; default mark is a small bullet.
.T *string*	*String* is printed as an over-size, centered title.
.I [*in*] [*a* [*x*]]	Change the current text indent (does not affect titles); *in* is the indent (in inches unless dimensioned, default is 0); if *in* is signed, it is an increment or decrement; the presence of *a* invokes the **.A** macro (see below) and passes *x* (if any) to it.
.S [*p*] [*l*]	Set the point size and line length; *p* is the point size (default is "previous"); if *p* is 100, the point size reverts to the *initial* default for the current foil-start macro; if *p* is signed, it is an increment or decrement (default is 18 for **.VS**, **.VH**, and **.SH**, and 14 for the other foil-start macros); *l* is the line length (in inches unless dimensioned; default is 4.2″ for **.Vh**, 3.8″ for **.Sh**, 5″ for **.SH**, and 6″ for the other foil-start macros).

.DF *n f* [*n f* ...] Define font positions; may not appear within a foil's input text (i.e., it may only appear after all the input text for a foil, but before the next foil-start macro); *n* is the position of font *f*; up to four "*n f*" pairs may be specified; the first font named becomes the *prevailing* font; the initial setting is (**H** is a synonym for **G**):

.DF 1 H 2 I 3 B 4 S

.DV [*a*] [*b*] [*c*] [*d*] Alter the vertical spacing between indentation levels; *a* is the spacing for **.A**, *b* is for **.B**, *c* is for **.C**, and *d* is for **.D**; all non-null arguments must be dimensioned; null arguments leave the corresponding spacing unaffected; initial setting is:

.DV .5v .5v .5v 0v

.U *str1* [*str2*] Underline *str1* and concatenate *str2* (if any) to it.

The last four macros in the above list do not cause a break; the **.I** macro causes a break only if it is invoked with more than one argument; all the other macros cause a break.

The macro package also recognizes the following upper-case synonyms for the corresponding lower-case *troff* requests:

.AD .BR .CE .FI .HY .NA .NF .NH .NX .SO .SP .TA .TI

The **Tm** string produces the trademark symbol.

The input tilde (~) character is translated into a blank on output.

See the user's manual cited below for further details.

FILES

/usr/lib/tmac/tmac.v
/usr/lib/macros/vmca

SEE ALSO

eqn(1), mmt(1), tbl(1), troff(1) in the *UNIX Programmer's Manual—Volume 1: Commands and Utilities.*

BUGS

The **.VW** and **.SW** foils are meant to be 9″ wide by 7″ high, but because the typesetter paper is generally only 8″ wide, they are printed 7″ wide by 5.4″ high and have to be enlarged by a factor of 9/7 before use as viewgraphs; this makes them less than totally useful.

NAME

prof − profile within a function

SYNOPSIS

#define MARK
#include <prof.h>

void MARK (name)

DESCRIPTION

MARK will introduce a mark called *name* that will be treated the same as a function entry point. Execution of the mark will add to a counter for that mark, and program-counter time spent will be accounted to the immediately preceding mark or to the function if there are no preceding marks within the active function.

Name may be any combination of up to six letters, numbers or underscores. Each *name* in a single compilation must be unique, but may be the same as any ordinary program symbol.

For marks to be effective, the symbol MARK must be defined before the header file *<prof.h>* is included. This may be defined by a preprocessor directive as in the synopsis, or by a command line argument, i.e:

```
cc −p −DMARK foo.c
```

If MARK is not defined, the *MARK*(name) statements may be left in the source files containing them and will be ignored.

EXAMPLE

In this example, marks can be used to determine how much time is spent in each loop. Unless this example is compiled with *MARK* defined on the command line, the marks are ignored.

```
#include <prof.h>

foo( )
{
        int i, j;

        .
        .
        .
        MARK(loop1);
        for (i = 0; i < 2000; i++) {
```

```
                . . .
        }
        MARK(loop2);
        for (j = 0; j < 2000; j++) {
                . . .
        }
}
```

SEE ALSO

profil(2), monitor(3C).
prof(1) in the *UNIX Programmer's Manual—Volume 1: Commands and Utilities.*

NAME

regexp − regular expression compile and match routines

SYNOPSIS

#define INIT <declarations>
#define GETC() <getc code>
#define PEEKC() <peekc code>
#define UNGETC(c) <ungetc code>
#define RETURN(pointer) <return code>
#define ERROR(val) <error code>

#include <regexp.h>

char *compile (instring, expbuf, endbuf, eof)
char *instring, *expbuf, *endbuf;
int eof;

int step (string, expbuf)
char *string, *expbuf;

extern char *loc1, *loc2, *locs;

extern int circf, sed, nbra;

DESCRIPTION

This page describes general-purpose regular expression matching routines in the form of *ed*(1), defined in **/usr/include/regexp.h**. Programs such as *ed*(1), *sed*(1), *grep*(1), *bs*(1), *expr*(1), etc., which perform regular expression matching use this source file. In this way, only this file need be changed to maintain regular expression compatibility.

The interface to this file is unpleasantly complex. Programs that include this file must have the following five macros declared before the "#include <regexp.h>" statement. These macros are used by the *compile* routine.

GETC() — Return the value of the next character in the regular expression pattern. Successive calls to GETC() should return successive characters of the regular expression.

PEEKC() — Return the next character in the regular expression. Successive calls to PEEKC() should return the same character (which should also be the next character returned by GETC()).

UNGETC(*c*) — Cause the argument *c* to be returned by the next call to GETC() (and PEEKC()). No more that one character of pushback is ever needed and this character is guaranteed to be the last character read by GETC(). The value of the macro UNGETC(*c*) is always ignored.

RETURN(*pointer*) — This macro is used on normal exit of the *compile* routine. The value of the argument *pointer* is a pointer to the character after the last character of the compiled regular expression. This is useful to programs which have memory allocation to manage.

ERROR(*val*) — This is the abnormal return from the *compile* routine. The argument *val* is an error number (see table below for meanings). This call should never return.

ERROR	MEANING
11	Range endpoint too large.
16	Bad number.
25	"\digit" out of range.
36	Illegal or missing delimiter.
41	No remembered search string.
42	\(\) imbalance.
43	Too many \(.
44	More than 2 numbers given in \{ \}.
45	} expected after \.
46	First number exceeds second in \{ \}.
49	[ ] imbalance.
50	Regular expression overflow.

The syntax of the *compile* routine is as follows:

```
compile(instring, expbuf, endbuf, eof)
```

The first parameter *instring* is never used explicitly by the *compile* routine but is useful for programs that pass down different pointers to input characters. It is sometimes used in the INIT declaration (see below). Programs which call functions to input characters or have characters in an external array can pass down a value of ((char *) 0) for this parameter.

The next parameter *expbuf* is a character pointer. It points to the place where the compiled regular expression will be placed.

The parameter *endbuf* is one more than the highest address where the compiled regular expression may be placed. If the compiled expression cannot fit in (*endbuf−expbuf*) bytes, a call to ERROR(50) is made.

The parameter *eof* is the character which marks the end of the regular expression. For example, in *ed*(1), this character is usually a /.

Each program that includes this file must have a **#define** statement for INIT. This definition will be placed right after the declaration for the function *compile* and the opening curly brace ({). It is used for dependent declarations and initializations. Most often it is used to set a register variable to point the beginning of the regular expression so that this register variable can be used in the declarations for GETC(), PEEKC() and UNGETC(). Otherwise it can be used to declare external variables that might be used by GETC(), PEEKC() and UNGETC(). See the example below of the declarations taken from *grep*(1).

There are other functions in this file which perform actual regular expression matching, one of which is the function *step*. The call to *step* is as follows:

```
step(string, expbuf)
```

The first parameter to *step* is a pointer to a string of characters to be checked for a match. This string should be null terminated.

The second parameter *expbuf* is the compiled regular expression which was obtained by a call of the function *compile*.

The function *step* returns non-zero if the given string matches the regular expression, and zero if the expressions do not match. If there is a match, two external character pointers are set as a side effect to the call to *step*. The variable set in *step* is *loc1*. This is a pointer to the first character that matched the regular expression. The variable *loc2*, which is set by the function *advance*, points to the character after the last character that matches the regular expression. Thus if the regular expression matches the entire line, *loc1* will point to the first character of *string* and *loc2* will point to the null at the end of *string*.

Step uses the external variable *circf* which is set by *compile* if the regular expression begins with ^. If this is set then *step* will try to match the regular expression to the beginning of the string only. If more than one regular expression is to be compiled before the first is executed the value of *circf* should be saved for each compiled expression and *circf* should be set to that saved value before each call to *step*.

The function *advance* is called from *step* with the same arguments as *step*. The purpose of *step* is to step through the *string* argument and call *advance* until *advance* returns non-zero indicating a match or until the end of *string* is reached. If one wants to constrain *string* to the beginning of the line in all cases, *step* need not be called; simply call *advance*.

When *advance* encounters a * or \{ \} sequence in the regular expression, it will advance its pointer to the string to be matched as far as possible and will recursively call itself trying to match the rest of the string to the rest of the regular expression. As long as there is no match, *advance* will back up along the string until it finds a match or reaches the point in the string that initially matched the * or \{ \}. It is sometimes desirable to stop this backing up before the initial point in the string is reached. If the external character pointer *locs* is equal to the point in the string at sometime during the backing up process, *advance* will break out of the loop that backs up and will return zero. This is used by *ed*(1) and *sed*(1) for substitutions done globally (not just the first occurrence, but the whole line) so, for example, expressions like **s/y*//g** do not loop forever.

The additional external variables *sed* and *nbra* are used for special purposes.

EXAMPLES

The following is an example of how the regular expression macros and calls look from *grep*(1):

```
#define INIT            register char *sp = instring;
#define GETC()          (*sp++)
#define PEEKC()         (*sp)
#define UNGETC(c)       (--sp)
#define RETURN(c)       return;
#define ERROR(c)        regerr()

#include <regexp.h>
...
    (void) compile(*argv, expbuf, &expbuf[ESIZE], '\0');
...
```

```
                    if (step(linebuf, expbuf))
                                    succeed();
```

FILES

/usr/include/regexp.h

SEE ALSO

bs(1), ed(1), expr(1), grep(1), sed(1) in the *UNIX Programmer's Manual—Volume 1: Commands and Utilities.*

BUGS

The handling of *circf* is kludgy.

The actual code is probably easier to understand than this manual page.

NAME

stat – data returned by stat system call

SYNOPSIS

#include <sys/types.h>
#include <sys/stat.h>

DESCRIPTION

The system calls *stat* and *fstat* return data whose structure is defined by this include file. The encoding of the field *st_mode* is defined in this file also.

```
/*
 * Structure of the result of stat
 */
struct    stat
{
          dev_t     st_dev;
          ino_t     st_ino;
          ushort    st_mode;
          short     st_nlink;
          ushort    st_uid;
          ushort    st_gid;
          dev_t     st_rdev;
          off_t     st_size;
          time_t    st_atime;
          time_t    st_mtime;
          time_t    st_ctime;
};

#define S_IFMT    0170000 /* type of file */
#define S_IFDIR   0040000 /* directory */
#define S_IFCHR   0020000 /* character special */
#define S_IFBLK   0060000 /* block special */
#define S_IFREG   0100000 /* regular */
#define S_IFIFO   0010000 /* fifo */
#define S_ISUID   04000   /* set user id on execution */
#define S_ISGID   02000   /* set group id on execution */
#define S_ISVTX   01000   /* save swapped text */
#define S_IREAD   00400   /* read permission, owner */
#define S_IWRITE  00200   /* write permission, owner */
#define S_IEXEC   00100   /* exec/search permission, owner */
```

FILES

/usr/include/sys/types.h
/usr/include/sys/stat.h

SEE ALSO

stat(2), types(5).

NAME

term − conventional names for terminals

DESCRIPTION

These names are used by certain commands (e.g., *tabs*(1), *man*(1) and are maintained as part of the shell environment (see *sh*(1), *profile*(4), and *environ*(5)) in the variable **$TERM**:

1520	Datamedia 1520
1620	DIABLO 1620/others using the HyType II printer
1620−12	same, in 12-pitch mode
2621	Hewlett-Packard 2621 series
2631	Hewlett-Packard 2631 line printer
2631−c	Hewlett-Packard 2631 line printer - compressed mode
2631−e	Hewlett-Packard 2631 line printer - expanded mode
2640	Hewlett-Packard 2640 series
2645	Hewlett-Packard 264n series (other than the 2640 series)
300	DASI/DTC/GSI 300 and others using the HyType I printer
300−12	same, in 12-pitch mode
300s	DASI/DTC/GSI 300s
382	DTC 382
300s−12	same, in 12-pitch mode
3045	Datamedia 3045
33	TELETYPE® Model 33 KSR
37	TELETYPE Model 37 KSR
40−2	TELETYPE Model 40/2
40−4	TELETYPE Model 40/4
4540	TELETYPE Model 4540
3270	IBM Model 3270
4000a	Trendata 4000a
4014	TEKTRONIX 4014
43	TELETYPE Model 43 KSR
450	DASI 450 (same as Diablo 1620)
450−12	same, in 12-pitch mode
735	Texas Instruments TI735 and TI725
745	Texas Instruments TI745
dumb	generic name for terminals that lack reverse line-feed and other special escape sequences
sync	generic name for synchronous TELETYPE 4540-compatible terminals
hp	Hewlett-Packard (same as 2645)

lp	generic name for a line printer
tn1200	User Electric TermiNet 1200
tn300	User Electric TermiNet 300

Up to 8 characters, chosen from [−a−z0−9], make up a basic terminal name. Terminal sub-models and operational modes are distinguished by suffixes beginning with a −. Names should generally be based on original vendors, rather than local distributors. A terminal acquired from one vendor should not have more than one distinct basic name.

Commands whose behavior depends on the type of terminal should accept arguments of the form **−T***term* where *term* is one of the names given above; if no such argument is present, such commands should obtain the terminal type from the environment variable **$TERM**, which, in turn, should contain *term*.

SEE ALSO

profile(4), environ(5).
man(1), mm(1), nroff(1), tplot(1G), sh(1), stty(1), tabs(1) in the *UNIX Programmer's Manual—Volume 1: Commands and Utilities*.

BUGS

This is a small candle trying to illuminate a large, dark problem. Programs that ought to adhere to this nomenclature do so somewhat fitfully.

NAME

troff — description of output language

DESCRIPTION

The device-independent *troff* outputs a pure ASCII description of a typeset document. The description specifies the typesetting device, the fonts, and the point sizes of characters to be used as well as the position of each character on the page. A list of all the legal commands follows. Most numbers are denoted as *n* and are ASCII strings. Strings inside of **[ ]** are optional. *Troff* may produce them, but they are not required for the specification of the language. The character **\n** has the standard meaning of "newline" character. Between commands white space has no meaning. White space characters are spaces and newlines. All commands which have an arbitary length numerical parameter or word must be followed by white space. For example, the command to specify point size, **s###**, must be followed by a space or newline.

s*n* The point size of the characters to be generated.

f*n* The font mounted in the specified position is to be used. The number ranges from 0 to the highest font presently mounted. 0 is a special position, invoked by *troff*, but not directly accessible to the troff user. Normally fonts are mounted starting at position 1.

c*x* Generate the character *x* at the current location on the page; *x* is a single ASCII character.

C*xyz* Generate the special character *xyz*. The name of the character is delimited by white space. The name will be one of the special characters legal for the typesetting device as specified by the device specification found in the file *DESC*. This file resides in a directory specific for the typesetting device. (See *font*(5) and **/usr/lib/font/dev*.**)

H*n* Change the horizonal position on the page to the number specified. The number is in basic units of motions as specified by *DESC*. This is an absolute "goto".

h*n* Add the number specified to the current horizontal position. This is a relative "goto".

V*n* Change the vertical position on the page to the number specified (down is positive).

v*n* Add the number specified to the current vertical position.

nnx This is a two-digit number followed by an ASCII character. The meaning is a combination of **h***n* followed by **c***x*. The two digits *nn* are added to the current horizontal position and then the ASCII character, *x*, is produced. This is the most common form of character specification.

n*b a* This command indicates that the end of a line has been reached. No action is required, though by convention the horizontal position is set to 0. *Troff* will specify a resetting of the *x*,*y* coordinates on the page before requesting that more characters be printed. The first number, *b*, is the amount of space before the line and the second number, *a*, the amount of space after the line. The second number is delimited by white space.

w A **w** appears between words of the input document. No action is required. It is included so that one device can be emulated more easily on another device.

p*n* Begin a new page. The new page number is included in this command. The vertical position on the page should be set to 0.

{ Push the current environment, which means saving the current point size, font, and location on the page.

} Pop a saved environment.

t*xxxxx* Print the string of characters, *xxxxx*, using the natural width of each character to determine the next x coordinate. *Troff* does not currently produce this form of command. It is not recommended. The characters will probably be too close together.

.... **\n** — A line beginning with a pound sign is a comment.

Dl *x y*\n — Draw a line from the current location to *x*,*y*. At the end of the drawing operation the current location will be *x*,*y*.

Dc *d*\n — Draw a circle of diameter *d* with the leftmost edge being at the current location (x, y). The current location after drawing the circle will be x+*d*,y, the rightmost edge of the circle.

De *dx dy*\n — Draw an ellipse with the specified axes. *dx* is the axis in the x direction and *dy* is the axis in the y direction. The leftmost edge of the ellipse will be at the current location. After drawing the ellipse the current location will be x+*dx*,y.

Da *x y r*\n — Draw a counterclockwise arc from the current location to *x*,*y* using a circle of radius *r* . The current location after drawing the arc will be *x*,*y*.

D~ *x y x y*...\n — Draw a spline curve (wiggly line) between each of the *x*,*y* coordinate pairs starting at the current location. The final location will be the final *x*,*y* pair of the list. Currently there may be no more than 36 *x*,*y* pairs to this command.

x i[nit]\n — Initialize the typesetting device. The actions required are dependent on the device. An **init** command will always occur before any output generation is attempted.

x T *device*\n — The name of the typesetter is *device*. This is the same as the argument to the **−T** option. The information about the typesetter will be found in the directory **/usr/lib/font/dev**{*device*}.

x r[es] *n h v*\n The resolution of the typesetting device in increments per inch is *n*. Motion in the horizontal direction can take place in units of *h* basic increments. Motion in the vertical direction can take place in units of *v* basic increments. For example, the APS-5 typesetter has a basic resolution of 723 increments per inch and can move in either direction in 723rds of an inch. Its specification is:
x res 723 1 1

x p[ause]\n Pause. Cause the current page to finish but do not relinquish the typesetter.

x s[top]\n Stop. Cause the current page to finish and then relinquish the typesetter. Perform any shutdown and bookkeeping procedures required.

x t[railer]\n Generate a trailer. On some devices no operation is performed.

x f[ont] *n name*\n Load the font *name* into position *n*.

x H[eight] *n*\n Set the character height to *n* points. This causes the letters to be elongated or shortened. It does not affect the width of a letter.

x S[lant] *n*\n Set the slant to *n* degrees. Only some typesetters can do this and not all angles are supported.

NAME

types — primitive system data types

SYNOPSIS

#include <sys/types.h>

DESCRIPTION

The data types defined in the include file are used in UNIX system code; some data of these types are accessible to user code:

```
typedef struct { int r[1]; } *      physadr;
typedef long             daddr_t;
typedef char *           caddr_t;
typedef unsigned int     uint;
typedef unsigned short   ushort;
typedef ushort           ino_t;
typedef short            cnt_t;
typedef long             time_t;
typedef int              label_t[10];
typedef short            dev_t;
typedef long             off_t;
typedef long             paddr_t;
typedef long             key_t;
```

The form *daddr_t* is used for disk addresses except in an i-node on disk, see *fs*(4). Times are encoded in seconds since 00:00:00 GMT, January 1, 1970. The major and minor parts of a device code specify kind and unit number of a device and are installation-dependent. Offsets are measured in bytes from the beginning of a file. The *label_t* variables are used to save the processor state while another process is running.

SEE ALSO

fs(4).

NAME

values — machine-dependent values

SYNOPSIS

#include <values.h>

DESCRIPTION

This file contains a set of manifest constants, conditionally defined for particular processor architectures.

The model assumed for integers is binary representation (one's or two's complement), where the sign is represented by the value of the high-order bit.

BITS(*type*)	The number of bits in a specified type (e.g., int).
HIBITS	The value of a short integer with only the high-order bit set (in most implementations, 0x8000).
HIBITL	The value of a long integer with only the high-order bit set (in most implementations, 0x80000000).
HIBITI	The value of a regular integer with only the high-order bit set (usually the same as HIBITS or HIBITL).
MAXSHORT	The maximum value of a signed short integer (in most implementations, 0x7FFF ≡ 32767).
MAXLONG	The maximum value of a signed long integer (in most implementations, 0x7FFFFFFF ≡ 2147483647).
MAXINT	The maximum value of a signed regular integer (usually the same as MAXSHORT or MAXLONG).
MAXFLOAT, LN_MAXFLOAT	The maximum value of a single-precision floating-point number, and its natural logarithm.

MAXDOUBLE, LN_MAXDOUBLE The maximum value of a double-precision floating-point number, and its natural logarithm.

MINFLOAT, LN_MINFLOAT The minimum positive value of a single-precision floating-point number, and its natural logarithm.

MINDOUBLE, LN_MINDOUBLE The minimum positive value of a double-precision floating-point number, and its natural logarithm.

FSIGNIF The number of significant bits in the mantissa of a single-precision floating-point number.

DSIGNIF The number of significant bits in the mantissa of a double-precision floating-point number.

FILES

/usr/include/values.h

SEE ALSO

intro(3), math(5).

NAME

varargs — handle variable argument list

SYNOPSIS

#include <varargs.h>

va_alist

va_dcl

void va_start(pvar)
va_list pvar;

type **va_arg(pvar,** *type***)**
va_list pvar;

void va_end(pvar)
va_list pvar;

DESCRIPTION

This set of macros allows portable procedures that accept variable argument lists to be written. Routines that have variable argument lists (such as *printf*(3S)) but do not use *varargs* are inherently nonportable, as different machines use different argument-passing conventions.

va_alist is used as the parameter list in a function header.

va_dcl is a declaration for *va_alist*. No semicolon should follow *va_dcl*.

va_list is a type defined for the variable used to traverse the list.

va_start is called to initialize *pvar* to the beginning of the list.

va_arg will return the next argument in the list pointed to by *pvar*. *Type* is the type the argument is expected to be. Different types can be mixed, but it is up to the routine to know what type of argument is expected, as it cannot be determined at runtime.

va_end is used to clean up.

Multiple traversals, each bracketed by *va_start* ... *va_end,* are possible.

SEE ALSO

exec(2), printf(3S).

EXAMPLE

This example is a possible implementation of *execl*(2).

```
#include <varargs.h>
#define MAXARGS     100

/*      execl is called by
                execl(file, arg1, arg2, ..., (char *)0);
*/
execl(va_alist)
va_dcl
{
        va_list ap;
        char *file;
        char *args[MAXARGS];
        int argno = 0;

        va_start(ap);
        file = va_arg(ap, char *);
        while ((args[argno++] = va_arg(ap, char *)) != (char *)0)
                ;
        va_end(ap);
        return execv(file, args);
}
```

BUGS

It is up to the calling routine to specify how many arguments there are, since it is not always possible to determine this from the stack frame. For example, *execl* is passed a zero pointer to signal the end of the list. *Printf* can tell how many arguments are there by the format.

It is non-portable to specify a second argument of *char*, *short*, or *float* to *va_arg*, since arguments seen by the called function are not *char*, *short*, or *float*. C converts *char* and *short* arguments to *int* and converts *float* arguments to *double* before passing them to a function.